AUGUST 24, 1814

WASHINGTON IN FLAMES

By
Carole L. Herrick

ISBN: 0-914927-50-7

Publish by:

Higher Education Publications, Inc.
6400 Arlington Boulevard, Suite 648
Falls Church, VA 22042
(703) 532-2300

This book is dedicated to my mother
Edna Newman-Doolittle Loop

"…the capture of Washington was
more owing to the blindness of the
Americans than to any other cause."

George Gleig, 1814

ACKNOWLEDGMENTS

The story of the British invasion and burning of America's seat of government was a mere grain of sand in the annals of history, but its occurrence was significant, for the outrage that unfolded afterward brought the fledging nation together. In a period of approximately eight hours, American troops were routed at Bladensburg, Washington was evacuated without any show of resistance, the nation's leaders fled to four different locations and the seat of government of the United States was set ablaze by British troops. President James Madison and his wife Dolley found safety in the Northern Virginia countryside, as did Secretary of State James Monroe, Attorney General Richard Rush and Navy Secretary William Jones. Considerable use of legend and misinterpretation of facts has flavored the story over the years, particularly regarding the flights of the Madisons.

Virginia's preparation for celebrating the 400th anniversary of the founding of Jamestown in 1607 was the impetus for writing this book. In order to highlight the commonwealth in 2007, The Jamestown/Yorktown Foundation created a "pilot community program" throughout Virginia with the intention that each community would complete a legacy project. This book was written as one of McLean/Great Falls Celebrate Virginia 1607-2007 legacy projects. The goal of this writing was to separate fact from fiction. The story needed to be clarified. For this reason, surviving primary sources such as letters, diary entries and newspaper accounts were used extensively. Their content has been quoted at length, rather than partially, in order to give the reader a more accurate account of the terror and tragic events surrounding Washington, August 24, 1814.

The quoted material was kept as written in the source text. Often it was a diary entry, or a hastily written note, and words were abbreviated misspelled or unreadable. The diary of Michael Shiner, a freed slave, is noteworthy. He taught himself to write, but wrote phonetically as he heard the words. Dates and times were often confusing for the same event, particularly when it came to individuals recalling something many years later. Various timelines were made so that individuals could be placed in the appropriate spot at the proper time.

I am indebted to many people for their assistance in acquiring material for this project. I am especially grateful to the Fairfax County Public Library system, in particular, the information staff at the Dolley Madison Library McLean, Virginia. Its head librarian, Carolyn Heyer listened to my thoughts and read many of the chapters as the project advanced. Bonnie Fiori, Margie Schoenberg, Lorraine Maetzold and Bonnie Weston were never too busy to assist me with my numerous requests. Sources of information were the following:

Arlington County Public Library, Arlington, Virginia
Dolley Madison Library, McLean, Virginia
Georgetown Neighborhood Library, Washington D. C., Peabody Room
Library of Congress
Lloyd House, Alexandria Public Library, Virginia
Mary Riley Styles Public Library, Falls Church, Virginia
Prince George's County Historical Society Library
Thomas Balch Library, Leesburg, Virginia
Tysons-Pimmit Regional Library, Falls Church, Virginia
Virginia Room, Fairfax County Public Library, Fairfax, Virginia

The National Archives
Archives Division, Fairfax County, Virginia

The Great Falls Historical Society
The Historical Society of Kent County
The McLean Historical Society
The Maryland Historical Society
The New York Historical Society
The Pennsylvania Historical Society
The Virginia Historical Society
The Washington D. C. Historical Society
The White House Historical Society

Dunbarton House, Washington, D.C.
Fort Belvoir, Virginia
Gunston Hall, Fairfax County, Virginia
James Madison University, Virginia
Marymount University, Arlington, Virginia
University of Virginia, Charlottesville, Virginia

Riverbend Park, Great Falls, Virginia

I am further indebted to many friends who generously gave of their time. From the beginning of the project Page Shelp assisted with the chapters that pertained to McLean and Great Falls. Along with Judy and Armand Weiss, she helped with the painful task of editing. The advice, perceptions, criticisms and insights of these three individuals are ingrained throughout the story. Phyllis Verhalen was a wealth of information when it came to Dolley Madison. Evelyn Fox, Barbara Smith and Karen Washburn were continually supportive and offered much needed encouragement from the book's conceptual beginning to the finished product. Alfred Brown, John Hansan, Diane Perrine, Gustav

Person, Francine Proulx, Joan and Cort Randell, Mayo Stuntz and David Whiteree all went the extra step to lend a helping hand in various ways. I am appreciative.

However, as in any publication, my greatest thanks must go to my family. Besides devouring many hastily prepared meals, my husband Philip spent a few Sunday afternoons viewing various locations that were a part of the British invasion and used for the escapes of the populace and government officials. His knowledge about such places as the Conn's Ferry Landing and Chain Bridge is far more than he ever wanted to know. My son Charles is a graphic design artist and works for a major consulting firm located at Tyson's Corner in Northern Virginia. It is his handiwork that brings this story alive. My mother Edna Loop lives in California. Our phone conversations often revolved around my latest trip to the Library of Congress. After reading much of the text, she concluded that "Dolley Madison must have been a very brave woman." The reader can decide this for himself. I can never thank them enough.

Carole L. Herrick

CONTENTS

INDEX TO ILLUSTRATIONS AND PICTURES

PROLOGUE

It was the summer of 1814. James Madison was serving a second term as the fourth President of the United States, a country that had been at war with Great Britain for over two years in a conflict known as the War of 1812, or referred to by the Federalists as "Mr. Madison's War." The nation's young capital, which had relocated from Philadelphia in November, 1800, was still under construction. Ten square miles of timbered land along the Potomac River had been had been set aside by the states of Virginia and Maryland to serve as the federal territory for the District of Columbia. The basic blueprint that had been drawn up by Major Charles Pierre L'Enfant, under the directorship of President George Washington, was slowly being molded by Andrew Ellicott and Benjamin Banneker into what was envisioned to become a magnificent city. Planned were broad diagonal boulevards, intersected by a grid of north-south streets, that were joined at key points with circles or squares designed to accept monuments or fountains. Included in the design were innovative features such as open space, symbolic vistas and strategically placed buildings that would create an expansive style vision for the new Republic. There was no nucleus in L'Enfant's plan. The government buildings were scattered. The site selected for the Capitol, designed by William Thornton, was on top a rise called "Jenkins Hill." The Executive Mansion, designed by architect James Hoban, was built to its west. The two buildings were 1.8 miles apart from each other, with the wide, mile long Pennsylvania Avenue connecting the two properties. From New York, L'Enfant wrote to Washington September 11, 1789:

"Sir: The late determination of Congress to lay the foundations on a city which is to become the capital of this vast empire offers so great an occasion of acquiring reputation to whoever may be appointed to conduct the execution of the business that your Excellency will not be surprised that my ambition and the desire I have of becoming a useful citizen should lead me to wish a share in the undertaking.

No nation, perhaps, had ever before the opportunity offered them of deliberately deciding on the spot where their capital should be fixed.... And, although the means now within the power of the country are not such as to pursue the design to any great extent, it will be obvious that the plan should be drawn on such a scale as to leave room for that aggrandizement and embellishment which the increase of the wealth of the nation will permit it to pursue at any period, however remote. Viewing the matter in this light, I am fully sensible of the extent of the undertaking."

The President's House received its first cornerstone in 1792. Washington laid the cornerstone for the Capitol in 1795 and, five years later, the second session of the Sixth Congress convened in the Senate (north) wing of the unfinished building. The new permanent seat of government was basically a metropolitan wilderness. There was no city. The roads were not paved. There were few houses; however, there was a section of row houses along Pennsylvania Avenue between 19th and 22nd Streets, known as the Six and the Seven Buildings where many government officials were able to reside. Others, if they were lucky, took up residence in the few hotels or boarding houses that were available at that time. Distinguished citizens lived in homes located in such nearby previously established communities such as Georgetown, Alexandria or Bladensburg. Albert Gallatin, then Secretary of Treasury, wrote January 15, 1801:

"Our local situation is far from being pleasant or even convenient. Around the Capitol are seven or eight boarding houses, one tailor, one shoemaker, one printer, a washing woman, a grocery shop, a pamphlets and stationery shop and an oyster house. This makes the whole of the federal City as connected with the Capitol."

In 1800 President John and First Lady Abigail Adams had the misfortune to relocate into a Presidential Palace that was still under construction and continually smelled of wet plaster. Not one room was finished and the main staircase had not been completed. Life in the new capital city was inconvenient and basically rural. Even though there was timber everywhere, wood had not been stockpiled for the winter. The yard did not have a fence around it. The Adamses found it difficult to take on social responsibilities with enthusiasm. Not wanting the world to view what was hanging outside on her clothesline to dry, Abigail converted what became known as the East Room into a drying room to pin up the damp clothes. Their residency in the White House was brief.

It was less than four months before Thomas Jefferson, a widower, was sworn in as the third President of the United States. Abigail described the White House to her daughter Abigail "Nabby" Smith:

"November 21, 1800

My Dear Child,... The house is upon a grand and superb scale, requiring about thirty servants to attend and keep the apartments in proper order, and perform the ordinary business of the house and stables; an establishment very well proportioned to the President's salary. The lighting the apartments, from the kitchen to parlors and chambers, is a tax indeed; and the fires we are obliged to keep to secure us from daily agues is another very cheering comfort. To assist us in this great castle, and render less attendance necessary, bells are wholly wanting, not one single one being hung through the whole house, and promises are all you can obtain. This is so great an inconvenience, that I know not what to do, or how to do....

If they will put me up some bells, and let me have wood enough to keep fires, I design to be pleased. I could content myself almost anywhere three months; but surrounded with forests, can you believe that wood is not to be had, because people cannot be found to cut and cart it!...

The house is made habitable, but there is not a single apartment finished, and all with- inside, except the plastering, has been done since Briesler came. We have not the least fence, yard, or other convenience, without, and the great unfinished audience-room I make a drying room of, to hang up the clothes in. The principal stairs are not up, and will not be this winter....

If the twelve years, in which this place has been considered as the future seat of government, had been improved, as they would have been in New England, very many of the present inconveniences would have been removed. It is a beautiful spot, capable of every improvement, and, the more I view it, the more I am delighted with it...."

From the very beginning, the planners, builders, government officials and citizens were visionaries who imagined a new, fresh capital that represented the people, yet offered magnificence and sophistication. They realized that such a city required more than just buildings, monuments and fountains. In July of 1800, Congress, while still at Philadelphia, authorized payment of eight hundred dollars to purchase the full length portrait of the late George Washington by Gilbert Stuart, including its frame, to be displayed in the White House. The Statement of Appropriations and Expenditures from the National Treasury in 1800 included the purchase of the painting:

"To Henry Lee, for the cost of a portrait, full length, of the late General Washington, purchased by him for the President's House.

July 9, 1800   Warrant No. 988 $800"

It wasn't until 1809, when President James Madison and his wife, Dolley, moved into the White House, that Washington City began to acquire some of the formal characteristics and ceremonies that are a part of a nation's capital. Jefferson, a widower, had been extremely hospitable as President, but etiquette was not his forte. There was an official lack of pomp, something the developing capital much needed. His tastes remained steadfastly rural. He did not want America to take on the formality of the European courts. Mrs. Madison, as the wife of the Secretary of State, was often asked to assist as hostess with many of Jefferson's dinners, but serving the nation as the First Lady, Dolley enthusiastically took on the responsibilities of establishing culture and a social life in the new city. The first inaugural ball was held at Long's Hotel in 1809. Four hundred people attended. Formal receptions, elegant dinner parties and weekly levees were initiated. Dolley, a Quaker, loved fashionable clothes and dressed stylishly, if not lavishly. In this department, she was a trendsetter, for what Mrs. Madison wore was always noticed and often copied, whether it was a turban or ostrich plumes covering a very large hat. Funds had been provided by Congress for decorating and furnishing the Presidential Mansion. The First Lady lost no time in improving the interior of the White House and directed the work that was done by Benjamin Latrobe, the Surveyor of Public Buildings. Latrobe wrote:

"Philadelphia, April 21st. 1809.

> Madam
>
> Today I was so fortunate as to get on board Captain Hand, 4 Chimney pieces, 2 for the dining room, 1 for the Antichamber and one for the drawing room.
>
> I am sorry to have counteracted any wish of yours as to Genl. Washington's picture. The dining room is properly the picture room, and in speaking to the president as to the furniture of the room, I understood it to be arranged that not only the Genl., but the succeeding Presidents should have a place there. I therefore intended him to occupy either the place at the West end of the room between the Windows, or the fire place at the East end. Over the drawing room Chimney piece, I intended my best looking glass, opposite to the door, and over the fire place (that is to be) of the dining room my squarest Glass, to repeat the Landscape through the Center window.
>
> But if you have the slightest wish to the contrary remember that the motto of my family, of my art, and of my duty, is *tutto si fa, tour se fait*. Mr. Bridport, the decorator to whom I have committed this business, is a man of great taste and talents and the first line of his instructions is, do as Mr. and Mrs. Madison wish.

iv

The curtains! Oh the terrible velvet curtains! Their effect will ruin me entirely, so brilliant will they be.

I shall certainly not be here another week. Your liveries are now the only things in my department not accomplished, and they are attended and tomorrow I report upon them."

Throughout the early formation of America's permanent seat of government Europe was involved with the Napoleonic Wars. The United States tried desperately to remain neutral, but by 1812, the political situation between America and Great Britain had deteriorated so badly that Congress declared war against England. This action stemmed from such issues as impressing American seamen, harassing American shipping along the eastern coast, plundering American ships on every sea and Orders in Council against neutral trade. During 1813 British war ships, led by Rear Admiral George Cockburn in his seventy-four gun flagship *Albion*, were constantly seen throughout the Chesapeake Bay region. Raiding parties traveled up and down the various rivers that flowed into the bay, pillaging villages, taking prisoners and burning houses and public buildings to the ground. Washingtonians were nervous about a destructive invasion to their city. At one point, the English ships sailed up the Potomac, sounding the river and taking notes, but turned back before reaching the capital. Apprehensive as early as May 12, 1813, Dolley summarized her fears to Edward Coles, Madison's Private Secretary:

"And now if I could I would describe to you the fears and alarms that circulate around me. For the last week all the city and Georgetown (except the Cabinet) have expected a visit from the enemy, and were not lacking in their expressions of terror and reproach. Yesterday an express announced the pause of a frigate at the mouth of the Potomac. The commander sent his boats to examine a Swedish ship that lay near, but our informer was too frightened to wait for further news. We are making considerable efforts for defense. The fort is being repaired, and five hundred militia, with perhaps as many regulars, are to be stationed on the Green, near the Windmill, or rather Major Taylor's.

The twenty tents already look well in my eyes, who have always been an advocate for fighting when assailed, though a Quaker. I therefore keep the old Tunisian sabre within reach. One of our Generals has discovered a plan of the British, - it is to land as many chosen rogues as they can about fourteen miles below Alexandria, in the night, so that they may be on hand to burn the President's house and offices. I do not tremble at this, but feel hurt that the admiral (of Havre de Grace memory) should send me word that he would make his bow at my drawing-room soon."

Cockburn's raiding parties in the Chesapeake Bay continued into the following year, staying away from Washington. Congress recessed. Residents remained guarded, but never truly believed the enemy would actually invade the District. They thought of Washington as more of an unfinished village and, despite some notable buildings, it was not elegant or worth plundering. Then, Thomas Swann, a volunteer observer for the United States Army at Point Lookout, Maryland sighted on August 17, a British armada that had arrived in force....

1

ALARM

One of the least understood chapters in American history occurred August 24, 1814, during the War of 1812, when British troops marched unopposed into the nation's capital and set fire to the Capitol, the Executive Mansion and other public buildings, forcing an exodus of panicked citizens, government officials and Cabinet appointees, to all seek safety in the surrounding countryside. The President, First Lady and Secretary of State James Monroe found shelter in Virginia at separate locations. Nothing parallels this episode in the history of the United States. The horrific events of Pearl Harbor and 9-11 were basically surprise attacks; the invasion and burning of Washington D.C., was definitely preventable! Seeking to end the War, five peace commissioners, John Quincy Adams, James Bayard, Henry Clay, Jonathan Russell and Albert Gallatin, had been sent to Ghent, Belgium, in the spring of 1814, to negotiate a treaty with British ambassadors. While the negotiations were underway, ominous signals were reaching Washington, suggesting that Great Britain was preparing for a full-scale invasion of the capital of the United States. With Napoleon's abdication in Europe, England now had available the necessary seasoned veterans for such an engagement. President James Madison was alarmed, but few inhabitants took the warnings seriously; after all, the capital, built at the headwaters of the Potomac River, was only fourteen years old. Many reasoned that because of its lack of commercial activity, the new capital had no strategic importance. At this time even William Jones, Secretary of the Navy, did not share Madison's view, because he reasoned that Baltimore or Annapolis were more likely targets. In his account of the events to the Congressional Investigative Committee that looked into the causes of the successful British invasion Jones wrote in October, 1814:

> "The serious apprehensions of invasion and devastation, which succeeded the knowledge of those extraordinary events, which liberated the powerful naval and military forces of the enemy from European hostility, and the temper of the British, nation, as displayed in the language of its journals and conduct of its Government, in relation to the pacific mission which it had invited, were deeply felt, and frequently discussed, in occasional conversations which the probable points of attack were variously considered. My own impression inclined to the opinion that there were some points more exposed, less difficult of access, and more inviting to the enemy, upon the system of warfare he had adopted, than the metropolis; the only important objects which it presented, according to my view being the naval depot and public shipping.
>
> I recollect, on one of those occasions, that the President expressed very great solicitude for the safety of the metropolis; his belief that the enemy would attempt its invasion, and urged the expediency of immediate defensive preparations, with all the disposable force that could be conveniently collected. I accorded in the expediency of the preparation, but must confess I was not equally impressed with the apprehension of immediate danger, as well from the reasons I have before assigned, as from the then existing fact, that the force of the enemy, in the waters of the Chesapeake, was entirely naval, and apparently very satisfactorily engaged in conflagrating farm houses, and depredating upon slaves and tobacco, on the shores of the Patuxent. In this sentiment I was not alone."

The peace negotiations never got off the ground. Two of the American commissioners, Gallatin and Bayard, were sent to London seeking a solution to the stalemate. While there Gallatin wrote Monroe in June, 1814, warning him of vindictive sentiments in England that called for a full-scale attack upon America, even while the peace negotiations were taking place! He had received intelligence that the United States was to be treated severely for what the English felt was its indirect roll in delaying the defeat of Napoleon. Gallatin suggested that the Federal City was in danger and its citizens should expect heavy destruction if the capital were captured. He further added that America would not receive any assistance from Europe:

> "London, June 13, 1814
>
> Sir:
> The armament fitted against America will enable the British, besides

providing for Canada, to land 15 to 20,000 men on the Atlantic coast. Whether the ministry be nevertheless disposed for peace a few weeks will determine. It may be intended to continue the war for the purpose of effecting a separation of the Union, or with a view of promoting the election of a President of the Federal party, or in the hope of imposing conditions which will curtail the territory, the fisheries, and diminish the commerce of the United States; but even with the intention of a speedy and equal peace, the pride and vindictive passions of the nation would be highly gratified by what they would consider a glorious termination of the war, by an expedition that may console them for the mortification of naval defeats, retrieve the disgrace of the campaign in the Chesapeake, cripple the naval and commercial resources as well as the growing manufacturers of the United States. To use their own language, they mean to inflict on America, a chastisement that will teach her that war is not declared against Great Britain with impunity.

This is a very general sentiment of the nation, and that such are the opinions of the Ministry was strongly impressed on the mind of _____ by a late conversation he had with Lord Castlereagh. Admiral Warren also told Levett Harris, with whom he was intimate at St. Petersburg, that he was sorry to say instructions given to his successor on the American station were very different from those under which he had acted, and that he feared very serious injury would be inflicted on America.... I think it probable that Washington and New York are the places the capture of which would most gratify the enemy, and that Norfolk, Baltimore and the collected manufacturing establishments of the Brandywine and Rhode Island are also in danger. The ostensible object everywhere will be the destruction of the public naval magazines and arsenals, and of all the shipping, whether public or private; but heavy contributions, plunder, and whatever marks a predatory warfare must be expected.... whatever may be the object and duration of the war, America must rely on her resources alone. From Europe no assistance can, for some time, can be expected."

Madison was one of the few who understood the seriousness of the situation and feared such an attack. Because there had been previous warnings, he felt that Gallatin's alarm, received the 26th of June, was not to be taken lightly. Enlisting the support of Monroe, he convened an emergency Cabinet meeting on July 1, 1814, at the Executive Mansion. Madison explained the danger to Washington and presented a defense plan, which the Cabinet members unanimously approved. It called for establishing a camp of 2000 to 3000 regular troops between Washington and Baltimore. An additional 10,000 to 12,000 militia would be put on standby in neighboring states, ready to assemble and march when necessary. Jones continued in his report to the Investigative Committee:

"On the 30th day of June, the members of the cabinet were invited to attend a meeting, at the President's mansion, on the following day at noon. At or near the time appointed, the Secretaries of State, Treasury, War, and Navy, and the Attorney General assembled.

The President stated the object of the meeting to be the consideration
of the menacing aspect of things in consequence of the augmented
power of the enemy by the great political changes which had taken
place in Europe; and the disposition manifested by the Government
and people of Great Britain, to prosecute the war with the most
vindictive and devastating spirit; represented the motives and
inducements, which, he conceived, the enemy had to prefer the
invasion of the capital rather than any other immediate enterprise;
and urged the necessity of speedy and efficient preparation for the
defence of the district and capital; inquired into the existing state of
its military and naval defences, and the extent of the disposable force
which it would be practicable to concentrate in the District....

To the regular force, the President proposed to add ten thousand
militia; to be designated, and held in readiness, in such neighboring
districts as should be found most convenient. He also suggested the
propriety of depositing, at a suitable place, contiguous to the metropolis, a supply of arms, ammunition, and camp equipage."

Since the plan was designed to defend the nation's capital, the
group gave it special status by creating a new military district,
comprising Maryland, the District of Columbia, and the portion of
Virginia lying between the Rappahannock and Potomac Rivers. The10th
Military District became official the following day, with the whole area
placed under the command of an officer in the regular army. Madison
named Brigadier General William H. Winder, a Baltimore lawyer
recently released from captivity on the Canadian front, as the commander
to defend Washington. Winder's immediate superior, Secretary of War
John Armstrong, had championed Major General Moses Porter for the
position, and strongly opposed Winder's appointment. Richard Johnson,
thought to have killed the Shawnee Chief Tecumseh, was Chairman of
the House of Representatives Committee of Inquiry that investigated the
causes of the success of the British invasion. He said in his report:

"The next day, July the 2d, by a general order of the War
Department, the 10th military district was created, to embrace the
State of Maryland, the District of Columbia, and that part of Virginia
lying between the Rappahannock and Potomac, under the command
of Brigadier General Winder, who, being then in Baltimore, was
advised of the fact by a letter from the Secretary of War from the
same date."

Two days later, on Independence Day, the government sent out a
levy to the governors in all the fifteen states specifying the amount of
their quotas to be included in an extra militia force that would total
93,500 men. These troops would be organized at home, but held in
readiness. The requisition requested was as follows: Connecticut, 3000;
Delaware, 1000; Georgia, 3500; Kentucky, 5500; Louisiana, 1000;
Maryland, 6000; Massachusetts, 10,000; Mississippi Territory, 500; New

Hampshire, 3500; New Jersey, 5000; New York, 13,500; North Carolina, 7000; Pennsylvania, 14,000; Rhode Island, 500; South Carolina, 5000; Tennessee, 2500; Virginia, 12,000. Johnson further added:

> "On the 4th of July, a requisition was made on certain States for a corps of ninety-three thousand five hundred men, designating the quota of each, with a request to the Executive of each state to detach, and hold in readiness for immediate service, their respective detachments, recommending the expediency of fixing the places of rendezvous, with a due regard to points, the importance or exposure of which would most likely attract the views of the enemy."

Winder's job to arm and fortify the 10th Military District proved challenging. The principal defense to be relied upon was the militia, yet the requested militia forces never materialized. Everything was subject to Armstrong's orders. The General could not actually call any of the supposedly citizen soldiers into federal service until the Secretary of War gave him permission. He had no authority over any detachment until it was organized, equipped and formally turned over to him by the War Department. There were about 500 regulars at Winder's disposal, but most of them were already assigned to protecting various forts, particularly Fort Warburton (also known as Fort Washington), which was located on the Maryland shore of the Potomac, about twelve miles south of the capital. Winder found a stubborn opponent in the Secretary of War, who maintained the opinion that Washington was not in any danger and kept his attention focused on Canada. He told Winder that militia forces should only be called upon in the face of sudden emergencies. In a letter to Armstrong dated July 9, Winder related that he had listened to Armstrong's position concerning the militia, and presented an opposing view, suggesting that militia forces needed to be called in preparation for the supposed invasion, otherwise a lack of cohesiveness would result when undisciplined troops were needed. Armstrong never responded to Winder's letter. Winder suggested:

> "In conversation with you at Washington, I understood the idea, at present entertained, relative to the auxiliary militia force, proposed for the District, to be, that it shall be draughted and designated, but that no part of it is to be called into the field until the hostile force, now in the Chesapeake, shall be reinforced to such an extent as to render it probable that a serious attack is contemplated....
>
> What time will this allow us to hear of his arrival, to disseminate through the intricate and winding channels the various orders to the militia, for them to assemble, have their officers designated, their arms, accoutrements, and ammunition, delivered, the necessary supplies provided, or for the commanding officer to learn the different corps and detachments, so as to issue orders with the promptitude and certainty so necessary in active operations? If the enemy's force should be strong, which, if it come at all, it will be,

sufficient numbers of militia could not be warned and run together
even as a disorderly crowd, without arms, ammunition, or
organization, before the enemy would already have given his blow....

Allow me, sir, respectfully to propose that four thousand militia be
called out without delay. I propose to station these in equal
proportions, in the most eligible positions between South river and
Washington, and in the vicinity of Baltimore...."

On July 12, Armstrong did grant Winder authority to issue a call
for six thousand militia troops from Maryland to be mustered into service
and held in readiness. Armstrong followed this five days later on July
17, by giving Winder permission to call for additional increments from
the District of Columbia, 2000, Pennsylvania, 5000, and Virginia, 2000,
so that the number of militia he could legally call into federal service
totaled 15,000. These forces were included with about one thousand
regulars from the 36th and 38th U. S. Infantry Regiments. Armstrong's
letters were as follows:

> "War Department, July 12, 1814
> SIR: You will receive herewith the copy of a circular letter, addressed
> to the governors of certain States, requiring a body of militia to be
> organized and equipped, and held in readiness for future service.
>
> In case of actual or menaced invasion of the District you command,
> you will call for a part, or for the whole of the quota assigned to the
> State of Maryland, which shall have been organized and equipped
> under the aforesaid requisition.
>
> In performing this duty, you will be careful to avoid unnecessary
> calls, to proportion the call to the exigency, and to have inspected,
> without delay, all corps entering on service, to the end that men, who
> from any cause are unfit therefor, be promptly discharged, and that a
> due proportion, in all cases, be maintained between officers and
> privates."

> "War Department, July 17, 1814
> SIR: In addition to my circular letter of the 12th inst., which subjects
> to your call the quota of Maryland militia, you are also authorized to
> draw from that of Virginia 2000 men, and from the quota of
> Pennsylvania 5000. The whole of the militia of the District of
> Columbia, amounting to about 2000, is kept in a disposable state, and
> subject to your orders."

Armstrong's attitude for the defense of the District of Columbia
was one of extraordinary apathy. Winder had an army that existed on
paper only. Orders were issued by Armstrong that implied organization
and readiness of militia troops, when, in fact, these forces never existed

or materialized. The numbers that were collected never exceeded a few hundred. Virginia and Maryland were unable to fulfill their quota. Both states had already mobilized large numbers of troops on their own authority to protect their coastlines from continual raids by the English. Authorities in Pennsylvania informed the United States government that their state could not compel any man to serve because of a new militia law which temporarily deprived Governor Simon Snyder of his authority to enforce the draft. The legislature at its last session had revamped its militia laws, the result being that none of the standing militia could be compelled to serve and nothing could be done about the matter until October. On behalf of the Governor, Pennsylvania's State Secretary, N. B. Boileau, responded to Armstrong on July 25, 1814:

> "The repeal of our militia law of 1807, and its several supplements, on the 1st of August next; the disannulling of all militia commissions on that day, by a new law of the last session, granted under the old law, except the commissions of such officers as may then be in actual service; the ordering by the new law; the holding of elections of officers by the militia, after the said 1st of August; the notice of election; returns to be made; and the protracting to the 4th Monday of October next; the classification of the militia; causes an utmost total disorganization of our militia system, between the 1st of August and the 4th of October, and presents difficulties, in yielding perfect compliance with the requisition of the President, insurmountable.
>
> It is hoped, however, that the patriotism of the people will obviate the difficulty, by a voluntary tender of services, which the Governor has invited, growing out of this unaccountable oversight of the Legislature. It is strongly doubted whether any orders can be enforced under the present state of things.
>
> The requisition refers to the act of Congress, passed 28th February, 1795; under, which militia can be held in service three months only; and to the law of 1814, which authorized the President to keep them six months in service. The law of Pennsylvania, passed at the last session of its Legislature, requires the Governor to mention, in general orders, the period for which any militia ordered into service is to remain on duty. It is desirable, therefore, to know whether the requisition is intended for three or six months' service."

Citizens in Washington formed a "Committee of Safety," headed by the Mayor, James H. Blake, which spoke to Armstrong on July 18, expressing concern for the city's safety. The militia commander of the District of Columbia, Major General John P. Van Ness, president of the Bank of the Metropolis, suggested that the two brigades under his command be called up on a rotational basis so that at least some force would be on available if a crisis arose. Armstrong did not authorize the request. Van Ness approached the Secretary a second time, after the British fleet had begun collecting ships in the Chesapeake, and received a response that the enemy would not come to Washington, but would strike Baltimore. Van Ness stated to the Investigative Committee:

> "...and I suggested the utility and propriety of ordering out our militia in successive or alternate detachments. I further informed him (which I was authorized to do, by the pressing, voluntary offers of many of my fellow-citizens) that both the citizens and the troops of the District of Columbia, were ready and anxious to be made use of, in any way that the Government might prescribe or direct, for the public good....
>
> At length, in August last, when the increased and reinforced fleet, with the troops, ascended the Chesapeake, and were known, from authentic information, to have entered the Patuxent, I called on Secretary Armstrong again and expressed, as usual, my apprehensions, arising from want of means and preparations, adding that, from the known naval and reputed land force of the enemy, he probably meant to strike a serious blow.
>
> His reply was, 'oh yes! by G__d, they would not come with such a fleet without meaning to strike somewhere, but they certainly will not come here; what the d___ l will they do here,' &c. After remarking that I differed very much from him, as to the probable interest they felt in destroying or capturing our seat of Government, and that I believed a visit to this place would, for several reasons, be a favorite object with them, he observed, 'no, no! Baltimore is the place, sir; that is of so much more consequence.'"

Residents of Alexandria were also very concerned for the lack of solid defensive measures concerning their town, part of the District of Columbia at that time. The town's main protection against an invasion was a river defense, provided by the guns at Fort Warburton, located on the east bank of the Potomac south of their city. As early as May of 1813, doubts were registered to the President that the fort could not withstand a strong attack because the necessary naval arrangements were not in place to stop a British advance. As fears increased the following summer that the English might actually attack the District of Columbia, Alexandria's committee of vigilance sought out Winder and apprised him of the precariousness of Alexandria's defensive position and offered suggestions to better fortify the garrison. The committee requested providing more ammunition, bringing in larger guns, and building additional forts along the Potomac. Israel Thompson, clerk of the Common Council of Alexandria, told the Investigative Committee:

> "In consequence of reports that the enemy contemplated an attack upon the city of Washington, the municipal authority of Alexandria thought it advisable to appoint a committee of vigilance, for the purpose of procuring information of the approaches of the enemy, and of obtaining assistance and advice as to the measures which it might be proper to pursue for protection and defense. As soon as this

committee was appointed, they caused representations to be made to General winder, of the defenceless condition of the town, and earnestly entreated that some measures should be taken for its protection.

General winder was called on, because it had been distinctly understood that the Secretary of War would receive our communications through this channel only. From General Winder every assurance was made that could have been wished, that every thing in his power should be done for the protection of the town. His means, however, were very inconsiderable: he had no money to expend in fortifications, or even in the erection of batteries; and unless some defence of this sort could be obtained, the town would be exposed to the mercy of the enemy if he should approach by water, and should succeed in passing the fort."

The General listened to the committee's concerns and contacted the Secretary of War about Fort Warburton July 25, 1814. He pointed out that the garrison was incomplete in its preparedness for any engagement that might take place against enemy forces and made several requests to remedy the situation. In early August, Winder, the President, and some Cabinet members, inspected the garrison. Winder assured all that he would do everything in his power to protect Alexandria. Yet, Armstrong remained unconvinced of the precariousness of Alexandria's situation and did not devote any energy to improving its defense. He considered improvements to the fort, along with building other batteries along the Potomac, as too expensive. In his opinion, bayonets were all that was required. Armstrong told the Investigative Committee:

"The considerations which governed my own opinion on this subject, and which may have governed that of others, were, that to put Washington *hors d'insulte*, by means of fortifications, would from physical causes, among which is the remoteness from each other of the several points to be defended, have exhausted the treasury; that bayonets are known to form the most efficient barriers:…"

Madison expected his Secretary of War to ensure the safety of the nation's capital from foreign attack, but Armstrong treated the defense of Washington with indifference. He issued orders based on his own judgment, implying the organization and readiness of militia, when only a mere shadow of such forces existed. He was convinced that there was absolutely no direct threat to Washington and felt that keeping militia men in camps, equipping them and drilling in the heat of summer, was expensive and unnecessary. The President, very concerned with Armstrong's attitude about an invasion to the Federal City, had also grown extremely dissatisfied with the Secretary's performance about matters along the Canadian border. He recognized that Armstrong was exceeding the duties of his office by not consulting him on major policies concerning strategy and promotions on the northern front. Even though public confidence in the Secretary of War began to decline, Madison did not dismiss him. On August 13, however, the President sent Armstrong a lengthy letter chastising him for usurping Presidential authority. He outlined specific guidelines concerning the duties of the Secretary of War and ordered Armstrong to clear all future decisions with him:

> "On viewing the course which the proceedings of the War Department have not unfrequently taken, I find that I owe it to my own responsibility as well as to other considerations, to make some remarks on the relations in which the Head of the Department stands to the President, and to lay down some rules for conducting the business of the Department, which are dictated by the nature of those relations.
>
> In general the Secretary of War, like the Heads of the other Depts as well by express statute as by the structure of the constitution, acts under the authority & subject to the decisions & instructions of the President, with the exception of cases where the law may vest special & independent powers in the head of the Department....
>
> Instructions to military Commanders relating to important plans & operations have been issued without any previous or even any subsequent communication thereof to the Executive, and letters expressly intended & proper for the knowledge & decision of the Ex have been recd & acted on without being previously communicated or the measures taken being made known to him....
>
> These rules may omit cases falling within, and embrace cases not entirely within, the reason of them. Experience therefore may improve the rules. In the meantime, they will give a more suitable order & course to the business of the Dept., will conduce to a more certain harmony & cooperation in the proceedings of the several Departments, and will furnish the proper opportunity for the advantage of cabinet consultations on cases of a nature to render them expedient."

The Secretary of War did not resign, but choose a more passive role. Winder, however, understood the seriousness of his appointment, but was inexperienced and lacked forcefulness. In a brief period of time, he traveled to every corner of the Washington-Baltimore-Annapolis triangle inspecting various forts and checking possible positions that could be taken in defense of the capital. He further looked at numerous landing sites, campgrounds and roads that could be used by the enemy in approaching any of the three cities. The General was a whirlwind of activity. He remained in daily communication with Washington by writing copious letters, offering suggestions, giving information and sounding alarm. Yet, no overall plan for defending the 10th Military District ever actually developed. Washington had little in the way of fortifications. Alexandria, the most important city near Washington, was left to fend for herself. He was desperate for men, but did little to get them. He never collected the promised 15,000 militia or 1000 regulars. There was little available ammunition, guns or flints. While some citizen efforts were underway to provide defensive measures for Washington, enemy ships appeared in strong force in mid-August on the Chesapeake Bay. The General reported that he had only been able to collect about 3250 militia troops by this time:

> "When the enemy arrived at the mouth of Potomac, of all the militia which I had been authorized to assemble there were but about 1,700 in the field, from 13 to 1400 under general Stansbury near this place, and about 250 at Bladensburg, under lieutenant colonel Kramer; the slow progress of draft, and the imperfect organization, with the ineffectiveness of the laws to compel them to turn out, rendered it impossible to have procured more."

In expressing his thoughts to Thomas Jefferson later in the year, (December 21, 1814), Monroe wrote that he believed Washington might have been saved if the plans of July 1 had been implemented. He was highly critical of Armstrong. Monroe's view was that there was plenty of time for preparation, but Armstrong refused to recognize the danger to the city. He pointed out that the citizens were divided and their opinions were not taken into consideration. Nothing had been done to stop the advance of the enemy. The day before the fall of Washington was one of extreme alarm, yet, Armstrong continued to treat the matter of an attack with contempt and the forces necessary to defend the nation's capital had not been collected at the assigned locations and formed into an army. Monroe wrote:

> "This city might have been sav'd, had the measures proposed by the President to the heads of depts. on the 1st of July, and advised by them, and order'd by him, been carried into effect. For this there was full time before the attack was made. Whatever may be the merits of General Winder, who is undoubtedly intelligent & brave, an infatuation seemed to have taken possession of Genl. Armstrong, relative to the danger of this place. The representatives of corporate bodies, committees of citizens &c, were slighted & divided both before & after the first of July. As late as the 23 of Aug. when the enemy were within 10 miles, by a direct route & marching against it, he treated the idea with contempt altho there was no serious impediment in their way, for the force intended for its defense, was then to be collected at the places of rendevouz & formed into an army. The battle of the next day gave the city to the enemy."

General William H. Winder (1775-1824), Commander of the 10th Military District, could not make up his mind where the British were headed and kept his forces divided. Many troops were still rushing to Bladensburg when the battle commenced.

As the British advanced, Secretary of War John Armstrong (1758-1843) remained stubbornly consistent in his opinion that they would not attack Washington - Baltimore was their target.

2

THE ENEMY LANDS

The alleged impetus for the invasion was probably the destruction that resulted from several American raids along the Canadian front, particularly the burning and pillaging of public buildings at York, the capital of Upper Canada, in April, 1813. At York, American forces attacked and overwhelmed the British, and the defenders of Fort York withdrew. As the Yankees approached the garrison, the stone magazine blew up, killing at least thirty eight and injuring over two hundred others. Brigadier General Zebulon Pike was among those killed in the explosion. The story that unfolded claimed that angry American soldiers, believing that the fort had been rigged, immediately retaliated on their own initiative, and not under any orders, by burning the public buildings. However, Irving Brant in his book *The Fourth President: The Life of James Madison*, suggested that retaliation on the part of Americans was not anywhere near the excesses as generally described:

> "The truth can be found in official records *of that time*, both Canadian and American. The city was captured on April 27 and capitulated on the 28th. *The Parliament House burned on April 30.* On April 27, a party of sailors looted the public library located in the Elmsley House. There is no doubt about the date. The Reverend John Strachan of York wrote that Commodore Chauncey had gathered up and promised to return the books carried away '*on the 27*

April.' On that same day a detachment of sailors *entered* Parliament House. Commodore Chauncey sent to Secretary Jones 'the British standard taken at York *on the 27th of April* last, accompanied by the mace over which hung a human scalp.' These articles, said Chauncey, 'were taken from the Parliament House *by one of my officers* and presented to me.'

All this was three days before the Parliament House burned. When that fire broke out, Major Grafton, commander of the American detachment *guarding York*, was on horseback less than 300 yards away. He rode over to the burning building, about which a crowd was standing, and asked how the fire started. Nobody knew. 'At this time there was not in sight an American soldier.'

General Dearborn inferred from the reports to him that the building – two connected Wooden 24 X 40 foot halls – was burned by 'some exasperated subjects of Canada.' Of these there were plenty. The general's proclamation against disorder, wrote a York magistrate, 'produced a good effect on the turbulent minds of some wretches of our own population, whose thirst for plunder was more alarming to the inhabitants than the presence of the enemy.'

Citing the fire, the magistrates unitedly requested General Dearborn to restore their civil Functions – a move (as they described the situation to General Sheaffe) to deal with 'a great number of traitorous people who had come from the country.' At the end of the occupation the magistrates sent a message to Dearborn gratefully acknowledging 'a line of conduct so conducive to the protection of a number of individuals, and so honorable to himself.'"

The following summer Governor General George Prevost told Cochrane to raid communities throughout the Chesapeake to retaliate for the depredations at York by "inflicting that measure of retaliation which shall deter the enemy from the repetition of similar outrages." After terrorizing and pillaging the coastal towns, the British developed an amphibious plan to capture the American capital. It was twofold. The first part was to pursue and destroy a very strong American gunboat flotilla, commanded by Commodore Joshua Barney. This flotilla had been harassing the Royal Navy throughout the Chesapeake during the early summer, but was now trapped in the Patuxent River near its head. Once the gunboats were rendered useless, the decision would be made whether to pursue the second part of the plan: the grand attack, the taking of Washington. Occupation was never a consideration. Cochrane wrote to the Secretary of the Admiralty September 27, 1814:

"...and as I had gained information from Rear-Admiral Cockburn, whom I found in the Potowmack, that Commodore Barney, with the Baltimore flotilla, had taken shelter at the head of the Patuxent, this afforded a pretext for ascending that river to attack him near its source, above Pig Point, while the ultimate destination of the combined force was Washington, should it be found that the attempt might be made with any prospect of success."

A three-pronged attack was put into motion. Captain Sir Peter Parker in the 38-gun frigate *Menelaus* was sent into the Upper Bay to prevent Eastern Shore forces from being sent to defend the Federal City. At the same time, Captain James Gordon, in the 38-gun frigate *Seahorse*, led warships up the Potomac River, with the task of destroying Fort Warburton and supporting the army if needed in its attack on the capital. Cochrane, who directed the operations, entered the Patuxent River in his 80-gun warship *Tonnant* with the main thrust of the British fleet under cover of darkness on Thursday, August 18, 1814. With him were two subordinates who would lead the invasion by land and water: Major General Robert Ross and Rear-Admiral Sir George Cockburn. Cochrane continued in the above summarization to the Secretary of the Admiralty:

> "Previously to my entering the Patuxent, I detached Captain Gordon, of his Majesty's ship Seahorse, with that ship and the ships and bombs named in the margin, up the Patowmack, to bombard Fort Washington (which is situated on the left bank of that river, about ten or twelve miles below the city), with a view of destroying that fort, and opening a free communication above, as well as to cover the retreat of the army, should its return by the Bladensburg road be found too hazardous from the accession of strength the enemy might obtain from Baltimore; it was also reasonable to expect, that the militia from the country to the northward and westward would flock in, so soon as it should be known that their capital was threatened.
>
> Captain Sir Peter Parker, in the Menelaus, with some small vessels, was sent up the Chesapeake above Baltimore, to divert the attention of the enemy in that quarter; and I proceeded with the remainder of the naval force and troops, up this river, and landed the army upon the 19th and 20th at Benedict."

As the Patuxent narrowed and became shallower, Cochrane found it necessary to anchor the heavier ships. Before dawn he shifted his troops to lighter vessels, such as frigates, brigs and schooners. He remained behind aboard the *Tonnant*. The invaders sailed further up the river as far as the depth of the water would allow. They anchored that evening roughly eight miles short of Benedict, one of the older settlements in Maryland, located on the west bank of the river. At dawn Friday morning the troops were transferred into boats and barges, and rowed against the flow to the deserted village of Benedict. There an expeditionary force of British regulars, under Ross's command, disembarked. According to George Gleig, a subaltern in the British army, the total number of troops that landed at Benedict amounted to about four thousand five hundred and twenty. He included in his diary:

> "The whole infantry may, therefore, be estimated at four thousand

and twenty men. Besides these, there were landed about a hundred artillery-men, and an equal number of drivers; but for want of horses to drag them, no more than one six-pounder and two small three-pounder guns were brought on shore. Except those belonging to the general and staff-officers, there was not a single horse in the whole army. To have taken on shore a large park of artillery would have been, under such circumstances, absolute folly; indeed, the pieces which were actually landed, proved in the end of very little service, and were drawn by seamen sent from the different ships for the purpose. The sailors thus employed, may be rated at a hundred, and those occupied in carrying stores, ammunition, and other necessaries, at a hundred more; and thus by adding these, together with fifty sappers and miners, to the above amount, the whole number of men landed at St. Benedict's may be computed at four thousand five hundred."

The British made camp at Benedict. The remainder of Friday and most of the following day was spent unloading the ships, resting the troops and organizing them into three brigades. All this was done unhurriedly without any opposition from the Americans. Gleig, who later became a chaplain in the British army, hinted that the delay to move forward was caution on the part of the General, who had a reputation of being a hesitant commander. He wrote:

"As the evening closed in, all the arrangements, customary in bivouacs, were effected. The troops, assembling near their arms, trimmed and enlarged their fires, and sat down by companies and sections on the ground beside them....

Stores continued to be carried from the ships to the shore long after nightfall, and the cry of the seamen on the docks, the splash of oars in the water, and the heavy noise of casks and carriages, as they were rolled into the bivouac, all had an effect in keeping alive the excitement, which men ever experience on first taking the field, after a long interval of quiet.... Nevertheless, we rose in excellent spirits and high good humour, and took post beside our men, in confident expectation that an immediate advance would occur as soon as there should be light enough to direct our steps....

Contrary to the expectations which had been formed, no hint was dropped about moving, and as we all knew General Ross sufficiently to be aware, that there could be no disinclination on his part to carry on the war with vigor, we looked now for some other cause of a delay, which, on every account, we united in deploring. Long previous to the disembarkation, - as early, indeed, as the entrance of the fleet into the bay, - the several regiments had received instructions as to their order; and to each of the three brigades into which the army was divided, a commandant had been appointed. It could not, therefore, be for the purpose of organizing his troops that our leader abstained from advancing. But there were stores to be landed, a medical and commissariat department to be arranged, and dispositions to be made for a speedy and safe reshipment, in case of any reverse or check in our operations.

Besides, it was not quite certain that the end of the debarkation had as yet been determined on. The most prevalent rumour, indeed, spoke of a flotilla of gun-boats on the river; and of the necessity of a co-operation between the fleet and the army, to secure its capture; but whether even now, the general or admiral were not calculating their means for the attainment of a higher object, is, to say, the least of it, doubtful. Be this, however, as it may, one thing appeared very certain, namely, that there was but a slender chance of our effecting anything, or making any progress, during the day."

Unexpectedly the bugle sounded late Saturday afternoon. The three brigades quickly formed into a column, with Ross leading on horseback. Wearing their traditional scarlet woolen uniforms, British soldiers began marching north under a shimmering August sun. In concert with the column, a miniature fleet of armed boats, tenders and other small craft loaded with seamen and marines under the command of Cockburn began moving up the Patuxent in the direction of Nottingham, in pursuit of Barney's gunboats. The British column stayed near the riverbank, marching parallel to the ships in case the army was needed in capturing the American flotilla. The march that afternoon in the heat and humidity was of short duration - about four miles from Benedict; however, the task was made more difficult by the weight of at least sixty pounds of food, clothing, weapons and ammunition carried by each soldier. There were no supply wagons. Each soldier carried his own provisions. Gleig continued:

"Our messes were just laid upon the grass, and we had taken our seats beside them, when the bugles suddenly sounded. Mortified, as it was but natural that we should be, at an occurrence so ill-timed, there remained for us only one course to pursue. We took each in his hand as much meat and bread as he believed that he should be able to consume whilst on the march, and the rest was unceremoniously bestowed in our own and our men's haversacks; we buckled on our accoutrements, and slung our baggage on our backs and hurried off to our stations.... The different corps had already taken their stations, and were in anxious expectation of the word to march, when, about four o'clock in the afternoon, General Ross, accompanied by his aides-de-camp and staff, rode up. No preconcerted plan had been arranged, nor had the slightest wish been expressed on the part of the officers; but his appearance among them was hailed by loud and reiterated shouts from the men. The thing was wholly involuntary, and it failed not to cause the gratification which it was calculated to produce. The General pulled off his hat, smiled and bowed to the soldiers; and then addressing himself to the officer in command, desired that he would lead on. Another hearty cheer followed the delivery of this order, and the march, began."

Courtesy Naval Historical Center

Commander Josuha Barney (1759-1819) was ordered to destroy his gunboat flotilla trapped at Pig Point in the Patuxent to keep it from falling into enemy hands.

Courtesy Naval Historical Center

The Naval Secretary William Jones (1760-1831) ordered both the flotilla and navy yard burned. Naval protection was not provided for the capital area as enemy ships steadily advanced up the Potomac River and captured Alexandria.

3

ACTING SCOUT MONROE

Even though there was uncertainty about the objective of the invading forces, inhabitants of Washington were hastily boarding up their homes and leaving the city. Armstrong continued to take lightly the ominous signals of an impending attack upon the nation's capital, still insisting that Washington had no strategic value and Baltimore, America's fourth largest city, was the intended target, or possibly Annapolis. Both the President and the Secretary of State, held a different opinion - the destruction of the capital of the United States was the intended goal. At this time, officials had received only basic information from spies near the bay that foreign ships were ascending both the Potomac and Patuxent Rivers. Since the government had no official intelligence operations at this time, Monroe, who had scouted under Captain William Washington during the Revolutionary War, volunteered his services in this capacity:

> "Calling on the President on the morning of the 18th of August, he
> informed me that the enemy had entered the Patuxent in considerable
> force, and were landing at Benedict. I remarked that this city was
> their object. He concurred in the opinion. I offered to proceed
> immediately to Benedict, with a troop of horse, to observe their force,
> report it, with my opinion of their objects, and, should they advance
> on this city, to retire before them, of communicating regularly their

movements to the Government. This proposal was acceded to."

Monroe, hoping to set out Thursday evening, promptly contacted the Secretary of War and the Commander of the 10th Military District, requesting cavalry support for a mission to scout the movements of the British and send back information to the government. In his letter to Armstrong, he again stressed that he felt Washington was in greater danger than any other place:

> "Washington, Aug. 18, 1814
>
> Dear Sir, - The movements of the enemy menaces this place among others, and this, I conceive, in a more imminent degree than any other. In aid of the measures of the Government I should be happy to proceed with a troop of horse to the coast opposite the enemy, from which point I will advise you of their force & objects so far as I may be able to collect them, & should they land, retire before them. It would be agreeable to me to set out this evening. Should you approve the suggestion, I will thank you to give an order to Genl. Van Ness to supply the force necessary."

Both men agreed to Monroe's request and quickly sent him to reconnoiter the enemy, also supplying him with needed cavalry support from Captain William Thornton's Alexandria troops of the Columbian Dragoons. Monroe left the city on Friday and arrived near Benedict within sight of the enemy's squadron the following morning, where he established an observation operation. So desperate was the need for accurate information that none thought it strange that a Cabinet official, the Secretary of State, led a scouting party. Winder later reported to the Investigative Committee:

> "On Thursday evening, Colonel Monroe proposed, if I would detach a troop of cavalry with him, to proceed in the most probable direction to find the enemy, and reconnoitre him. Captain Thornton's troop from Alexandria, was detailed on this service, and, on Friday morning, the Colonel departed with them. At this time, is was supposed the enemy intended coming up the Bay, as one of his ships was already in view from Annapolis, and his boats were sounding South river. It was Colonel Monroe's intention to have proceeded direct to Annapolis, but before he had got without the city, he received intelligence that the enemy had proceeded up the Patuxent, and were debarking at Benedict. He therefore bent his course to that place."

Lookouts for Barney, whose flotilla of gunboats was now hidden near the village of Nottingham, had been closely observing the British activities throughout the Chesapeake. Once the enemy fleet entered the Patuxent, a count was taken of the various ships and sent to the Commodore. Most alarming was a statement confirming Barney's view that Cockburn was after the flotilla, but that the Admiral also planned to dine in the nation's capital on Sunday. Even though it was unclear how the information was obtained, its detail appeared credible. Barney forwarded the intelligence gained to the Navy Secretary Friday morning:

"Nottingham, August 19 - 9 A.M.
Sir - One of my officers has this moment arrived from the mouth of the Patuxent, and brings the enclosed account. I haste to forward it to you; the Admiral said, he would dine in Washington on Sunday, after having destroyed the flotilla, &c.

One 80 or 90 gun ship, flag at the main.

Four 74 gun ships, one flag at mizzen.

Six frigates.

Ten ships, about 32 guns.

Five small ships.

Two brigs.

One large schooner, 16 guns.

Two smaller schooners about 10 guns.

Thirteen large bay craft.

A large number of small boats are now under way, standing up the Patuxent, with a number of men, with a determination to go to the city of Washington, as they said yesterday."

Monroe set up his reconnaissance position on Saturday nearly three miles from the village port. He observed the landing, but had difficulty estimating the enemy's strength because he did not have a telescope. That afternoon he reported from Aquasco Mills to Madison that the British were debarking their ships in force at Benedict. His opinion was that America's seat of government was the target and suggested that preparations promptly be undertaken for its defense:

"Acquasco Mills, seven miles from Benedict,
August 20, 1814, one o'clock, P. M.
Dear Sir:
I arrived here this morning at eight o'clock, and have been since within four miles of Benedict, at Butler's mill, where it was reported the enemy, on their march, had arrived. The report was unfounded. The enemy landed yesterday at Benedict, and had advanced their pickets within a mile and a half of that mill, for security only. From a height between that mill and the Patuxent, I had a view of their shipping; but being at the distance of three miles, and having no glass, we could not count them. We shall take better views in the

course of the evening, and should anything be seen, material, I will immediately advise you of it. The general idea is, that they are still debarking their troops, the number of which I have not obtained any satisfactory information of. The general idea also is, that Washington is their object, but of this I can form no opinion at this time. The best security against this attempt is an adequate preparation to repel it."

The above note was written three hours before the British broke camp and left Benedict at four o'clock on Saturday. Monroe apparently thought that the British would remain at that location until the next day and, unable to do much without his much needed spyglass, rode to Charlotte Hall, a nearby school, where he spent the night. When he returned the following morning to view the activities at Benedict, he was surprised that he saw no enemy troops. He carefully counted twenty-three square rigged anchored vessels, which were the main part of the fleet left behind under the command of Cochrane, but few barges. This confirmed his suspicion that the invading forces were intent on destroying Barney's flotilla before attempting an attack on Washington. He wrote again to the President apprising him of the situation:

"Horse Road, 21st, August, 1814
Dear Sir, - I quartered last night near Charlotte Hall, and took a view this morning at 8 oclock, from a commanding height, below Benedict creek, of all the enemy's shipping near the town, and down the river to the distance at least of 8 or 10 miles. I counted 23 sq: rigged vessels. Few others were to be seen, & very few barges. I inferred from the latter circumstance that the enemy had moved up the river, either against Com: Barry's flotilla at Nottingham, confining their views to that object, or taking that in their way & aiming at the city, in combination with the force on Powtowmac, of which I have correct information.

I had, when I left Aquasco Mills last night, intended to have passed over to the Powtowmac, after giving you an account of the vessels from the height below Benedict: but on observing the very tranquil scene which I have mentioned, I was led by the inference I draw from it to hasten back to take a view of the enemy's movements in this quarter, which it might be more important to the govt. to be made acquainted with. I am now on the main road from Washington to Benedict, 12 miles from the latter, & find that no troops have passed in this direction. The reports make it probable that a force by land and water has been sent against the flotilla. I shall proceed with Capt. Thos. Trist immediately to Nottingham, and write you thence whatever may be deserving notice.

The enemy have plundered the country to the distance of 3 or 4 miles of all their stock &c. The intelligence of the enemy's force in the Potowmack varies here as much as in Washington. I have had no means of forming a correct estimate of it."

4

BARNEY'S FLOTILLA DESTROYED

The Redcoats began their march early Sunday and, keeping a steadily amphibious advance up the Patuxent, headed toward the hamlet of Nottingham, where they thought Barney's gunboats were hidden. The August heat and humidity, combined with the lengthy confinement of the troops onboard the English ships, soon began to show. Mixed with the sixty pounds of weight each soldier carried and their heavy uniforms, men lagged behind or simply dropped by the wayside. Ross never slowed the advance. After an exhausting march, including a few rounds fired at American riflemen, they reached a completely deserted Nottingham, only to discover that the flotilla was not there. Gleig described the area and the disappointment of not finding Barney's fleet of boats:

> "For several miles in every direction the country was in a high state of cultivation; though, instead of the maize and wheat which we had hitherto seen, the fields were covered with an abundant and luxuriant crop of tobacco. This plant seems, indeed, to be at all times the staple commodity of that district; for, besides what was growing and unripe, we found numerous barns filled with the remains of last year's crop; the whole of which was, of course, seized in the name of His Majesty King George the Third.

But in the main object of our pursuit we were disappointed. The flotilla, which had been stationed opposite to Nottingham, retired, on our approach, higher up the stream; and we were consequently in the situation of a huntsman who sees his hounds at fault, and has every reason to apprehend that his game will escape."

Before the enemy reached Nottingham, Barney, recognizing that his flotilla was trapped and there was no escape, moved his boats as far up the Patuxent as practical. This was Pig Point, located on the eastern side of the river, closer to Upper Marlborough. There he had his boats rigged for demolition. Then, with four hundred of his crewmen, he abandoned his vessels and, taking as much equipment as possible, headed inland to join the American forces gathering at the Wood Yard, under Winder's command. A skeleton crew, with Lieutenant Solomon Frazier in charge, was left behind with orders to destroy the entire flotilla if necessary, per the instructions of the Naval Secretary. Jones offered:

> "On the 18th of August the Secretary received the first intelligence of the reinforcement of the enemy; the day on which they landed at Benedict. Commodore Barney was ordered to destroy his flotilla whenever it appeared certain that it would otherwise be captured, and to unite and co-operate with the forces under command of General Winder."

Monroe was able to precede the invading forces into Nottingham Sunday afternoon. He found a good position to watch their movements, and patiently waited until the enemy came into view. It was dusk before the head of the exhausted, perspiring column of enemy soldiers, finally came into his sight. This was followed by three British barges rowing up the Patuxent. As the scout for the government, this was his first glimpse of the enemy. He quickly wrote alerting Winder, who was assembling American forces at the Wood Yard, roughly midway from Bladensburg in the north and Benedict in the south. Before sending his message, the river became alive with further activity as more of Cockburn's small fleet advanced and he added another two lines, reporting that there were more foreign vessels than what was first observed:

> "Nottingham, August 21, 1814
>
> Sir:
>
> The enemy are now within four hundred yards of the shore. There are, but three barges at hand, and their force in view is not considerable. If you send five or six hundred men, if you could not save the town, you may, perhaps, cut off their retreat or rear.
>
> P.S. Ten or twelve more barges in view. There are but two muskets in town, and a few scattering militia.
>
> Five o'clock. Thirty or forty barges are in view."

Monroe correctly assumed that this amphibious movement was the same force that disembarked at Benedict. He conferred with Colonel William Beall of Annapolis, who had also been watching the advancing Redcoats, but from a more commanding height. Together they were able to form a fairly accurate idea of the enemy numbers and strength. They concluded that the British infantry consisted of an amount between four and five thousand soldiers and there were possibly another one thousand men in the barges. Before fleeing from Nottingham later that night for the American camp at the Wood Yard, Monroe informed the President of the estimated strength of the enemy:

> "In retiring from Nottingham, late in the evening of the 21st, after writing a note to the President, I observed a column of the enemy in the rear of the town, which I concluded had passed from Benedict by a road near the river, moving in concert with the barges. The number I could not ascertain, having seen its head only. I went immediately to Mr. Oden's, where I met Colonel Beall, whom I had before seen at Nottingham. He had taken a view of the enemy's column from a commanding height contiguous to the town. From his statement we both concluded that it must have amounted to between four and five thousand men. The force in the barges was supposed to exceed one thousand; so that the whole force of the enemy might be estimated at about six thousand.
>
> Hearing that General Winder was at the Woodyard, I hastened to him. He had there about two thousand two hundred men, consisting of the marines, Colonel Lavall's cavalry, and the city and Georgetown militia. I understood that he either then gave orders, or repeated those he had before given, to a part of the militia at Baltimore, and to Colonel Beall, who commanded six or seven hundred at Annapolis, to move towards Bladensburg to his support."

Monroe, in his efforts to fully access the strength of the invading forces, remained in Nottingham, observing the advance as long as possible. The *Richmond Enquirer* reported that he was almost captured when exiting the town:

> "Colonel Monroe was near being taken, having been at Nottingham, when they arrived, got out of one side of the town while they were marching at the other."

Madison upon receiving Monroe's dispatch from Nottingham late that night immediately responded, expressing surprise that the invasionary force was not larger than previously estimated and at their lack of any cavalry support. He commented that if there were to be an invasion, the British had separated themselves a good distance from their ships. Even more interesting, was the President's remark that he had received little information about Gordon's squadron ascending the Potomac:

                                                                    "August 21, 1814
Dear Sir: I recd. yours of 11 P. M. about 20 minutes ago. You will
hear from Genl. A. or myself by other express who will leave this
about 9 or 10 o'C. If the force of the Enemy be not greater than yet
appears, & he be without Cavalry, it seems extraordinary that he shd.
venture on an enterprize to this distance from his shipping. He may
however count on the effect of boldness & celerity on his side, and
the want of precaution on ours. He may be bound also to do
something, & therefore to risk everything. We know little of what is
passing in the Potowmac. A company of regular recruits from Va.
arrived here last evening. Nothing new from the North or from
abroad."

Ross set up headquarters Sunday night at Nottingham, but was
cautious and, as Madison had observed, concerned that his troops were
some distance from the main fleet anchored on the Patuxent below
Benedict. The British had not yet found Barney. The General's orders
were that he was "not to engage in any extended operations at a distance
from the coast." An inland campaign without cavalry, little artillery,
minimal number of troops, vague intelligence and no support from
Cochrane's guns would be putting the British forces at great risk.
Returning to the fleet seemed appropriate. Coming ashore, Cockburn
argued that they couldn't turn back because they had encountered little
resistance and he felt Barney's flotilla was within their grasp. The
General acquiesced and the next day, continued moving his infantry
forward. Gleig's observations were the following:

> "In this posture the army continued during the night, having its right
> defended by the river, and its left extending considerably beyond the
> town, and secured, as usual, by a connected chain of outposts; nor
> was it put in motion, as had been done the day before, as soon as
> there was sufficient light to distinguish objects. There seemed,
> indeed, to be something like hesitation as to the course to be pursued,
> - whether to follow the gun-boats, or to return to the shipping; but, at
> last, the former proceeding was resolved upon, and the column set
> forward about eight o'clock, in the direction of Marlborough, another
> village, about ten miles beyond Nottingham."

Receiving the combined report offered by Monroe and Beall at
the Wood Yard, Winder promptly acted by again calling for additional
forces. Thus far, he had been able to gather a little over 2000 troops. He
could not make up his mind where the British were headed, but was of
the opinion that they would march west toward the Potomac River, attack
Fort Warburton and join Gordon's forces ascending the river before
striking at Washington. Sunday night he sent orders to Brigadier General
Tobias Stansbury and Lieutenant Colonel Joseph Sterett, who were
commanding separate contingents of Maryland Militia, to move south
from their camps near Baltimore to Bladensburg so that they would be in

positions to defend Washington from that end if necessary. Stansbury's brigade arrived the following evening, but it was not until Tuesday night that Sterett's regiment of about eight hundred reached Bladensburg. Stansbury reported:

> "August 22, at ten o'clock A.M. received from General Winder letter
> No 3, dated at the Woodyard, the 21st, ten o'clock P.M. directing me
> to advance with all speed to Bladensburg. In consequence thereof,
> the line of march was taken up immediately, and at seven o'clock
> P.M. we arrived at Bladensburg."

Winder considered a surprise attack. This was put into motion early Monday even though he was greatly outnumbered. He began by sending an advance corps of infantry, artillery and cavalry units in the direction of Nottingham to take positions and observe the approaching enemy. The General, his staff and Monroe followed in that direction, headquartering at Benjamin Oden's farmhouse, located about a half mile short of a fork in the road - the junction of the Wood Yard and Marlboro Roads. The west prong of the fork, down which the Americans had marched, connected with Washington, the east prong went to Upper Marlboro, and the road that the enemy was advancing upon came from Nottingham. Winder reasoned that if the British chose the right hand fork to Upper Marlboro, then the flotilla and possibly Baltimore were the targets; but if they chose the left hand fork, then they were headed for Fort Warburton and the capital. His remaining troops were positioned in line of attack down the Wood Yard Road in expectation that the British would take the western fork and march in the direction of Washington. The Americans patiently waited for the arrival of the enemy. John Law, a Baltimore artilleryman, wrote:

> "The main body of the enemy stayed that night at or near
> Nottingham, having an advance party stationed at a church about
> three miles this side of that town. About one o'clock the same night,
> our troops were beat up and ordered to strike their tents; although the
> principal part of the force did not move until nine or ten o'clock the
> next morning. About sunrise the regulars, together with a small
> detachment of about three hundred men, consisting of Captain Peter's
> company of artillery, Captain Stull's rifle corps, and Captain
> Davidson's light infantry, were sent in advance on the road to
> Nottingham. About nine or ten o'clock the same day, the remainder
> of our force marched about a mile, to an elevated position near the
> dwelling house of Mrs. West, and remained there about two hours,
> under the expectation that the enemy would take that road on his way
> from Nottingham to Washington."

After reaching an agreement with Cockburn to maintain the amphibious advance, Ross abandoned Nottingham early Monday morning to continue the pursuit of Barney's flotilla. The column had difficulty keeping up with Cockburn's squad because the road gradually cut inland from the river. Long before reaching the fork in the road, an advance team encountered Yankee cavalry, under the command of Lieutenant Colonel Jacint Lavall. An inauspicious confrontation took place, without injury to either side. The American horsemen retired. Gleig continued:

> "The advance parties having arrived at the more open country which surrounds Marlborough , found themselves suddenly in the presence of two squadrons of well-mounted, and handsomely-appointed cavalry. They were composed, as we afterwards learned, of gentlemen volunteers in the service of their country. To do them justice, the troopers no sooner saw our men, than they made a spirited effort to cut down one or two files, which appeared to be separated from their companions, and at a distance from the wood. But a single discharge from another party which they had not observed, instantly checked them; and they galloped off."

When the Redcoats arrived at the fork in the road, Ross halted the march, while deciding which route to take. While he was consulting with advisors and making up his mind, American forces were forming battle positions further down the Wood Yard Road. Both Winder and Monroe believed that the enemy was in full march for Washington with the intention of attacking the American army. Ross finally did turn his column west down the Wood Yard Road in the direction of Washington, but, realizing that he was leading his men away from Cockburn's boats, he changed his mind and redirected his column towards Upper Marlboro. Unfortunately Monroe had already apprised the President of the situation by writing:

> "The enemy are advanced six miles on the road to the Wood Yard, and our troops retiring. Our troops were on the march to meet them, but in too small a body to engage. general W. proposes to retire till he can collect them in a body. The enemy are in full march for Washington. Have the materials prepared to destroy the bridges."
>
> Monday, 9 o'clock. You had better remove the records."

The American troops were eager for an engagement. To their dismay, Winder did not attack or even pursue the unsuspecting enemy. Instead, the General hastily withdrew the American forces back to the Wood Yard, where they were joined by Barney and his sailors. Later that day, the entire American Army was moved from the Wood Yard to Long Old Fields (now Forestville), roughly equidistant from both Washington and Bladensburg. Law continued:

> "It was, however, ascertained that the enemy had taken the road to Upper Marlborough, and that the detachment of our troops, who had

been sent that morning in advance, were retreating. All the troops were then ordered to retreat; and, instead of being marched towards Upper Marlborough, where the enemy remained that night, (waiting, it is presumed, to be joined by the detachment which had been sent against Commodore Barney's flotilla) we were marched to the Battalion Old Fields, about eight miles distant from Upper Marlborough, and about the same distance from Washington. The same day we were joined by the crews of Commodore Barney's flotilla."

After observing the enemy throughout the morning, Winder concluded that the surprise engagement was too great a risk. Being heavily outnumbered (over two to one) was certainly a consideration in his decision, but perhaps he simply realized that at this time his untrained militia troops were no match for the seasoned veterans. Thus, while the American army was retreating, the enemy forces continued to advance in the summer's humidity and heat of the August sun. After retiring his troops back to the Wood Yard, Winder left with a few cavalry scouts and spent further hours observing the British at Upper Marlboro before returning to the camp. Winder wrote:

"A doubt, at that time, was not entertained by any body of the intention of the enemy to proceed direct to Washington, and the advantage of dividing their force, and proceeding on two roads running so near each other, to the same point, so obvious, that I gave orders to Scott and Peter to retire, and occupy the first eligible position between the junction of that road and the one we were on, and the Woodyard; dispatched a patrol of cavalry to observe that road, and give the earliest notice of any advance of the enemy upon it. I still continued the observation of the enemy myself, and he turned a part of his column into the road to the Woodyard, and penetrated a skirt of wood, which hid the junction of the Marlborough and Woodyard road from view, and there halted it within a quarter of a mile of Oden's house....

It appeared afterwards that his whole force halted here for an hour or upwards, and thus continued in an uncertainty as to his intended route. I had, in the mean time, rode back and assisted Peter and Scott to post their detachments in a favorable position, from whence I entertained a hope to have given the enemy a serious check, without much risk to this detachment.... As soon as I had satisfied myself as to the position and disposition of Scott's and Peter's detachments, I advanced again towards the enemy, to ascertain his situation and intentions. It had now become certain that he had taken the road to Marlborough; and Colonel Monroe crossed over to that place, to join Lieutenant Colonel Tilghman, and observe his movements.

I sent an order immediately to Scott and Peter, to retire back to General Smith, and the latter to take post the points where the roads from Washington city and the Woodyard, to Marlborough, unite.... It further became necessary to retire still further back, and the only position where the troops could be tolerably accommodated, or posted to advantage, was at Dunlap's, or, as it is generally called, the Long, or Battalion Old Fields"

As Winder's forces were returning to the Wood Yard and Ross's troops were advancing towards Upper Marlboro, distant explosions reverberated throughout the countryside. Both armies knew what this meant: Cockburn, with his Marines, had finally found the flotilla. Barney was nowhere in sight. After preparing seventeen boats for demolition Sunday evening, the Commodore had left with most of his flotillamen to link up with Winder's army, leaving behind a skeletal crew. The seamen arrived at the Wood Yard Monday about noon, to meet the bulk of the militia forces just returning from its uneventful march to and from Nottingham. As the British closed in on the flotillia "for the kill," Cockburn realized that the boats were rigged to explode. He halted his approach as the remaining flotillamen began blowing up their abandoned boats one by one, beginning with the *Scorpion*, to prevent their capture. Sixteen vessels of the flotilla were destroyed. One boat survived and was seized, along with thirteen merchant ships found nearby. A few American seamen were captured. The way was now open for the invaders to begin their assault on Washington City. That evening, Cockburn sent his report to Cochrane informing him of the complete annihilation of the American flotilla:

> "On approaching Pig Point, where the enemy flotilla is said to be, I landed the Marines under Captain Robyns on the left bank of the river and directed him to march round and attack on the land side of the town situated on the point, to draw from us the attention of such troops as might be there for its defence and the defence of the flotilla. I then proceeded with the boats, and as we opened the reach above Pig Point I plainly discovered Commodore Barney's broad pendant in the headmost vessel, a large sloop, and the remainder of the flotilla extending in a long line astern of her.
>
> Our boats now advanced towards them as rapidly as possible, but on nearing them we observed the sloop bearing the broad pendant to be on fire, and she very soon afterwards blew up. I now saw clearly that they were all abandoned and on fire with trains to their magazines, and out of the seventeen vessels which composed this formidable and so much vaunted flotilla, sixteen were in quick succession blown to atoms, and the seventeenth, in which the fire had not taken, we captured.
>
> The Commodore's sloop was a large armed vessel, the others were gun boats all having a long gun in the bow and a cannonade in the stern, but the caliber of the guns and members of the crew of each differed in proportion to the size of the boat, varying from 32 pounders and 60 men to 18 pounders and 40 men. I found here laying about the flotilla under its protection, thirteen merchant schooners, some of which not being worth bringing away. I caused to be burnt. Such as were in good condition, I directed to be moved

to Pig Point. Whilst employed taking these vessels, a few shots were fired at us by some of the men of the flotilla from the bushes on the shore near us, but Lieutenant Scott whom I had landed for that purpose soon got hold of them and made them prisoners. Some whose men likewise shewed themselves on the neighbouring heights, but a rocket or two dispersed them, and Captain Robyns who had got hold of Pig Point without resistance, now spreading his men through the country. The enemy retreated to a distance and left us in quiet possession of the town, the neighborhood and our prisoners."

In a letter, later printed in the *Niles Register*, to James Pleasants, a Congressman from Virginia, Barney described the destruction of the flotilla. He pointed out that the enemy was firing on the Americans with cannon and rockets when the order was given to blow up the vessels. He reconfirms that his orders from the Secretary of the Navy were to keep the boats above the enemy and destroy them if attacked:

"Baltimore, Oct. 30th, 1814

Hon. Mr. Pleasants,

Sir --- It was not until this morning that I saw a short sketch of the debate of the 'Flotilla bill.' I was much surprised at what was said on that occasion; for it was well known when *orders* were given to *blow up* the flotilla, that the enemy were firing upon them from 40 barges with cannon and rockets, and had landed a body of marines at Pig Point, within a mile of the flotilla. The orders from the Secretary of the Navy to me, were to keep the flotilla above the enemy, and if they attempted to march for Washington, to land my men, leaving sufficient to destroy the flotilla if attacked....

On Sunday, 21st of August, finding the enemy on the road to the Wood-Yard direct for Washington, I landed upwards of four hundred men, leaving only eight men in each barge to take care of them or *destroy them* as the case might be, but by no means to suffer them to fall into the hands of the enemy;... On Monday morning the 22nd, we joined the army at the Wood-Yard, where I found the marine corps and five pieces of heavy artillery, which the secretary of the navy had the precaution to send forward from Washington and place under my command....

So far from being able to get 'farther up the river,' as was said, the vessels were aground, and blown up in that situation; and as to having time to save the baggage, so contrary is the truth, that several of the men were taken prisoners in the act of destroying the flotilla, and still remain so. Much more might be said on this subject, but the winter coming on imperiously calls for some assistance to these unfortunate men."

Upon receiving Monroe's hasty message Monday morning, that the British were advancing down the Wood Yard Road and Winder had fallen back, an alarmed President lost no time in responding, confirming that plans to secure the official documents were already underway. He further added that as soon as any assistance was available, he would hurry it on, but felt that any encounter with the enemy would be over before such help would arrive. Madison included his latest information concerning Gordon's squadron ascending the Potomac, but these reports continued to be sketchy and unreliable. Armstrong remained passive and Winder focused his attention on the amphibious advance up the Patuxent. The area surrounding the village of Bladensburg had emerged as the most likely spot where a battle would take place. Madison included in his letter that Colonel Decius Wadsworth was supervising defensive measures in that locality. Madison wrote:

"August 22, 1814
10 O'C. A.M.

Dear Sir:

Since nine of this morning Tatham has come and speaks of reinforcements to the first Column of the Enemy at Nottingham. Taylor, I understand is also here just from Parker, with a report that the Enemy have 3000 in the Potowmac. This must be a great exaggeration, if there be not more shipping than we know of. It wd. seem not improbable that if they have land force of any sensible importance, that it would be equal to some distinct object, otherwise it wd. not be taken from the real operative force. It is sd. Parker is moving up parallel with the frigates; but at what point they were I do not learn.

I take for granted that there are arrangements where you are for quick intelligence from every important point. The papers of all the Officers are underway to retired places. I fear not much can be done more than has been done to strengthen the hands of Genl. W. As fast as succorers arrive here they be will hastened on, but the crisis I presume will be of such short duration, that but few Even from the neighboring County will be on the ground before it is over. Genl. Douglas's Brigade will receive another spur, so will the Militia who are to rendevouz at a Church in Fairfax near this. Wadsworth is taking measures for defensive works on the road about Bladensbg.

It appears that the reinforcements in Canada, amount to 8 or 10,000."

5

PANIC IN WASHINGTON

Residents still in the Federal City, who had been fearful, now panicked. Most who had not already left, hastily bundled what they could gather together, boarded up their homes and fled into the wooded countryside. The dry and dusty August roads were completely clogged with desperate refugees clinging to any belongings they could wheel or carry. Wagons, carts, mules and horses were at a premium. The banks sent their specie away. On Monday, lawyer Francis Scott Key somehow obtained two wagons in Fredericktown, Maryland where he had sent his children, and brought them back to his home in Georgetown to take his papers and personal belongings out of the city. On Tuesday the president of the Bank of Washington Samuel Smith, and his wife Margaret, sent household items to the Quaker village of Brookville, Maryland. That night they fled the city with their family and servants after being roused in the middle of the night by Willie Bradley, a messenger who informed them that the enemy had arrived. It sounded ominous. He announced that Winder had retreated and explicitly told them they should go. Mrs. Smith was a copious letter writer. In writing to her sister, Jane Bayard Kirkpatrick, she said that by Tuesday the women and children were removed from the city, but most of its inhabitants were convinced that the Americans would win. She further wrote:

"The alarm was such that on Monday a general removal from the city and George Town took place. Very few women or children remain'd in the city on Tuesday evening, altho' the accounts then received were that the enemy were retreating. Our troops were eager for an attack and such was the cheerful alacrity they display'd, that a universal confidence reign'd among the citizens and people. Few doubted our conquering. On Tuesday we sent off to a private farm house all our linen, clothing and other movable property….

We were roused on Tuesday night by a loud knocking, - on the opening of the door, Willie Bradley called to us, 'The enemy are advancing, our own troops are giving way on all sides and are retreating to the city. Go, for Gods sake go'…. We immediately rose, the carriage and horses were soon ready, we loaded a wagon with what goods remained and about 3oclock left our house with all our servants, the women we sent to some private farm houses at a safe distance, while we pursued our course."

A fifteen year old teenager from New England was visiting Washington during the spring and summer of 1814. She arrived in May and stayed at the residence of Benjamin Homans, chief clerk at the Navy Department. Miss. Brown, whose given name remains unknown, later related through a personal interview many of her adventures during the invasion. She recalled:

"These festival times did not last long. The news soon came that the British had landed at Benedict, the scene of former ravages, about thirty miles below us on the river. Then we hear of fifty-one British ships in Chesapeake Bay. The military are ordered out, those of Pennsylvania, Maryland, and Virginia, by order of General Armstrong, Secretary of War, commanded to be in readiness in case an attack should be made. The public officials began packing up their valuable papers to be removed to places of safety. Now all is hurry and panic, armies gathering, troops moving in all directions, the citizens trying to secure such things as were most valuable and most easily transported, and flying from their homes to the country, Mr. Homans, in whose family I was a visitor, among the number.

What became of the Secretary of State I do not remember, but much of his household furniture, together with the books and papers of the Department, were put on board of sundry flour boats and committed to the guardianship of Mr. Homans, who sent them up the Potomac. Himself and family, including myself, retreated to the residence of Mr. Obed Rich on the Georgetown Heights. There in that lovely retreat it was decided to tarry and watch the further development of affairs, while the boats rested at the entrance of the canal round the Little Falls of the Potomac, ready at any alarm to push up the river to a more remote place.

My mother and sister had been invited to sojourn with some English friends in Georgetown and were enabled to visit us while we remained at the house of Mr. Rich. My brother had been entrusted with the books and papers of the Post Office with which he was connected. He was a youth of about nineteen years, this circumstance affords fine illustration of the panic which overwhelmed the minds of public men. After he had seen his important charge safely deposited in the cellar of a farmhouse far from all suspicion of the enemy he with the ardor of youth made frequent visits to the city to see for himself what was going on.

Mr. Madison was with the army and Mrs. Madison, with such assistance as in the confusion could be obtained, was bravely endeavoring to secure what she could in the White House."

Officials at government agencies had been preparing for this moment once the enemy landed at Benedict, and they were doing their utmost to hastily pack documents and transport them away from the capital for hiding. At the Senate, Lewis Machen placed documents into the single wagon he was able to obtain and secured them near Brookville. Captain Elias Caldwell, the chief clerk, was unavailable to help because he had been called to ready the District's cavalry. William Thornton, designer of the Capitol building, supervised the packing and moving of Patent Office papers and had them hauled to his farm located in what later became Bethesda, Maryland. Thornton was unable to remove the patent models to safety because they were too numerous and cumbersome. These remained behind in Blodgett's Hotel, located at the northeast corner of 8th and E Streets, which housed both the Patent Office and the Post Office. J. T. Frost and Samuel Burch, clerks at the House of Representatives, were able to secure some records from the House beginning Monday and took them to a location outside the city. Both later stated that everything could possibly have been saved, including the contents of the Library of Congress, had they been able to obtain carts and wagons. Clerks at the Navy Department received notice by Saturday to secure documents so that they could be ferried up the Potomac River. On Tuesday the cargo bypassed the Little Falls, going through the locks of the two and a half mile Little Falls Skirting Canal, which was completed in 1795. The boats remained hidden on the river above the Little Falls until brought back to Washington. Homans described the following:

"In obedience to the instructions from the Secretary of the Navy, to prepare for the removal and safety of the public documents and archives of the Navy Department, on Saturday the 20th day of August, 1814, anticipating a difficulty in procuring wagons, he sanctioned the transportation by water, in boats up the Potomac river.

On Sunday, three of the clerks were employed packing up in boxes and trunks, all the books of record, papers, library, maps, charts, plans, stationary, trophies, various valuable instruments, paintings, prints, &c. ready for removal on the next day; and in the evening of

Sunday, the 21st of August, two river boats, with their crews were engaged for the purpose at the ordinary pay and wages.

On Monday, the 22d August, two of the city carts were engaged, and all the boxes and articles in the Navy Department (heavy desks and furniture excepted,) were put on board a boat at the nearest wharf to the offices, and at 4 P.M. proceeded up the river as far as Georgetown....

On Tuesday, the 23d August, the chief clerk, with one of the clerks of the Department, proceeded up the river Potomac, and passed through the locks and canal to a place of safety. There was no difficulty in procuring more boats and men to navigate them up the river above the falls."

Mordecai Booth, a clerk with the Navy Department, received instructions from the Commandant of the Washington Navy Yard, Commodore Thomas Tingey, for the dangerous job of procuring wagons and removing the powder from the Naval Magazine to a place of safety. Booth spent a difficult Monday trying to find and impress wagons. There were not many to be had and his job became even more difficult when the Navy Secretary told him to impress additional teams and take supplies to Barney and his flotillamen. He returned to the navy yard that evening after only obtaining five wagons. Booth later wrote a lengthy, descriptive report to Tingey of his activities during the invasion. In his account of hiding the powder, Booth reported:

"Navy Yard Washtn Monday 22nd, August 1814
In pursuance to your instructions to me of this day, to procure Waggons to remove the powder from the Naval Magazine, I proceeded forthwith, to the execution of your order, after borrowing the Horse of Thomas Murray, Master Cooper of the Yard, in consequence of your regret, at my being obliged to ride one of the public Horses of the Yard, then so much wanted. Murrays Horse was borrowed of his wife.

I was aware of the demand for Waggons - from the alarm then created by the removal of public, as well as private property - and my direction was to the Turnpike road leading into the City from Baltimore. I met with no waggons, but left directions at Long's Hotel on Capitol Hill, that from four to five wagons should be directed to the Navy Yard to you, should that number pass, that would be disposed to engage in public employment....

On my way, I overtook the Honbl Wm. Jones, Secretary of the Navy - He enquired where I was going - I informed him of your orders, and was on my way to Geo: town in pursuit of waggons - He asked me if you had wagons to dispatch provisions to Comdr Barney. I replied I did not believe you had - He then ordered me to impress all I could get....

The five wagons, to wit Thomas Wade, three negroes under his charge, and Thomas Cowthon, I arrived with, a little before sunset at the Yard.

Tuesday 23rd. Today I was in the Yard before sunrise - and proceeded to have the Teams appraised etc: and as soon as practicable, got off Thos. Cowthon and Wm. Barnett with provisions for Commdr Barney. The other four - Wade and the three Negroes - I caused to go to the Magazine, where were they loaded with one hundred and twenty four Barrels, and two quarter casks of Powder. Being without a Horse - and having to attend to securing the powder, and understanding that Murray had objected to his wife's lending his horse - and finding him in his stable, I impressed him, with a saddle and bridle - Before I left the City, I impressed the waggon & team of four horses, of John Bair an old Dutchman, to whom I gave a Certificate of impressment, and got him into the Yard.

I then followed the Waggons, and the powder, and overtook them before they crossed the Potomac Bridge. On the south side, and as I was about to ascend the ridge from the Causeway, I met Col. Minor's Regiment of Fairfax Militia - The Colonel recommended six persons as a competent guard to take charge of the powder, and that night, I reached Wrens Tavern at the falls Church, late at night, within one mile of the farm of Daniel Dulany, Esq., where the powder was to be deposited....

Wednesday 24th. Desirous of having the powder delivered and under guard, I was on my horse at the dawn of the day, and ordered the waggons to gear up, and follow me. On getting to the Farm, I found seventy five barrels of Powder had been deposited - the Barn in which it was, open, and much out of order - I went to the house of Mr. Dozier Bennett, a respectable Citizen recommended by Col Minor, in whom I might confide, for its care. He agreed to have my orders attended to, and to have collected a competent guard, on my stipulating to allow him, two dollars pr. day for his services, and one & a half dollars, for each person employed to aid him; until I could relieve them by sending a guard over; which Col Wharton had promised me would be done - As soon as I had completed my orders, and directed the Waggons to hasten their return to the City - I set out to attend you."

Monroe kept his staff at the State Department informed of the enemy's advance. Soon after the Benedict landing he advised that the national documents and records archived at the State Department needed to be properly secured. Stephen Pleasonton, a senior clerk, immediately set about purchasing coarse linen and had it made into bags. With the help of others in his office, he placed into them treasured documents, such as the original Declaration of Independence written on parchment. Other national valuables secured in the handmade bags included the correspondences of George Washington, the letter in which Washington resigned his commission, international treaties, and secret, unpublished journals of Congress. At one point, while packing the priceless documents, Pleasonton encountered the Secretary of War in the hallway, who chastised him for being unnecessarily alarmed. At that time the State and War Departments were housed in the same building on Seventeenth Street, separated by a hallway. In a written description of the packing events thirty-four years later, Pleasonton related his recollections to William Winder, the son of the Commander of the 10th Military District, who had inquired about the State Department archival activities during the British invasion:

> "Washington City, August 7, 1848
> Soon after learning that the British fleet were in the Chesapeake, we learned also that they were ascending the Patuxent, evidently with the view of attacking this city. Upon receiving this information, which was about a week before the enemy entered Washington, Col. Monroe, then Secretary of State, mounted his horse, and proceeded to Benedict, a small village on the Patuxent, where the British forces were being landed. From an eminence within a quarter of a mile of the village, Col. Monroe could distinctly see the number and kind of troops of which their army was composed; and recollecting the threats held out in the British papers, and believing that we had no force which could successfully resist them, he sent a note, either to Mr. John Graham, the chief clerk of the office, or myself, (I do not remember which,) by a vidette, advising us to take the best care of the books and papers of the office which might be in our power. Whereupon I proceeded to purchase coarse linen, and cause it to be made into bags of convenient size, in which the gentlemen of the office, assigned by me, placed the books and other papers, after which I obtained carts, and had them conveyed to a grist mill, then unoccupied, belonging to Mr. Edgar Patterson, situated a distance on the Virginia side of the Potomac, beyond the chain bridge, so called, two miles above Georgetown.
>
> While engaged in the passage way of the buildings with the papers, the Department of State being on one side, and the War Department on the other side of the passage, General Armstrong, then Secretary of War, on his way to his own room, stopped a short time, and observed to me, that he thought we were under unnecessary alarm, as he did not think the British were serious in their intentions of coming to Washington."

Fortunately, Pleasonton did not pay attention to Armstrong's optimistic view. On Tuesday, August 23, the secured items were loaded into carts and wagons and taken across the Potomac and hidden in an abandoned grist mill, recently purchased by Edgar Patterson, located at the Falls Bridge. As fears increased overnight that the Redcoats would actually invade Washington, Pleasonton became uneasy about the mill's location because it was dangerously close to Foxall's Foundry, an ammunition and cannon factory located along the Potomac just west of Georgetown. He worried that if the British captured the city, they would certainly destroy the weapons foundry, or that a traitor might lead them from Foxall's to the vacant mill site. The following day, he reloaded the valuable cargo into wagons impressed from Virginia farms, and accompanied it thirty-five miles further inland to Leesburg, where everything was deposited in an empty farmhouse. The keys were entrusted to the Reverend John Littlejohn, minister of the Old Stone Methodist Church and Leesburg's Collector of Internal Revenue. It is thought that the archival documents were stored in a walk-in, arched-brick basement vault at a 200 acre farm that acquired the name "Rokeby" in 1830. Pleasonton's correspondence continued:

> "... it was the part of prudence to preserve the valuable papers of the Revolutionary Government, comprising the Declaration of Independence, the laws, the secret journals of Congress, then not published, the correspondence of General Washington, his commission resigned at the close of the war, the correspondence of General Greene, and other generals, as well as all the laws, treaties, and correspondence of the Department of State since the adoption of the Constitution down to that time.

> Considering the papers unsafe at the mill, as, if the British forces got to Washington, they would probably detach a force for the purpose of destroying a foundry for cannon and shot in the neighborhood, and would be led by some evil disposed person, to destroy the mill and papers also. I proceeded to some farm houses in Virginia, and procured wagons, in which the books and papers were deposited, and I proceeded with them to the town of Leesburg, a distance of 35 miles, at which place an empty house was procured, in which, the papers were safely placed, the doors locked, and the keys given to the Rev. Mr. Littlejohn, who was then, or had been, one of the collectors of internal revenue.

> Being fatigued with the ride, and securing the papers, I retired early to bed, and was informed next morning by the people of the hotel where I staid, that they had seen, the preceding night, being the 24th of August, a large fire in the direction of Washington, which proved to be a light from the public buildings the enemy had set on fire, and burned them to the ground."

After the collapse of two wooden bridges built across the Potomac River at the Little Falls, one with four and a half foot chains anchored in stone towers was built in 1808. It became known as Chain Bridge, but it was swept away by flood waters after two years on November 24, 1810. A fourth bridge was built in similar fashion in 1811, and was used by Dolley in her flight into Virginia. The view is from the Maryland shore, going north to south. Included is Patterson's milling operations, the site of the abandoned grist mill where Pleasonton first hid valuable national documents.

6

WINDER RETREATS

The first part of the British invasionary agenda, the destruction of Barney's gunboats, had been achieved with practically no resistance on the part of the Americans. This surprised Ross, who ordered a halt at Upper Marlborough Monday afternoon, where he was later joined by the victorious Cockburn. The Redcoats remained at that location about twenty-four hours. With the flotilla now out of the way, they were ready to finalize their plans for the attack on America's seat of government. The Admiral dispatched his aide, Lieutenant James Scott, to ride back to Benedict and report the news to Cochrane that the American flotilla was no longer a threat and that the British forces were now preparing to invade Washington. Meanwhile, Ross found comfortable headquarters in the residence of a hospitable prominent medical practitioner, Dr. William Beanes, a Federalist with British sympathies. Gleig's narrative in *A Subaltern in America* discussed the generosity offered the enemy forces by Beanes:

> "The only inhabitants whom we found abiding in this house was a
> Doctor Bean, a medical practitioner, and the proprietor of a valuable
> farm in the neighbourhood. The Doctor was, in point of fact, a
> Scotchman; that is to say, he had migrated about twenty years ago
> from some district of North Britain, and still retained his native

dialect in all its doric richness. He professed, moreover, to retain the
feelings as well as the language of his boyish days. He was a
Federalist - in other words, he was hostile to the war with England,
which he still persisted in regarding as his mother country. Such, at
least, were the statements with which he favoured us, and we
believed him the more readily, that he seemed really disposed to treat
us as friends.

There was nothing about his house or farm to which he made us not
heartily welcome; and the wily emigrant was no loser by his civility.
We took, indeed, whatever we stood in need of, provisions, forage,
and even horses; but our commissary paid this man of professions the
full value of his commodities. From Doctor Bean, I however
scrupled not to accept a present. He offered me all that his house
contained; I took only a little tea, some sugar, and a bottle of milk;
and did not insult him by alluding to a remuneration."

Obviously, Monday had not been a good day for the Americans.
The surprise attack against the advancing army never materialized,
Barney's gunboats were destroyed and Winder pulled his troops back to
Old Fields. A very anxious President departed the capital that evening
for the American camp, to assist Winder with strategy and to review the
American troops. He traveled in the company of at least Rush, Jones and
General John Mason. Knowing he would spend the night with the army,
he told Dolley to take care of herself and urged her, if necessary, to
preserve the public and private cabinet papers. Left alone, except for a
few loyal servants, she began placing things into trunks, making choices
about what to take or what to leave. A guard of one hundred soldiers
was stationed around the White House. Madison stayed overnight at the
Williams farm about a mile from Old Fields. The General of the 10th
Military District met with the President at six the following morning.
Shortly afterwards, Madison, along with most of his Cabinet, reviewed
the American forces and later presided over a staff conference. Around
noon Tuesday, the President sent a hopeful note from the Williams' farm
to Dolley, indicating that the British forces were not as strong as
everyone first thought and that he probably would be back at the White
House that evening:

"My Dearest:
We reached our quarters last evening at the camp between 8 & 9 oC.
and made out very well. I have passed the forenoon among the
troops who are in high spirits & make a good appearance. The
reports as to the enemy have varied every hour. The last & probably
truest information is that they are not very strong, and are without
cavalry or artillery; and of course that they are not in a condition to
strike at Washington. It is believed also that they are not about to
move from Marlbro', unless it be from an apprehension of our
gathering force, and on a retreat to their ships. It is possible however
they may have a greater force or expect one, than has been
represented or that their temerity may be greater than their strength.

> I sent you a message last night by Col. M. and one to-day by a
> messenger of Genl. Winder who set out at a moment when it was
> impossible to write. I have detained Shorter, that I might give you by
> him some final & certain information. We expect any how to learn
> something further from the camp concerning the enemy. If it should
> be of a nature to make it advisable to return to the camp, you will not
> see me this evening; otherwise I hope I shall be with you in the
> course tho' perhaps later in the evening."

Reports received at this time about the strength and movements of the British were contradictory, but most of the information indicated to Winder that the enemy would remain at its current location at Upper Marlboro and await reinforcements. An advance detachment under Peter was ordered eastward to reconnoiter the area, as had been done the previous day around Nottingham. Meanwhile, an attack was again considered and battle plans were drawn up. This seemed reasonable. Fresh units for the defense of the capital were marshaling. Winder's army had grown in size from the previous day. Another 1000 men had rushed to Old Fields, so that his force there consisted of about 3000 troops. Stansbury had reached Bladensburg with 1400 men, Sterett was on his way there with another 800 and Beall had 800 near Annapolis. Including Barney's men, this added up to well over 6000 troops. Winder now had an army that outnumbered the enemy. Furthermore, the Americans had cavalry and artillery, plus even more troops were on the way. The British had about forty stolen horses for cavalry and, for practical purposes, no artillery. After considering the various alternatives, it was decided to concentrate the American forces and attack the British the following morning, Wednesday, while they remained bivouacked at Upper Marlboro. Winder reported:

> "I received constant intelligence that the enemy still remained in
> Marlborough; and, therefore, felt no doubt that, if he intended to take
> the road to Annapolis, any movement upon that road was only an
> advance party for observation, and preparatory to a general
> movement; and as the morning advanced, and the information
> brought still confirmed the impression that the enemy intended no
> movement from Upper Marlborough, I resolved to endeavor to
> concentrate the force (which I hoped had now considerably
> accumulated within my reach) down upon the enemy's lines near
> Marlborough "

Satisfied that things were under control, Winder left Old Fields for Bladensburg in order to confer with Stansbury about the battle plans. He placed General Walter Smith, Commander of the District Militia, in charge during his absence. Shortly after Winder left, Major Thomas McKenney .returned to the American headquarters, bringing with him two British deserters. McKenney, who had been scouting the enemy's movements, predicted that the Redcoats would strike the American forces within twenty-four hours. After listening to McKenney's report, Armstrong continued to remain stubbornly consistent in his opinion that the nation's capital was not under any threat. He adamantly informed everyone that the British had no intention of attacking, but if they did, he volunteered that Annapolis, rather than Baltimore, was the target of choice. The prisoners were then interrogated by the President and offered little information, except to say that the British forces were about the same size as the American army. McKenney recalled:

> "After Commodore Barney had been forced to blow up his flotilla in the Patuxet, and our troops being at the battalion Old Fields, and I had come in as a vidette, having rode along the enemy's flanks, for over a mile, and picking up, on my return to camp, two British deserters, whom I brought in with me, I found on horseback, in our camp, President Madison, General Armstrong, and two or three other persons, to whom, in presence of the Commanding General, I stated the position of the enemy, and what appeared to be their numbers, and gave it as my opinion that they would be at our encampment before daylight next morning. To which General Armstrong replied, 'They can have no such intention. They are foraging, I suppose; and if an attack is meditated by them, upon any place, it is Annapolis.'
>
> The deserters were then interrogated, chiefly by President Madison. But they knew not who commanded them; knew nothing of their destination, and as little of their numbers. I then asked them to look at our force, and say whether theirs was equal to it. They did so, and with a smile, said 'We think it is.'"

After interrogating the two British prisoners, there was little doubt in the President's mind as to the destructive intent of the enemy. He immediately sent Dolley a more ominous second message apprising her of eminent danger. He suggested that she should be ready to leave the city at a moment's notice because the enemy seemed stronger than was first reported. Under the impression that the British would remain at the Marlboro location for some time, and Winder would initiate a confrontation the following morning, Madison rode back into the city at two that afternoon, along with Armstrong and Jones, to meet and further strategize with various officials. It was about this time that Ross unexpectedly broke camp and began marching in the direction of Washington. The British forces had rested at Upper Marlboro over twenty-four hours. There appeared to be some hesitancy once again, according to Gleig, on the part of Ross about moving forward:

> "In Marlborough we remained not only during the night, but till past noon on the following day. The hesitation which had caused the loss of a few hours at Nottingham again interfered, and produced a delay which might have been attended with serious consequences. At length, however, orders were given to form, and we quitted Marlborough about two in the afternoon, taking the road to

Washington."

Winder had ridden about eight miles from his headquarters, when a messenger, sent by Smith, overtook him. The messenger was McKenney, who reported the unexpected news that the British had left Upper Marlboro and were marching in the direction of the American camp at Old Fields. McKenney stated that Peter's reconnoitering force had encountered the Redcoats along the Upper Marlboro Road. A skirmish had taken place; one man was wounded and Peter's troops were forced to withdraw back to Old Fields. He further related that Smith and Barney had hastily formed a line of battle across the road in anticipation of an immediate attack from the enemy. Completely taken by surprise, the General turned his horse around and galloped back to Old Fields. McKenney continued:

> "Whereupon my commanding officer, General Smith, ordered formed a line of battle, Commodore Barney's artillery being in advance of our main line, and near the wood that intervened between the two armies. The line being formed, I was ordered to go in quest of General Winder, General Smith remarking, 'I do not feel at liberty to take the responsibility of the fight, if the commander-in-chief of the forces can be had to give direction to it.'

> Putting spurs to my horse, I lost not a moment in reaching what I had learned was the position of General Winder. I met him about eight miles from our encampment, delivered the message with which I was charged, when, putting spurs to his horse, we galloped back to camp together.

> Riding round the field, and observing the line of battle, he remarked, 'It is all well arranged, but the manifest object of the enemy is, to attack us in the night. We have not the material for a night fight.' Whereupon, he gave orders to take up the line of march; cross the eastern branch bridge, and occupy the heights beyond. We did so. This was the evening of the 23d of August."

After breaking camp, the Redcoats did not march far and did not pursue. Their advance was halted Tuesday afternoon about three miles from Old Fields, where they bivouacked at the Melwood estate of Mary Digges, the widow of Dr. Ignatius Digges. This was a unique position because it gave the British a choice of roads that led to such places as Annapolis, Bladensburg, the Eastern Branch Bridge or Fort Warburton. Great doubt was still entertained by the American General as to which course the British intended to pursue. Winder incorrectly presumed that they were organizing for a night attack. He felt that his army was not prepared for such a situation. About five p.m., in a state of uncertainty and doubt, he gave the order to pull back. Once again the American army retreated, marching through the early evening, crossing over the lower bridge (also called Eastern Branch Bridge), before ending up at the Washington Navy Yard about one a.m. Wednesday, August 24. Law stated that officers hurried the men and the retreat basically became a run of eight miles:

> "The detachment of three hundred militia, which had been sent on the day before, were again ordered to advance towards the enemy. They met him on his march, about six miles in advance of our encampment, but with so great a disparity of force, that it was impossible for them to make a stand. After Captain Stull's rifle company had fired about four rounds, the detachment was compelled to retreat, to prevent being surrounded by the enemy. About five o'clock, P.M., after having remained some time in line of battle, we were ordered to retreat to Washington, and, although, our march on the retreat was extremely rapid, yet orders were occasionally given to the captains of companies to hurry on their men. The march, therefore, literally became a run of eight miles, and the propriety of this rapid movement, which unnecessarily fatigued and dispirited the men, may be tested by the fact, that the main body of the enemy *bivouacked* that night on the Melwood estate, more than three miles distant from the ground we had left."

While the American forces pulled back, Barney and his crew, remained behind for some hours, holding a defensive position, but the enemy never came. Before sunset Winder had the seamen withdraw across the Eastern Branch Bridge into Washington. A few men and one cannon were left behind to cover their retreat. Once back in the city, Barney was ordered to post his artillery in positions to guard the lower bridge over the Eastern Branch. Barney described his retreat from the Old Fields camp in his report to the Secretary of the Navy:

> "Farm at Elk Ridge, 29, August 1814
> This is the first moment I have had it in my power to make a report of the proceedings of the forces under my command, since I had the honour of seeing you at the camp at the 'Old Fields.' On the afternoon of that day, we were informed that the enemy was advancing upon us. The army was put under arms, and our positions taken; my forces on the right, flanked by the two battalions of the 36th and 38th, where we remained some hours; the enemy did not make his appearance. A little before sun-set general Winder came to me, and recommended that the heavy artillery should be withdrawn, with the exception of one 12 pounder to cover the retreat. We took up our line of march, and in the night entered Washington by the Eastern Branch bridge. I marched my men, &c. to the marine barracks, and took up quarters for the night, myself sleeping at commodore Tingey's in the navy yard. About 2 o'clock general Winder came to my quarters, and we made some arrangements for the morning."

7

ROSS'S DECISION

The second note the President sent to the First Lady from Old Fields, advising her to be ready to leave at a moment's notice, did not survive time; however, it is mentioned in a continuing letter to her sister, Lucy Payne Washington Todd that Dolley began Tuesday, August 23, 1814 describing the unfolding the drama at the White House. This famous narrative was written at intervals during a two day period and offered a detailed account of Dolley's activities during the final hours before the capital fell:

> "Tuesday Augt 23d 1814.
>
> Dear Sister
> My husband left me yesterday morng. to join Gen. Winder. He inquired anxiously whether I had courage, or firmness to remain in the President's house until his return, on the morrow, or succeeding day, and on my assurance that I had no fear but for him and the success of our army, he left me, beseeching me to take care of myself, and of the cabinet papers, public and private. I have since recd. two despatches from him written with a pencil; the last is alarming, because he desires I should be ready at a moment's warning to enter my carriage and leave the city; that the enemy seemed stronger than had been reported, and that it might happen that they would reach the city, with intention to destroy it.

I am accordingly ready; I have pressed as many cabinet papers into trucks as to fill one carriage; our private property must be sacrificed, as it is impossible to procure wagons for its transportation. I am determined not to go myself until I see Mr. Madison safe, and he can accompany me, as I hear of much hostility towards him. Disaffection stalks around us. My friends and acquaintances are all gone; Even Col. C with his hundred men, who were stationed as a guard in the enclosure. French John, with his usual activity and resolution, offers to spike the cannon at the gate, and lay a train of powder, which would blow up the British, should they enter the house. To the last proposition I positively object, without being able to make him understand why all advantages in war may not be taken."

In the midst of the mounting tensions on Tuesday, the First Lady also received a tactful letter of regret for a dinner engagement that evening at the Executive Mansion. This was written by a very frightened Eleanor Jones, wife of the Navy Secretary, who had begun preparations to leave the city, but had no transportation and did not know where to go. Mrs. Jones wrote:

"Washington, August 23, 1814
My Dear Madam, - In the present state of alarm and bustle of preparation for the worst that may happen, I imagine it will be more convenient to dispense with the enjoyment of your hospitality today, and, therefore, pray you to admit this as an excuse for Mr. Jones, Lucy, and myself. Mr. Jones is deeply engaged in dispatching the marines and attending to other public duties. Lucy and I are packing, with the possibility of having to leave; but in the event of necessity we know not where to go, nor have we any means yet prepared for the conveyance of our effects. I sincerely hope and trust the necessity may be avoided, but there appears rather serious cause of apprehension. Our carriage horse is sick, and our coachman absent, or I should have called last evening to see your sister. I feel great solicitude on her account."

After riding back to Washington Tuesday afternoon, Madison dined at the F Street home of his brother-in-law Richard Cutts, Superintendent General of Military Supplies and the husband of Dolley's sister, Anna. He then proceeded to the residence of the Secretary of State at 20th and I Streets to further strategize with Armstrong and Monroe. At this time the three men still thought the Americans would attack the enemy the following morning. When the meeting broke up, Armstrong went back to his residence, Madison returned to the Executive Mansion, and Monroe left to keep an eye on the enemy, accompanied by at least Rush, Thornton and Charles Carroll. Later in the evening Monroe learned of the skirmish that afternoon between Peter's troops and the British, but it was not until after midnight, when he was back in Washington, that he heard about Winder's retreat to the navy yard. Monroe stated to the Investigative Committee:

"In the afternoon of the 23d, the President, with the Secretaries of War and Navy, returned to Washington. The Attorney General, and several respectable friends from the city, proceeded with me to the road leading from Marlborough to Bladensburg. Late that evening I heard of the advance of the enemy on the party under Major Peter, and against General Winder.

Not knowing the result, I hastened to General Stansbury's quarters at Bladensburg, and found him encamped on the height beyond the village on the road leading to Marlborough. He had just heard of the enemy's movement, but was likewise unacquainted with the result.... I proceeded to the city, where I learned that General Winder had crossed the Eastern Branch, and taken post near the navy yard."

Meanwhile at the White House, the President met with Colonel George Minor of Falls Church, commander of the 60th Regiment of the Virginia Militia, consisting of about 600 infantry and 100 cavalry. Minor had rushed his men to the city after receiving a verbal message from the President the prior evening to hurry in defense of the District. The Colonel was seeking to equip his troops because many who had been called "rushed to serve" and did not have weapons or ammunition. Recognizing the urgency of the situation, Madison hastened Minor to the Secretary of War, to obtain the necessary equipment. Armstrong, who was boarding nearby in the Seven Buildings on Pennsylvania Avenue, had already retired for the evening. His response was that the armory was closed and Minor should wait until the following morning and report to Colonel Henry Carbery, who would supply everything his men needed. At this time both Madison and Armstrong were still unaware that Winder had pulled back to the navy yard, resulting in aborting the plans to attack at first light. Minor described his situation:

"Immediately issued orders for the regiment under my command to assemble at Wren's tavern on the Tuesday following, it being the nearest point of the county of Fairfax to the city; and, on Sunday the 21st, received orders, through Brigadier General Douglas, to repair with a detachment of ninety men, that had been previously placed in detail, to march at a moment's warning to the aid of General Hungerford, whose head quarters were either in the counties of Westmoreland, King George or Northumberland; and to make one other requisition of one hundred and forty men, exclusive of officers, and order them to the aid of General Winder, city of Washington; and on Monday evening the 22d, received a verbal message from the President, by Mr. John Graham, to hasten on the troops which had been ordered from my regiment, ... and, after informing Mr. Graham the purport of the orders, I had received, we both concluded it would be proper for him to return to Washington, and have the orders, first alluded to, countermanded; so as to justify me in marching with my whole force to the city; which consisted, as well as I can recollect, of six hundred infantry and about one hundred cavalry;...

On the receipt of which, I took up my line of marching immediately, and arrived at the capitol between sunset and dark, and immediately made my way to the President and reported my arrival, when he referred me to General Armstrong, to whom I repaired and informed him as to the strength of the troops, as well as to the want of arms, ammunition, &c. which made it as late as early candle light, when I was informed by that gentleman the arms, &c. could not be had that night, and directed me to report myself next morning to Colonel Carbery, who would furnish me with arms, and &c."

Winder obviously needed to confer with Madison. He arrived at the Executive Mansion soon after Minor had left, sometime after eight o'clock Tuesday evening, in order to update the President about the afternoon's skirmish, his decision for the retreat to the navy yard, and that he had lost all advantage for an attack the following morning. After updating Madison about the turn of events, he proceeded back to the camp on a borrowed horse, stopping first at the Upper Bridge over the Eastern Branch (also known as Stoddard's Bridge) to make certain that it was rigged for explosion. The bridge was blown up by the Americans a few hours later, sometime between three and four Wednesday morning. On his way back to headquarters, the General fell off his horse and badly injured himself, so that he was in great pain before the battle even began the following day. Winder's narrative to the Investigative Committee continued:

"Upon arriving at the bridge, about eight o'clock, I directed General Smith, to halt his men in the most convenient position near the bridge on this side; and I passed over and rode directly to the President's, and informed him of the then state of things…. I returned to the bridge to see that the different detachments which I had stationed there were upon the alert, and understood the objects for which they were detached. And I thence, returned to the camp, between three and four o'clock, much exhausted, and considerably hurt in the right arm and ancle from a severe fall which I had into a gully or ditch on my way to the navy yard."

Winder's troops were not concentrated. There was no advantage by taking a position at the navy yard. He could have retreated from Old Fields to Bladensburg, where Stansbury's Maryland Militia was camped, and united his army. Instead he preferred to protect Fort Warburton in case the Redcoats marched in that direction to link up with Gordon's fleet ascending the Potomac. With the defense of Washington now dependent upon a single battle, he needed to show a force of strength. Unfortunately, his troops remained divided, with half protecting the Eastern Branch of the Potomac, which was virtually impassable, except for the remaining Lower Bridge (the Upper was blown up) that was ordered to be demolished if necessary. The other half guarded the bridge across the Eastern Branch at Bladensburg, once a flourishing tobacco exporter established in 1742. Additional militia troops were steadily arriving, but they were not trained. Winder's army was disorganized and not ready for the engagement that took place. The Americans were opposed by 4500 tightly concentrated British regulars whose march thus far had been fairly free of opposition; however, Ross and Cockburn, faced their own set of problems - they had been ordered to return to their ships! Cochrane, upon receiving the news from messenger Scott that the flotilla was eliminated and the troops would attack Washington, issued orders for an immediate pull back to the ships! He recognized that by proceeding forward, the British forces were in jeopardy because they were too few in number, without cavalry and had little artillery. Furthermore, Gordon's squadron was still struggling up the Potomac and had not ascended far enough to be of any help in an engagement or retreat. He decided England had achieved enough by destroying Barney's flotilla. Scott was directed to hasten back to Ross's headquarters carrying the written orders; but before leaving he was required to memorize its contents and, if captured, he would destroy the letter. The orders according to Scott, who later put them on paper, in *Recollections of a Naval Life*, were basically the following:

> "The orders contained in that letter were to the following effect: That under all circumstances the Rear-admiral had already effected more than England could have expected with the small force under his orders; that he was on no account to proceed one mile farther, but, upon the receipt of that order, the army was immediately to return to Benedict to re-embark; that the ulterior and principal objects of the expedition would be risked by an attempt upon the capital with such inadequate means; - and concluded with a reiteration of the orders to return immediately."

Reaching the British camp, now at Melwood, about 2:00 a.m. Wednesday morning, August 24, 1814, Scott found the two commanding officers asleep on their cloaks in a shepherd's hut. Waking them up, he delivered Cochrane's packet to the Admiral, who read its contents, and handed it over to Ross. The two officers went outside and talked the matter over at length. The General was of the opinion there was no choice; they had to return. The Admiral argued that Cochrane's view was limited because he remained behind aboard the *Tonnant* and was not at the scene. Cockburn pointed out that they were in the field and had closely observed the American army which was not strong. They had met little or no resistance thus far, and Winder had already pulled back twice when confronted with adversity. Cockburn convincingly argued that they should continue to advance. Ross, as leader of the land forces, had rank over the Admiral, but he was persuaded to move forward and attack. Unbelievable! This was a flagrant disregard of written orders. How different history would have been had Ross directed the forces back to Benedict as ordered. Scott wrote:

> "I did not reach the spot till two o'clock in the morning;... I delivered my open packet to the Admiral; he read it, and handed it over to General Ross.
>
> It is not surprising that the latter, who had been so lately accustomed to the regular warfare carried on in the Peninsula, should have felt diffident in having with so small a force advanced thus far into an enemy's country, or that that diffidence should be increased upon the receipt of such a document as I have detailed. Having perused it, he remarked that there was now no other· alternative than to return. 'No,' replied the Admiral, 'we cannot do that; we are too far advanced to think of a retreat; let us take a turn outside, and talk the matter over.'
>
> Both officers left the hut. The general's aid-de-camp, the quarter-master-general, and myself, were at a short distance, and could not avoid occasionally hearing what passed as they walked to and fro in earnest conversation.
>
> 'If we proceed,' said our energetic commander, 'I'll pledge every thing that is dear to me as an officer that we shall succeed. If we return without striking a blow, it will be worse than a defeat - it will bring a stain upon our arms. I know their force - the militia, however great their numbers, will not - cannot stand against your disciplined troops. It is too late,' continued the Admiral - 'we ought not to have advanced - there is now no choice left us. We must go on.'
>
> The consultation lasted till the eastern sky became tinged with the blush of day. The General had been apparently much excited, and at this moment, striking his hand against his forehead, he exclaimed, 'Well, be it so, we will proceed.'"

The *National Intelligencer,* June 4, 1849, printed a letter written to the editor by J. S. Skinner, an American prisoner-of-war exchange agent at the time of the invasion. He related that in talking with Ross after the burning of the Federal City, the plan to take Washington was not finalized until after the flotilla was destroyed:

> "... for even when they ascended the Patuxent river, in pursuit of the Flotilla, which had retired, as it was supposed, to an inaccessible point above Nottingham, the expedition to Washington was not a part of their fixed design: nor was it decided on at last, as General Ross himself told the writer of this, until after the flotilla was blown up. Then, as he said, Admiral Cockburn urged him, he (Ross) having exclusive command of the land forces, to go ahead. 'Let us,' said he, 'now push on, so far as to feel their strength, at any rate, and, if circumstances require it, we can fall back on our shipping.'"

Ross indicated in his "Official Report of the Capture and

Destruction of the City of Washington" that he made the decision to attack after the gunboats were destroyed and deciding that the American forces were not very strong. This account was written and sent back to England before his death near Baltimore a few weeks later. In it he simply stated:

> "Having advanced to within 16 miles of Washington, and ascertaining the force of the enemy to be such as might authorize an attempt at carrying the capital, I determined to make it,…"

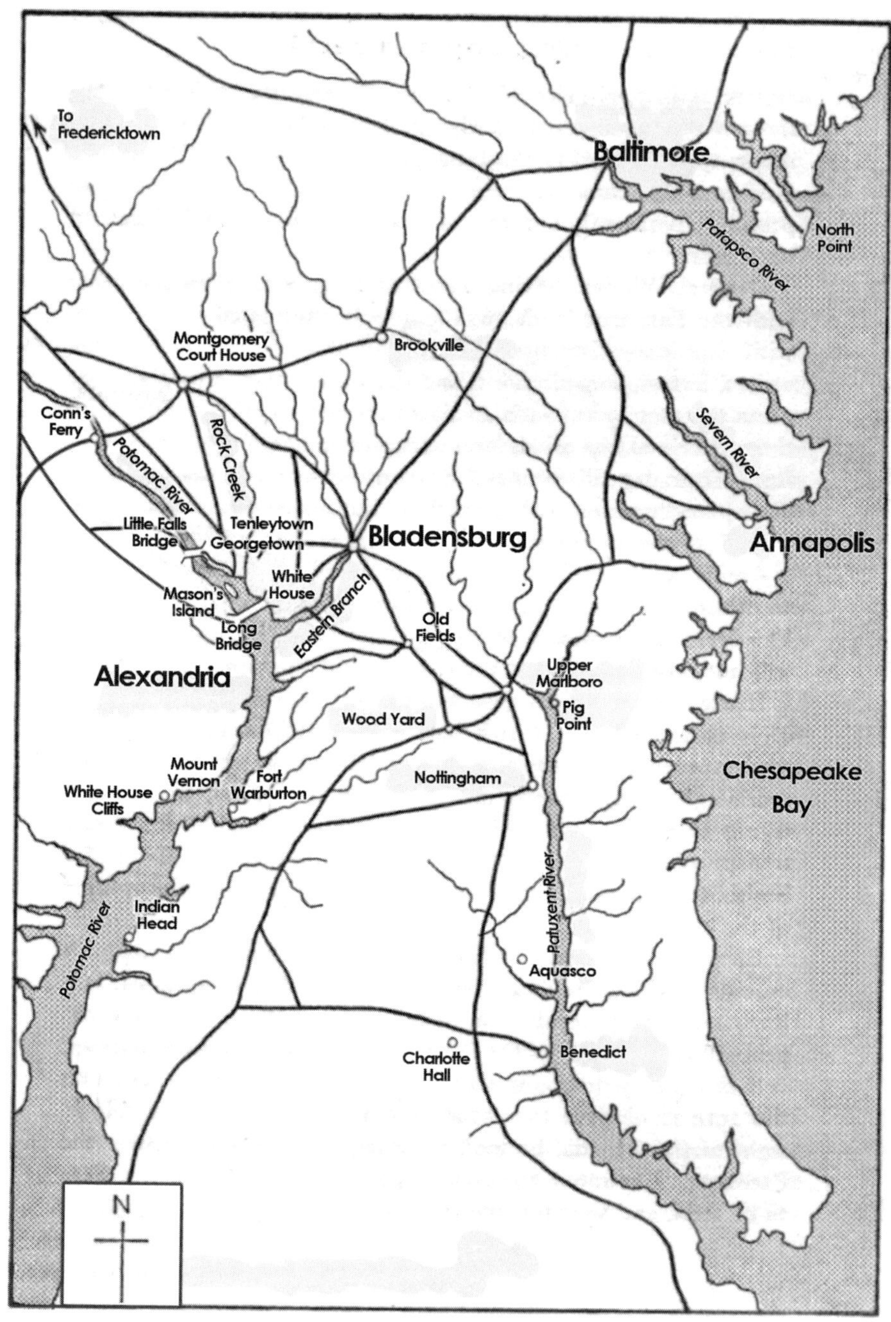

Map by Charles Herrick

This map shows the British theater of operations around Washington and Baltimore during the later part of the summer 1814. Included are the basic roads used by the invading army in their march to and from Washington.

8

AMERICAN UNCERTAINTY

The decision being made to attack, Ross broke camp at daybreak Wednesday, August 24, and began a forced march, not directly for Washington, but towards the village of Bladensburg northeast of the city. At this juncture five roads converged upon a single bridge that spanned the Eastern Branch of the Potomac. The enemy, having procured between forty to fifty horses from various farms, now had some cavalry support which patrolled the area as the column moved forward, giving their soldiers some degree of security. A rapid seven hour march to Bladensburg in the smothering August heat took a heavy toll from the brigades. Many men became exhausted and fell behind. Others found the ordeal too strenuous and simply left the ranks. Some simply dropped dead in their tracks. A fatigued Gleig struggled to keep up with the main part of the army. He later described the harrowing experience:

> "Having started on the 24th at an early hour, our march was for some time both cool and agreeable. The road --- if road it could be called --- wound for the first five miles through the heart of an immense forest, and being, in every sense of the word, a bypath, was completely overshadowed by projecting branches of trees, so closely interwoven, as to prevent a single sunbeam from making its way, even at noon, within the arch. But no sooner had we begun to emerge from the woods and to enter the open country, than an overpowering

change was perceived. The sun, from which we had been hitherto defended, now beat upon us in full force; and the dust rising in thick masses, from under our feet, without a breath of air to disperse it, flew directly into our faces, occasioning the greatest inconvenience both to the eyes and respiration. I have stated this at length, because I do not recollect a period of my military life during which I suffered more severely from heat and fatigue;...

It was now that we experienced the great usefulness of our badly mounted troopers, or as they were called by the private soldiers, our Cossacks.... They were divided into small parties of six or eight, and sent out in different directions to reconnoitre, two of them generally taking post at every suspicious corner, that one might give notice to the column, whilst the other watched the motions of an enemy. (It so happened that these precautions were unnecessary, for whatever might be the strength of the Americans in cavalry, their General did not think fit to employ it in harassing our march).

Numbers of men had already fallen to the rear, and many more could with difficulty keep up; consequently, if we pushed on much farther without resting, the chances were that at least one half of the army would be left behind.... Perhaps no halt ever arrived more seasonably than this, or bid fair to be productive or more beneficial effects; yet so oppressive was the heat, that we had not resumed our march above an hour, when the banks by the way side were again covered with stragglers; some of the finest and stoutest men in the army being literally unable to go on."

Winder received the news that the British were on the march, but remained uncertain as to where the enemy was headed. At this stage of the game, he still considered Baltimore or Annapolis as possible targets. The General continued to believe that if the destination was Washington, a direct approach would be taken to the city, so that Ross could link up with Gordon's squadron still ascending the Potomac; thus, he justified maintaining his position at the navy yard. Completely overwhelmed by the numerous conflicting reports coming in from his scouts, he sent an early morning dispatch to the Secretary of War describing the situation at the navy yard and requesting his advice or that of the government. This note was delivered by mistake to the President, who opened it, then sent it along to Armstrong, and lost no time in rushing to Winder's temporary headquarters in the home of Griffith Coombs near the navy yard:

"Wednesday morning, 24th of August, 1814
Sir: I have found it necessary to establish my head quarters here, the most advanced position convenient to troops, and nearest information. I shall remain stationary as much as possible, that I may be the more readily found, to issue orders, and collect together the various detachments of militia, and give them as rapid a consolidation and organization as possible.

P. S. - The news up river is very threatening. Barney's, or some other force, should occupy the battery at Greenleaf's Point and the Navy Yard. I should be glad of the assistance of counsel from yourself and the Government. If more convenient, I should make an exertion to go to you the first opportunity."

The President arrived at Winder's headquarters about 7:00 a.m. and was joined by all Cabinet members, except for Armstrong. For three hours they went over reports of British movements with Winder and other military leaders, most of which proved to be misinformation. At this time, it was decided that if the capital should fall to the enemy, Madison and his Cabinet would rendezvous at Fredericktown, Maryland about forty-five miles northwest of the city. Intelligence arrived about 10:00 a.m. that the British had taken the Bladensburg Road, leaving no doubt that Washington, and not Baltimore or Annapolis, was the target. It was clear they were not taking the more direct route over the Lower Bridge into the capital city, but would approach it from the north at Bladensburg. With everyone's approval, Monroe immediately left for that village, about five miles distant, to inform Stansbury that the Redcoats were marching in his direction and he should prepare for an engagement. Winder followed, after ordering the troops camped at the navy yard to proceed to the battle site without delay. By 11:00 a.m. his army was on the march, hoping to reinforce the Baltimore forces already at Bladensburg before the enemy arrived. Armstrong tardily arrived as the emergency meeting was breaking up. Monroe had already left and Winder was about to leave for the scene of the approaching battle. In his report to the Investigating Committee, Armstrong offered no apology for his tardiness:

> "On the morning of the 24th, I received a note from Gen. Winder, informing me of his retreat and the approach of the enemy, and asking counsel from me, or from the Government. This letter was late in reaching me. It had been opened and passed through other hands. The moment I received it I hastened, with the late Secretary of Treasury, to the General's head quarters. We found there, the President, the Secretary of the Navy, and the Attorney General. Gen. Winder was on the point of joining the troops at Bladensburg, whither, it was now understood, the enemy was also marching. I took for granted, that he had received the counsel he required; for, to me, he neither stated doubt or difficulty, nor plan of attack or defense."

Using precious time, the President quickly brought the Secretary of War up to date and inquired if he had any advice to offer. Armstrong replied that he had no additional advice, but was of the opinion that the coming battle would be between militia and regulars, and that the militia would be beaten. Madison included the following in his *Memorandum on the Battle of Bladensburg*:

"In the morning, a note, by an express from General Winder was handed me. It was addressed to the Secretary of War. Not doubting the urgency of the occasion, I opened and read it, and it went on immediately by the Express to Genl. Armstrong who lodged in the Seven buildings. Finding by the note that the General requested the speediest counsel, I proceeded to his Head Quarters on the Eastern Branch, trusting for notice to the Secretary of War to follow, to the note from Winder. On my reaching his quarters, we were successively joined by the Secretary of State {who soon with our approbation repaired to Bladensburg} the Secretary of the Navy, and Mr. Rush, the Attorney General. After an hour or so, the Secretary of Treasury arrived, and quickly after the Secretary of War.

The latter had been impatiently expected, and surprize at his delay manifested. Gen. Winder was, at the moment setting off to hurry on the troops to Bladensburg in consequence of certain intelligence that the Enemy had taken that direction. Barney's corps was also ordered thither, leaving the Bridge to be blown up if necessary. On Gen. Armstrong's coming into the room, he was informed of the certain march of the enemy for Bladensburg, and of what had passed before his arrival; and he was asked whether he had any arrangement or advice to offer in the emergency. He said he had not; adding, that as the battle would be between Militia and regular troops, *the former would be beaten*."

Barney, with his flotillamen, had been detailed by Winder to stay behind guarding the Eastern Branch of the Potomac, and ordered to blow up the Lower Bridge if necessary. Winder just could not let go of this spot and unify his army at Bladensburg. The Commodore, recognizing that his men could be put to better use, appealed to the Navy Secretary, who in turn looked to the President. Madison agreed with Barney's view that the bridge over the Eastern Branch could be defended just as easily with a few men, rather than five hundred. As Commander in Chief, he overruled Winder's orders and told Barney to hurry his seamen and artillery to Bladensburg. Barney continued in his letter to Jones from Elk Ridge:

"In the morning I received a note from general Winder, and waited upon him, he requested me to take command, and place my artillery to defend the passage of the bridge on the Eastern Branch, as the enemy was approaching the city in that direction. I immediately put my guns in position, leaving the marines and the rest of my men at the barracks, to wait further orders. I was in this situation when I had the honour to meet you, with the President and heads of departments, when it was determined that I should draw off my guns and men, and proceed towards Bladensburg, which was immediately put into execution. On our way, I was informed the enemy was within a mile of Bladensburg - we hurried on. The day was hot, and my men very much crippled from the severe marches we had experienced the days before, many of them being without shoes, which I had replaced that morning."

Astride their horses, ready to leave for the battle site, Secretary of the Treasury George Campbell took Madison aside and quietly spoke to him about Armstrong's behavior. Campbell suggested that the War Secretary was taking no part in the crisis because Armstrong insisted that he did not have the authority to voice opinions not specifically requested by the President. Campbell felt that the presence and advice of Armstrong in the field might be very useful. A surprised President agreed and, turning his horse, talked with Armstrong. The result of their deliberation was that the Secretary of War would assist Winder in any way he could and Madison would be on hand to back him up. In effect, this handed the command of the American forces over to Armstrong, who then exited the navy yard to communicate with Winder. Madison continued:

> "On coming out of the house and mounting our horses, the Secretary of the Treasury, who though in a very languid state of health had turned out to join us, observed to me privately that he was grieved to see the great reserve of the Secretary of War, who was taking no part on so critical an occasion; that he found him under the impression, that as the means of defending the District had been committed to Genl. Winder, it might not be delicate to intrude his opinions without the approbation of the President; tho' with that approbation he was ready to give any aid he could.

> Mr. Campbell said that notwithstanding his just confidence in Genl. Winder, he thought, in the present state of things which called for all the military skill possible, the military knowledge and experience of the Secretary of War ought to be availed of, and that no considerations of delicacy ought to jeopard the public safety....

> I told him I could scarcely conceive it possible that Genl. Armstrong could have so misconstrued his functions and duty as Secretary of War; that he could not but know that any proper directions from him would receive any sanction that might be necessary from the Executive; nor doubt that any suggestions or advice from him to Genl. Winder would be duly attended to.

> I told Mr. C. that I would speak to the Secretary of War explicitly on the subject; and accordingly turning my horse to him, expressed to him my concern and surprise at the reserve he shewed at the present crisis, and at the scruples I understood he had at offering his advice or opinions; that I hoped he had not construed the paper of instructions given him some time before, so as to restrain him in any respect from the exercise of functions belonging to his office; that at such a juncture it was to be expected that he should omit nothing within the proper agency of Secretary of War, towards the public defence; and that I thought it proper particularly that he should proceed to Bladensburg and give any aid to Genl. Winder that he could; observing that if any difficulty on the score of authority should arise, which was not likely, I should be near at hand to remove it.

He said in reply that he had put no such construction on the paper of instructions as was alluded to; and that as I thought it proper, he would proceed to Bladensburg, and be of any service to Genl. Winder he could."

The President arrived at the battle site shortly after noon astride a borrowed horse. At some point during the early morning, his horse had unexpectedly gone lame and he exchanged mounts with Carroll, of Bellevue. He sought out Armstrong, inquiring if the War Secretary had offered Winder any advice for the approaching engagement. To his amazement, Armstrong had not spoken with Winder. The President suggested that he promptly do so. Together they rode over to Winder, but the text of the conversation was lost to Madison because his horse became unruly. By the time he gained control the brief colloquy was over. Again, he asked if the Secretary had any advice to offer. Armstrong responded that everything seemed as good as circumstances permitted. Madison recorded the text of the conversation:

"I asked the latter whether he had spoken with Genl. Winder on the subject of his arrangements and views. He said he had not. I remarked that tho' there was so little time for it, it was possible he might offer some advice or suggestion that might not be too late, to be turned to account; on which he rode up to the General as I did myself. The unruliness of my horse prevented me from joining in the short conversation that took place. When it was over, I asked Genl. Armstrong whether he had seen occasion to suggest any improvement in any part of the arrangements. He said that he had not; that from his view of them they appeared to be as good as circumstances admitted."

For Madison, Armstrong's latest remark, coupled with his lack of initiative, must have been the "straw that broke the camel's back." The enemy was in sight, yet the Secretary of War remained passive. An outraged President countermanded the authority given to Armstrong earlier in the morning granting him authority to issue orders and told the Secretary that the military would handle its own duties and responsibilities. Armstrong later described his actions:

"This state of things gave occasion to a conversation, principally conducted by the President and the Secretary of the Treasury, which terminated in an understanding that I should repair to the troops, and give such directions that were required by the urgency of the case. I lost no moment in fulfilling this intention, and had barely time to reconnoitre the march of the enemy, and to inform myself of our own arrangements, when I again met the President, who told me that he had come to a new determination, and that the military functionaries should be left to the discharge of their own duties, on their own responsibilities. I now became, of course, a mere spectator of the combat."

About the hour the President and his contingent reached Bladensburg to view the battle and offer advice as needed, an anxious Dolley included a few more lines in her narrative to her sister Lucy. Not one to panic, she remained at the White House, now without guards, waiting for her husband. As did the President, she firmly believed that militia forces fighting for their hearths and homeland would courageously stop any invading army and was disappointed to detect this lack of spirit amongst the American troops. She told Lucy:

> "Wednesday morng., twelve o'clock. Since sunrise I have been turning my spy-glass in every direction, and watching with unwearied anxiety, hoping to discover the approach of my dear husband and his friends; but, alas! I can descry only groups of military, wandering in all directions, as if there was a lack of arms, or of spirit to fight for their own fireside."

Secretary of State James Monroe (1758-1831) was appointed acting Secretary of War after the American collapse at Bladensburg, holding two Cabinet posts simultaneously. His energetic spirit and decisive attitude lifted the moral of the dejected troops and helped restore confidence in the shattered administration. The military successes in the last phases of the War reflected positively on his performance as head of the War Department and led to his election as the fifth President of the Untied States.

9

THE BLADENSBURG RACES

At Bladensburg the American forces were obviously unprepared and hastily assembled. There was no coordination. Everything was in confusion. Stansbury's troops had neglected to blow up the Bladensburg Bridge that connected with the Washington and Georgetown Roads on the western side of the river. The American defense at Bladensburg was basically handled by the Baltimore militia and Barney's experienced flotillamen. Winder had been able to collect perhaps 7000 troops by this time, far more than the estimated 4500 of the British, but this figure was misleading because many of his men never saw action. Troops were still arriving when the battle commenced. The cavalry of nearly 400 horsemen was never used, Colonel William Scott's regulars were ordered to retreat before they had even fired a shot, and the 60th Virginia Militia totally missed the fight because Minor was still trying to procure weapons and ammunition from the munitions depot as suggested by Armstrong the prior evening. Monroe was the first official to arrive at the battle site. His first move was to inspect Stansbury's placement of 2200 Maryland militiamen and on his own initiative, he redeployed troops that were concealed by an apple orchard near the riverbank to more exposed positions on the sloping ground. This gave the appearance of more men on the field. The rearranged positions were Colonels John

Ragan's First Maryland, John Schutz's Second Maryland and Sterett's Fifth Maryland. The regiments were now a quarter of a mile farther back from their original stations and too spread out to effectively support the front line. Winder had been at the battle site less than twenty minutes when the enemy came into view. At this time, he was discussing the reformed line with Stansbury and Monroe, but was unable to address the concern because time had run out for any further planning. Events unfolded so quickly that the General was unable to even inspect his troops. Winder wrote:

> "I arrived at the bridge at Bladensburg about 12 o'clock, where I found Lieutenant Colonel Beall had that moment passed with his command, having just arrived from Annapolis.... Upon inquiry, I learned that General Stansbury was on a rising ground upon the left of his line. I rode immediately thither, and found him and Colonel Monroe together. The latter gentleman informed me that he had been aiding general Stansbury to post his command, and wished me to proceed to examine it with them, to see how far I approved of it.
>
> We were just proceeding with this view, when some person rode up and stated that news had just been received of a signal victory, obtained by General Izard over the enemy, in which one thousand of the enemy were slain and many prisoners taken. I ordered the news to be immediately communicated to the troops, for the purpose of giving additional impulse to their spirits and courage.
>
> The column of the enemy at this moment appeared in view, about a mile distant, moving up the Eastern Branch, parallel to our position. From the left, where I was, I perceived that, if the position of the advanced artillery were forced, that two or three pieces upon the left of Stansbury would be necessary to scour an orchard, which lay between his line and his artillery, and for another rifle company to increase the support of his artillery. These were promptly sent forward by General Smith, and posted as hastily as possible, and it was barely accomplished before I was obliged to give orders to the advanced artillery to open upon the enemy, who was descending the street toward the bridge. All further examination or movement was now impossible, and the position where I then was, immediately in rear of the left of Stansbury's line, being the most advance position was, which I could have any commanding view, I remained there."

Men were rushing in from the navy yard. American positions were still being deployed when the battle commenced. Winder's army had the advantage of rising ground and outnumbered the enemy, but it did not have the military knowledge or proper equipment necessary for victory. There was apprehension amongst officials about Winder's leadership skills, and now, at the critical moment, he did not inspire confidence with his officers and troops. The Commander of the 10th Military District was completely overwhelmed by the events. Three six-pounders that had been requested from Burch's artillery arrived, but they

were not set in place. With the enemy in sight, Burch went looking for
the General to receive orders as to where to put them, but could not find
him. One of his soldiers, Law, saw Winder nearby, approached him and
received the orders where to set up the guns. Shortly after they were in
place, Winder came by and told Law that when he retreated, he should
take the Georgetown Road. Law later stated:

> "At this time the advance of the British was just entering the outskirts
> of Bladensburg, and the arms of a large body of them were seen
> glittering in the sun, about a mile from the town. Finding that
> Captain Burch did not return as soon as might have been reasonably
> expected, and hearing that General Winder was a short distance from
> us, I marched our detachment of artillery towards the spot where he
> was, and, on coming up to him, inquired what position I should take
> with our artillery. He addressed me as Captain, and ordered me to
> place our pieces in battery on the left of the Baltimore line of
> infantry, which was immediately done. Shortly after he came up to
> us, and, again addressing me, said, 'When you retreat, take notice you
> must retreat by the Georgetown road.'"

It was approaching twelve thirty when the Americans spotted the
British marching up the southeastern side of the Eastern Branch toward
the Bladensburg Bridge. The river was shallow enough at this point to
ford easily. The two roads leading from Washington and Georgetown
formed a pie shaped wedge as they came together at the bridge on the
western side of the river. The Americans concentrated on that spot. The
plan was to deny the British access to the bridge and stop them as they
waded through the shallow water. The Baltimore artillery set up six
small cannons facing the bridge in an earthwork that Wadsworth's
civilian volunteers had preciously thrown together. Slightly behind to
the battery's left were two companies of Sterett's regiment and to its
right were Major William Pinkney's riflemen. Positioned about 500
yards behind this formation was Stansbury's Maryland Militia consisting
of 1400 troops, with Lavall's cavalry stationed considerably off to its
left. The enfilade formed a line that was thought to be sufficient to cover
the bridge, fordable water and both roads leading from it on the western
side. Two other lines were hastily arranging themselves behind the front
line as the troops reached the field. Beall's 800 Annapolis militiamen
had marched sixteen miles that morning, arriving at Bladensburg about
noon. They quickly assembled on the rising ground to the east of the
Washington Road, with Lieutenant Kramer's Maryland militia stationed
in front of them. Smith's District Militia hastily took positions on the
opposite side of the Washington Road near Tournecliffe's Bridge as the
men continued to pour in from the navy yard. Gleig put down his
thoughts at his first sight of the American army:

> "The corps which occupied the heights above Bladensburg, was

composed chiefly of militia; and as the American militia are not dressed in uniform, it exhibited to our eyes a very singular and a very awkward appearance. Sufficiently armed, but wretchedly equipped, clothed part in black coats, others in blue, others in ordinary shooting-jackets, and some in round frocks, the three motley lines of infantry, but that their order was tolerably regular, might have passed off very well for a crowd of spectators, come out to view the approach of the army which was to occupy Washington.

A few companies only, perhaps two, or at the most three battalions, wearing the blue jacket, which the Americans have borrowed from the French, presented some appearance of regular troops. The rest, as I have just mentioned, seemed country people, who would have been much more appropriately employed in attending to their agricultural occupations, than in standing, with muskets in their hands, on the brow of a bare green hill. There were, however, upon the right, some squadrons of horse, whose bearing was sufficiently warlike, whilst about twenty pieces of cannon, arranged at different points along the ridge, spoke of another and more serious affair, than a mere triumphal march through the middle of this levy.

I have seldom been more forcibly struck with anything than with the contrast, which a glance to the rear afforded at this moment, with the spectacle which was before me. A column of four thousand British soldiers, moving in sections of six abreast, and covering an extent of road greater than its windings would permit the eye to take in, met my gaze in that quarter. The dress, the perfect regularity of their step, the good order which they preserved, and, above all, the internal conviction, that they were only advancing to victory, excited in me feelings for which I have no words, and which he only can conceive who has stood in a similar situation."

Reaching the village, the British did not pause long. Ross took a brief look at the situation and ordered an immediate attack, even though he had only Colonel William Thornton's brigade of about twelve hundred men. The other troops had not yet arrived. He sent Thornton's Light Brigade to attack the bridge. At first, the American artillery and riflemen were able to slow the initial attack, felling those rushing the bridge. The enemy drew back and regrouped. Many began fording the shallow river on both sides. The Royal Marines quickly made it to the water's edge, set up their equipment and began setting off their latest weapon, the Congreve rocket. The rockets had an immediate impact along the Yankees' front line. The raw troops were terrified. Winder rushed about doing his utmost to calm the troops, pointing out that the rockets did little harm. The scholarly Madison, who took his role as Commander in Chief seriously, was positioned on horseback with his Cabinet directly behind the frightened line. It was at this time the President suggested that his entourage retire to a safer position on the field and leave the decisions to those who better understood warfare:

"When the Battle had decidedly commenced, I observed to the Secretary of War and Secretary of State that it would be proper to withdraw to a position in the rear, where we could act according to circumstances; leaving military movements now to the military functionaries who were responsible for them. This we did, Mr. Rush soon joining us. When it became manifest that the battle was lost; Mr. Rush accompanying me, I fell down into the road leading to the city and returned to it.

It had been previously settled that in the event of the enemy's taking possession of the city, and the necessity of Executive consultations elsewhere, Fredericktown would be the proper place for the assembling of the Cabinet."

Rush related to the Investigative Committee that before the battle commenced, Madison recognized that decisions during the engagement should be left to those who understood warfare. He was on the field only in an advisory position. The President's suggestion that Armstrong, Monroe and he retire further away from the line of fire, but remain on the field, had been decided during the ride to Bladensburg. The Attorney General stated:

"It had been the wish of the President, as signified to me, on the ride out, that, after every military arrangement for the battle had been made, on the best advice attainable, the civil functionaries should join him, and retire to the rear of the army, with a view to any ulterior deliberations which events might render necessary. I took it to be in conformity with this wish that the Secretary of State, the Secretary of War, and himself, retired at the time, and in the manner, I have stated, and it was in pursuance of it that I accompanied them.

Whilst still on the field, encompassed by part of our troops, I think I understood the two Secretaries to unite in opinion, that the mode in which they had been drawn up was as judicious as the time and circumstances allowed. But of this I do not speak with confidence, as my attention was partly taken up in viewing, from hill to hill, the contending movements. To me it appeared plain that entire ranks of our men, in front, were dispersed by the shock of the enemy, before any order for retreat was given by the commanding general."

It was not long before the remainder of Ross' army arrived. Reinforced, he ordered a second attack to the bridge. Thornton's Light Brigade again charged the bridge, rushing over the bodies of their own dead or wounded. Cannons roared and muskets fired, dropping many, but the British never ceased advancing. By the time the Americans were able to reload, the Redcoats were solidly across the bridge fanning out across the field with bayonets gleaming. The precision of the regulars and the screeching rockets proved too much for the militia troops. Even though this new weapon did little damage, the militiamen were terrified. The front line began to collapse. Without having been issued orders, the men simply fled the field. Others quickly followed. Winder tried to stem the tide, but it was too late. A universal flight took place. Through a messenger, Winder let Madison know that his forces were falling back and that he hoped to reform a second line with Smith's District Militia and make a stand near the Turnpike Gate. In this manner he tried to channel the retreat down the road towards Washington, but, most of the militia rushed down the Georgetown Road as instructed earlier to Law. Unfortunately, a rallying point had never been named in case of withdrawal and the fleeing troops, having nowhere specific to go, simply scattered all over the countryside. The initial engagement lasted less than an hour. It was a complete rout, prompting the battle to go down in history as "The Bladensburg Races." Winder reported:

> "The direct line of retreat to the whole of this first line being to the hill on which I had directed the artillery to halt, and immediately in connexion with the positions of General Smith's corps, which were not arrayed in line, but posted on advantageous positions in connexion with and supporting each other, according as the nature of the ground admitted and required; I had not for a moment, dispersed and disordered as was the whole of Stansbury's command, supposed that their retreat would have taken a different direction. But it soon became apparent that the whole mass were throwing themselves off to the right on the retreat towards Montgomery Court House, and flying wide of this point; the whole of the cavalry, probably, from the pressure of the infantry that way, were also thrown wide of this line of retreat toward the right.
>
> After making every effort to turn the current more toward General Smith's command and the city, in vain, and finding that it was impossible to collect any force to support the artillery, which I had directed to halt, and finding also that the enemy's light troops were extending themselves in that direction, and pressing the pursuit, I directed the artillery to continue their retreat, on the road they then were, toward the capitol, it being impossible for them to get across to the turnpike road or unite with General Smith's brigade.
>
> The hope of again forming the first line at this point, and there renewing the retreat, or, at all events, of being able to rally them between the capitol and that point, and renewing the contest, induced me, at the moment I directed the fifth regiment to retreat, to request Mr. Riggs, of Georgetown, to proceed to the President, and inform him that we had been driven back, but that it was my hope and intention to form and renew the contest between that place and the capitol."

So swift was the fall of Bladensburg that Barney and his seamen were still approaching when, to their astonishment, they encountered American infantry and cavalry racing from the battlefield in the direction of Washington or Georgetown. This was followed shortly thereafter by Madison and Rush who, upon receiving Winder's note of the fallback, retired, slowly down the road to Washington. The seamen had hauled five large cannons from the navy yard. Barney halted when he got within firing range of the enemy. He immediately ordered his guns set up in the road, and opened a destructive cannonading on the advancing troops, giving strength to Smith's militia forces. With the support of the experienced sailors and Marines under Captain Samuel Miller, a valiant, but futile, counterattack took place that lasted about an hour. Many militia troops shakily remained in position, but, to Barney's mortification, those who were running offered no assistance. His cannons roared, his seamen acting as infantry charged, and many British soldiers and officers were either killed or wounded. Financier Jacob Barker was at the White House later that afternoon, and heard the President remark on the extensive damage that Barney's cannons made to the advancing troops, and his astonishment that the enemy never stopped coming. Barker recalled:

> "The President had a full view of the conflict, and noticed the havoc made. He said the fire from Barney's guns made perfect lanes through the ranks of the enemy, but that the troops filled the voids thus created, without turning to the right or to the left to see whether their companions had lost a head, a leg, or an arm."

With the Americans in disarray, Ross and Cockburn rode into the fray, ordering in further reinforcements. The scarlet uniforms kept advancing. Winder ordered a retreat of what remained of his forces, but did not feel obligated to inform Barney because he had no authority over the navy. The General had thought nothing of keeping Barney's men behind, covering the army's retreat from Old Fields, or stationing the seamen in defense of the Lower Bridge while everyone was rushing to Bladensburg, but now amidst all the confusion, he more or less abandoned the flotillamen. Barney and his crew, obviously aware of the retreat, but not under the authority of the army, stood their ground and continued the fight. The drivers of the Commodore's ammunition wagon drove off with the retreat, leaving him without supplies. Barney received a wound in his thigh and many of his men went down. The enemy overran the battery and some of his sailors were bayoneted while still holding fuses in their hands. Completely outflanked, without militia support and out of ammunition, a badly wounded Barney ordered that the guns be spiked and his men retire. Three of his officers tried to help him from the field, but Barney was too weak to travel and remained behind. The Commodore surrendered to Captain John Wainwright, who then informed Ross and Cockburn that Barney had been taken prisoner. The two officers sought out Barney, who was paroled on the spot, and transported to a tavern near Bladensburg to have his wound properly dressed. Barney continued in his report from Elk Ridge to the Secretary of the Navy:

"The enemy from this period never appeared, in force, in front of us; they pushed forward their sharp shooters; one of which shot my horse under me, who fell dead between two of my guns. The enemy, who had been kept in check by our fire, for nearly half an hour, now began to out-flank us on the right; our guns were turned that way; he pushed up the hill, about two or three hundred, towards the corps of Americans stationed as above described; who, to my great mortification, made no resistance, giving a fire or two, and retired. In this situation we had the whole army of the enemy to contend with. Our ammunition was expended; and, unfortunately, the drivers of my ammunition wagons had gone off in the general panic. At this time, I received a severe wound in my thigh; Captain Miller was wounded; Sailingmaster Warner killed; Acting Sailingmaster Martin killed; and Sailingmaster Martin wounded; but to the honor of my officers and men, as fast as their companions and messmates fell at the guns, they were instantly replaced from the infantry.

Finding the enemy now completely in our rear, and no means of defence, I gave orders to my officers and men to retire. Three of my officers assisted me to get off a short distance, but the great loss of blood occasioned such a weakness that I was compelled to lie down. I requested my officers to leave me, which they obstinately refused; but upon being *ordered* they obeyed; one only remained. In a short time I observed a British soldier, and had him called, and directed him to seek an officer; in a few minutes an officer came, and, on learning who I was, brought General Ross and Admiral Cockburn to me. Those officers behaved to me with the most marked attention, respect, and politeness, had a surgeon brought, and my wound dressed immediately. After a few minutes conversation, the General informed me (after paying me a handsome compliment) that I was paroled, and at liberty to proceed to Washington or Bladensburg; as, also Mr. Huffington, who had remained with me, offering me every assistance in his power, giving orders for a litter to be brought, in which I was carried to Bladensburg; Captain Wainwright, first Captain to Admiral Cochrane, remained with me, and behaved to me as if I was a brother. During the stay of the enemy at Bladensburg, I received every marked attention possible from the officers of the army and navy."

Paul Jennings, an educated, intelligent household slave of the Madisons, was fifteen years old when the British captured Washington. He told his story about the British invasion many years later during 1865, in his manuscript *A Colored Man's Reminiscences of James Madison*. Jennings' narrative began with a description of the gallantry the Negro seamen displayed in defending Barney's battery:

"After the war had been going on for a couple of years, the people of Washington began to be alarmed for the safety of the city, as the British held Chesapeake Bay with a powerful fleet and army. Every thing seemed to be left to General Armstrong, then Secretary of war, who ridiculed the idea that there was any danger. But in August, 1814, the enemy had got so near, there could be no doubt of their intentions. Great alarm existed, and some feeble preparations for defence were made. Com. Barney's flotilla was stripped of men, who were placed in battery, at Bladensburg, where they fought splendidly.

A large part of his men were tall, strapping Negroes, mixed with white sailors and marines. Mr. Madison reviewed them just before the fight, and asked Com. Barney if his 'Negroes would not run on the approach of the British?' 'No Sir,' said Barney, 'They don't know how to run; they will die by their guns first.' They fought till a large part of them were killed or wounded; and Barney himself wounded and taken prisoner. One or two of these Negroes are still living here."

Charles Ball, an escaped slave, served under Barney and assisted in the demolition of the flotilla. He stood his post at Bladensburg and felt that the Americans could have won the battle had the militia not fled "like sheep chased by dogs." In 1837 a narrative of Ball's life, as told to a northern abolition group, was printed. Ball told the writer:

"When we reached Bladensburg, and the flotilla men were drawn up in line, to work at their cannon, armed with their cutlasses, I volunteered to assist in working the cannon, that occupied the first place, on the left of the Commodore. We had a full and perfect view of the British army, as it advanced along the road, leading to the bridge over the East Branch; and I could not but admire the handsome manner in which the British officers led on their fatigued and worn-out soldiers. I thought then and think yet that General Ross was one of the finest looking men that I ever saw on horseback.

I stood at my gun, until the Commodore was shot down, when he ordered us to retreat, as I was told by the officer who commanded our gun. If the militia regiments, that lay upon our right and left, could have been brought to charge the British, in close fight, as they crossed the bridge, we should have killed or taken the whole of them in a short time; but the militia ran like sheep chased by dogs."

Smith's District Militia received orders from Winder to fall back and take a stand near the Turnpike Gate. There his troops encountered Minor's 60th Virginia Regiment rushing to reach Bladensburg. Minor, who had requested weapons and ammunition from Armstrong the night before, finally was issued the necessary supplies late Wednesday morning. He had frantically sought out Carbery during the early hours, and unable to find him, located Winder near the Eastern Branch Bridge, who gave the necessary authority to draw weapons from the armory. But at the depot Minor encountered further bureaucratic delay as the clerk took a careful count before issuing any supplies. Finally drawing the requested supplies, Minor sent his men on to Capitol Hill, while he waited to sign receipts. By the time his troops were equipped and on their way towards Bladensburg, the battle was lost. They encountered fleeing troops near the tollgate on the Washington Road. There the

Virginians were ordered by an aide of Winder to halt and join the District Militia to cover the retreat of army. While the line was still forming, another order was given for Smith and Minor to retire their forces to Capitol Hill and prepare to take a stand there. Not one shot was fired by the Virginians. Minor continued in his report to the Investigative Committee:

> "… from early next morning, I diligently sought for, until a late hour of the forenoon, without being able to find him, and then went in search of General Winder, whom I found near the Eastern Branch; when he gave an order to the armorer for the munitions wanting, with orders to return to the capitol, there to await further orders.

> On my arrival at the armory, found that department in the care of a very young man, who dealt out the stores cautiously, which went greatly to consume time; as, for instance, when flints were once counted by my officers who showed every disposition to expedite the furnishing the men, the young man had to count them over again, before they could be obtained, and at which place I met with Colonel Carbery, who introduced himself to me, and apologized for not being found when I was in search of him, stating he had left town the evening before, and had gone to his seat in the country.

> After getting the men equipped, I ordered them on to the capitol, and waited myself to sign the receipts for the munitions furnished; and, on my arrival, was informed by Major Hunter, who commanded in my absence, orders had been given to march to Bladensburg, when we took up our march for that place and met the retreating army on this side of the turnpike gate, and was ordered by one of General Winder's aids to form the line of battle on a height near that place, and was soon after ordered by the General in person to throw back my regiment from that position, into sections, and to wait until the retreating army had passed, and cover their retreat; and immediately after sent his aid to direct me to countermarch immediately, and come on to the capitol."

Winder did his best to stem the rout. At first he tried to form a position about 500 yards behind the original line. When that failed, he tried to take a stand near the Turnpike Gate. When that failed, he hoped to make a stand at Capitol Heights. Even though troops were in flight towards Georgetown or Baltimore, he believed it was not too late to rally in defense of the city because he still, possibly, had a force of about 4000 troops. Monroe and Armstrong joined Winder at the Capitol for a hurried discussion about what to do. Armstrong wanted to use the unfinished Capitol building (two sections connected by a wooden walkway) as a fort and fight it out there. Troops that had hurried into the city assembled on the Capitol grounds waiting for the outcome. The decision finally reached was to continue the retreat to Tenleytown above Georgetown, where Winder could collect and reorganize his shattered army. This was an unpopular decision. The seat of government of the United States was now left open to the enemy! Any remaining semblance of discipline now vanished. The men fled the ranks and the commanding General was left without anything that resembled an army. Winder's explanation for not defending the nation's capital was lame and he did not dwell on this decision in his lengthy report to the Investigative Committee. Winder continued:

> "In a few moments the Secretary of State and the Secretary of War joined me, besides that they had been witnesses to the dispersion of the troops and the exhaustion of those just halted by me. I stated the diminution of my force, and the extent of the positions which rendered it impossible to place the force I then had in such a position as to prevent the enemy from taking me on the flank as well as on front, and that no reasonable hope could be entertained, that we had any troops who could be relied on to make a resistance as desperate as necessary, in an isolated building which could not be supported by a sufficiency of troops without; indeed it would have taken nearly the whole of the troops to have sufficiently filled the two wings, which would have left the enemy masters of every other part of the city, and given him the opportunity, without risk, in twenty-four hours, to have starved them into a surrender. The same objection equally applied to the occupation of any particular part of the city.

> Both these gentlemen concurred that it would subject the whole of my force to certain capture or destruction; and in its reduced and exhausted condition it was wise and proper to retire through Georgetown, and take post in the rear of it, on the heights, to collect my force."

Smith and the men who served under him were shocked that Winder did not put up a fight at Capitol Heights, but instead made the decision to continue a retreat, already put in motion, that took the American forces through the city. Recognizing that no attempt was going to be made to defend Washington, most of the troops comprising the District Militia began to think more about their own interests, such as protecting their families and homes, and simply left the ranks. Smith wrote:

> "Whilst the line was still forming, I received orders from General Winder to fall back to the capitol, and there form for battle. I took the liberty of suggesting my impression of the preferable situation we then occupied; but expecting that he might be joined there by some of the dispersed troops of the front line, he chose to make the stand there.

> Approaching the capitol, I halted the troops, and requested his orders as to the formation of the line. We found no auxiliaries there. He then conferred for a few moments with General Armstrong, who was a short distance from us, and then gave orders that the whole should

retreat through Washington and Georgetown.

> It is impossible to do justice to the anguish evinced by the troops of Washington and Georgetown on the receiving of this order. The idea of leaving their families, their houses, and their homes, at the mercy of an enraged enemy, was insupportable. To preserve that order which was maintained during the retreat, was now no longer practicable. As they retired through Washington and Georgetown, numbers were obtaining and taking leave to visit their homes, and again rejoining; and with ranks thus broken and scattered, they halted at night on the heights near Tenleytown, and, on the ensuing day, assembled at Montgomery Court House."

Lavall, whose mounted horsemen simply sat and watched the battle, ordered his cavalrymen to retreat when he saw the American forces collapse. He took his men to the Capitol grounds because he had heard Winder meant to put up resistance in defense of the city. When this did not happen he ordered his cavalrymen to follow the retreating army as it fled northwest to Tenleytown and later to Montgomery Court House. Lavall said:

> "The pleasing hope to meet all our forces collected at Washington, and that there we would be better able to receive the enemy, from various motives and resources which we could not have had at Bladensburg, filled my mind with anxiety, and helped to comfort me in our retreat; for it was not in the power of imagination to have indulged itself with a moment of doubt, whether we should fight or not at Washington, and defend the capitol to the last man. I have not met a man who was not of the same opinion with me on that score; by what fatality we were made to pass through the city and leave it unprotected I know not, nor is it within the reach of my comprehension."

Winder's report to Secretary of War Armstrong, written from Baltimore three days after the inglorious battle, was rather brief concerning the size of the American army. The General did his best to justify his decisions by presenting a simple scenario suggesting he had done everything that he could under the trying circumstances. Winder deftly underestimated the size of the American troops and overestimated the number of British soldiers wounded or killed, perhaps in hopes of gaining some slight respectability for the shameful conduct of the troops under his command. The General stated:

> "After all the force that could be put at my disposal in that short time, and making such dispositions as I deemed best calculated to present the most respectable force at whatever point the enemy might strike, I was enabled, by the most active and harassing movements of the troops, to interpose before the enemy at Bladensburg, about five thousand men, including three hundred and fifty regulars, and Commodore Barney's command. Much the larger portion of this

force arrived on the ground when the enemy were in sight, and were disposed to support in the best manner the position which General Stansbury had taken. They barely reached the ground before the action commenced, which was about one o'clock, P. M. of the 24th instant, and continued about an hour.

The contest was not as obstinately maintained as could have been desired, but was by parts of the troops sustained with great spirit and with prodigious effect, and had the whole of our force been equally firm, I am induced to believe the enemy would have been repulsed notwithstanding all the disadvantages under which we fought. The artillery from Baltimore, supported by Major Pinkney's rifle battalion, and a part of Captain Doughty's from the navy yard, were in advance to command the pass of the bridge at Bladensburg, and played upon the enemy, as I have since learned, with very destructive effect; but the rifle troops were obliged after some time to retire, and of course the artillery. Superior numbers, however, rushed upon them, and made their retreat necessary, not, however, without great loss on the part of the enemy....

The right and center of Stansbury's brigade, consisting of Lieutenant Colonel Ragan's and Shutz's regiments, generally gave way very soon afterwards, with the exception of about forty rallied by Colonel Ragan, after having lost his horse and a whole or a part of Captain Trower's company, both of whom General Stansbury represents to have made, even thus deserted, a gallant stand.... The 5th Baltimore regiment, under Lieutenant Colonel Sterret, being the left of Brigadier General Stansbury's brigade, still, however, stood their ground, and except for a moment, when part of them recoiled a few steps, remained firm and stood until ordered to retreat with a view to prevent them from being out flanked....

The reserve under Brigadier General Smith, of the District of Columbia, with the militia of the city and Georgetown, with the regulars, and some detachments of the Maryland militia, flanked on their right by Commodore Barney and his brave fellows, and Lieutenant Colonel Beall, still were to the right of the hill and maintained the contest for some time with great effect....

From the best intelligence there remains but little doubt that the enemy lost at least four hundred killed or wounded, and of these a very unusual portion killed. Our loss cannot, I think, be estimated at more than from thirty to forty killed, and fifty or sixty wounded. You will readily understand that it is impossible for me to speak minutely of the meritor demerit of particular troops so little known to me from their recent and hasty assemblage. My subsequent movements, for the purpose of preserving as much of my force as possible, gaining reinforcements and protecting this place, you already know."

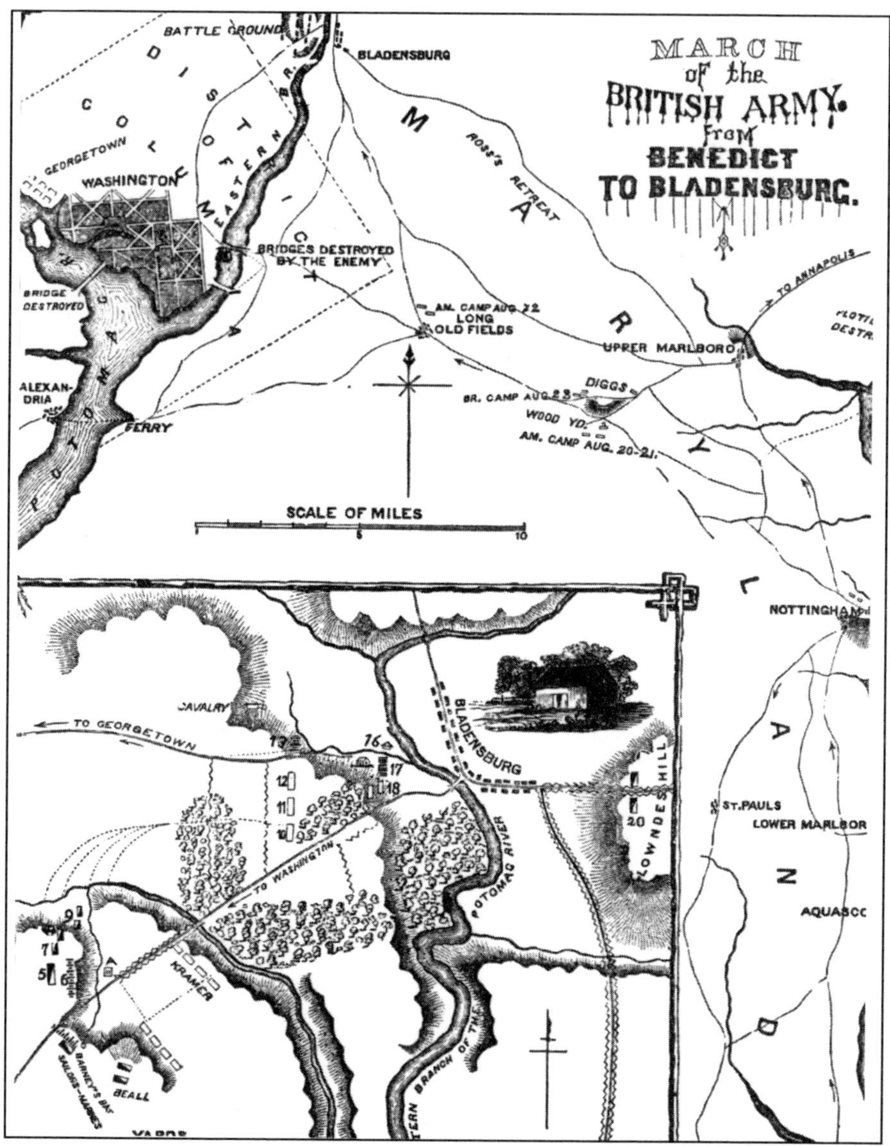

Lossing's Field Book of the War of 1812

The above shows the route taken by Brigadier General Robert Ross and Admiral George Cockburn from Benedict to and from Washington, including the theater of operations at the Battle of Bladensburg. The maps were drawn by Lieutenant George de Lacy Evans (1787-1870), a deputy quarter master general in the British army.

10

THE ESCAPES

Listening to the sounds of cannons booming from the not too distant fields of Bladensburg, Dolley asked Jennings to set the table for what was planned as an evening's victory party that was to include the entire Cabinet, their wives, military officers and other guests. As he was finishing this task, James Smith, a freed slave, galloped up to the mansion wildly waving his hat shouting for all to hear, "Clear out! Clear out! General Armstrong has ordered a retreat!" About this same time, the nervous First Lady received word from her husband that the battle was lost and she should abandon the Executive Mansion. A wagon was somehow obtained and hastily loaded with the numerous trunks already filled with national possessions to be deposited in the Bank of Maryland. The wagon contained such items as important Cabinet papers, White House silver, books, a few Madison belongings and the crimson velvet curtains that had hung in the oval drawing room for the past five years. Dolley's account to Lucy continued:

> "Wednesday Three O'clock. Will you believe it, my sister? We have had a battle, or skirmish, near Bladensburg, and here I am still, within sound of the cannon! Mr. Madison comes not. May god protect us! Two messengers, covered with dust, come to bid me fly; but here I mean to wait for him.… At this late hour a wagon has been procured,

and I have had it filled with the plate and most valuable portable articles belonging to the house. Whether it will reach its destination, the "Bank of Maryland," or fall into the hands of British soldiery, events must determine."

Earlier the First Lady received a panicked note from her sister Anna who resided on F Street in Washington. It has been given a date circa August 23, but the wording and tone of the letter suggests that it may have been sent after Anna learned that the battle had not gone well. The note was written in alarming haste. Clearly the Cutts were not prepared for Winder's swift defeat at Bladensburg. The Mr. C. referred to here was Anna's husband Richard. Anna wrote:

> "{ca. 23 August 1814}
>
> My Sister –
> Tell me for gods sake where you are and what {you are} going to do – I have only time to ask Mr. C. to take out the fore part of the carriage – put in the piano – and any thing he can get in there, or in a wagon if the British are coming – We can hear nothing but what is horrible here – I know not who to send this to – and will say but little-
>
> A Cutts"

Jennings related a picture of normalcy at the White House during Wednesday, until news arrived announcing the retreat. The daily tasks had continued as usual. The dinner that was customarily served at three in the afternoon was prepared. Jennings had set the table himself. Wine from the President's valued collection was placed in coolers. Armstrong, still not accepting that Washington was in jeopardy, stopped by earlier in the day and assured Dolley that there was no danger. Jennings related:

> "Well, on the 24th of August, sure enough, the British reached Bladensburg, and the fight began between 11 and 12. Even that very morning general Armstrong assured Mrs. Madison there was no danger. The President with General Armstrong, General Winder, Colonel Monroe, Richard Rush, Mr. Graham, Tench Ringgold, and Mr. Duvall rode out on horseback to Bladensburg to see how things looked. Mrs. Madison ordered dinner to be ready at 3, as usual; I set the table myself, and brought up the ale, cider and wine, and placed them in the coolers, as all the Cabinet and several military gentlemen and strangers were expected. While waiting, at just about 3, as Sukey, the house servant, was lolling out of a chamber window, James Smith, a free colored man who had accompanied Mr. Madison to Bladensburg, galloped up to the house, waiving his hat, and cried out, 'Clear out, clear out! General Armstrong has ordered a retreat!'"

Even though other messengers arrived, including Mayor James Blake, encouraging her to leave and not risk capture, Dolley was not to be hurried. By now panic had overtaken the city. The troops guarding the Presidential Mansion had long since fled. A good friend, Carroll, of

Bellevue, had arrived to help hasten her departure. Even though her carriage was ready, a determined Dolley insisted upon remaining until she was satisfied that Gilbert Stuart's full-length portrait of George Washington, purchased by Congress for the White House in 1800, would not fall into enemy hands. The picture was hanging on the west wall of the large dining room. Its gilded frame was tightly screwed to the wall. It was taking the combined efforts of the servants a long time to unscrew it, so for the sake of speed, she ordered that the frame be broken. This was done. The canvass, still attached to its stretcher, was taken out and laid on the dining room floor. The portrait's safekeeping was entrusted to Barker and Robert DePeyster, two longtime Quaker friends from New York who had stopped by the White House in the midst of the chaos to offer their assistance. Dolley told them to save Washington's picture if possible. If this were not feasible, then they should destroy it. Under no circumstances should they allow it to fall into the hands of the British. The two gentlemen hid the canvas at a Maryland farm for several weeks until Barker retrieved it and returned it to the First Lady. Before finally entering her coach, Dolley concluded her two day narrative to her sister Lucy:

> "Our kind friend, Mr. Carroll, has come to hasten my departure, and is in a very bad humor with me, because I insist on waiting until the large picture of General Washington is secured, and it requires to be unscrewed from the wall. This process was found too tedious for these perilous moments; I have ordered the frame to be broken, and the canvas taken out. It is done! and the precious portrait placed in the hands of two gentlemen of New York, for safe keeping. And now, dear sister, I must leave this house, or the retreating army will make me a prisoner in it by filling up the road I am directed to take. When I shall again write to you, or where I shall be tomorrow, I cannot tell!"

Jenning's description of salvaging Stuart's portrait of the first President paralleled the First Lady's account. He made it very clear that the painting was not cut from its frame, it was not rolled up, and Dolley did not carry it with her during her escape. For one thing, the oil was eight feet in length by five feet in width. It would have been awkward, difficult to roll up and the paint would have cracked. Jennings named Daniel Carroll, of Duddington, the brother of Bellevue's Carroll, as hastening Dolley into her coach. It was possible that both brothers were in attendance, but the few available accounts of the historic event have been consistent in describing only one Carroll at the White House – Charles Carroll, the owner of the Georgetown estate named Bellevue. Jennings continued:

> "All then was confusion. Mrs. Madison ordered her carriage, and passing through the dinning room, caught up what silver she could

crowd into her old-fashioned reticule, and then jumped into the chariot with her servant girl Sukey, and Daniel Carroll, who took charge of them; Jo Bolin drove them over to Georgetown Heights; the British were expected in a few minutes. Mr. Cutts, her brother-in-law, sent me to a stable on 14th Street, for his carriage. People were running in every direction. John Freeman (the colored butler) drove off in the coachee with his wife, child, and servant; also a feather bed was lashed on behind the coachee, which was all the furniture saved, except part of the silver and the portrait of Washington (of which I will tell you by-and-by)....

It has often been stated in print, that when Mrs. Madison escaped from the White House, she cut out from the frame the large portrait of Washington (now in one of the parlors there), and carried it off. This is totally false. She had no time for doing it. It would have required a ladder to get it down. All she carried off was the silver in her reticule, as the British were thought to be but a few squares off, and were expected every moment. John Suse' (a Frenchman, then door-keeper, and still living) and Magraw, the President's gardener, took it down and sent it off on a wagon, with some large silver urns and such other valuables as could be hastily got hold of. When the British did arrive, they ate up the very dinner, and drank the wines, &c., that I had prepared for the President's party."

In 1847, DePeyster wrote to Barker, who was then residing in Louisiana, requesting that he put into writing his recollection of the events relating to the saving of the portrait of the first President during the capture of Washington. Barker accommodated by writing a lengthy letter to DePeyster, who also wrote a brief description of the incident. Both letters were printed in the *New York Herald*, June 13, 1847. Barker was quite definite that the painting was not cut from its frame, that the gilded outside frame was broken, and that the painting remained intact on its stretcher on the floor of the room where it had been hanging before being transported by both men to a farmhouse in Maryland. Barker wrote:

"...when on the Pennsylvania Avenue, near the President's house, his servant came upon the full run, and said he was from the President, with a message to his lady to quit the city immediately; that the British had crossed the bridge at Bladensburg and were rapidly marching on to the city; that our troops had broken and run, without having made much opposition.

At the same time the servant requested me to go to the President's house, and render the necessary assistance. I immediately repaired there, and you joined me at the White House. On handing Mrs. Madison and Mrs. Cutts, her sister, into the carriage, Mrs. Madison said to me - 'Mr. Barker, I wish you, if you cannot save, to destroy, the portrait of Gen. Washington, the eagles which ornament the drawing room, and four cases of papers which you will find in the President's private room; the portrait I am very anxious to save, as it is the only original by Stuart; at all events, do not let them fall into the hands of the enemy, as their capture would enable them to make a great flourish.'

The carriage, with the ladies, accompanied by Mr. Cutts, took the direction of Georgetown - we immediately set about carrying into effect the directions of Mrs. Madison, whose admirable presence of mind, on that trying occasion, was of the most elevated character. It was with the greatest difficulty that we were enabled to procure a single horse and cart, with a driver, and another black boy, to assist us.

The cart we loaded with the most valuable articles to be found, and despatched it on the road taken by Mrs. Madison. About this time, the President came in with some others; he gave us an account of the battle which had been fought, and of the good conduct of Barney and his men. He then took some refreshments, and left, to join his lady....

Leaving the portrait on the floor of the room in which it had been hanging we removed the cases of papers to a distant house, concealing them in a cellar. The Eagles we also saved.... We took the portrait; you and I held each a corner of the light frame on which it was extended, having left the gilt frame on the floor of the room, my servant the third, and the hired black boy the other, and fell into the trail of the army, marched with them through Georgetown, and several miles on the road to Montgomery court house....

We were unable from fatigue to continue with the army, and, therefore, turned off into the woods, with the portrait. We were kindly received there at the residence of a widow lady, who had two sons in the army.... On the following morning, we arranged with our hostess to retain the portrait, until we, or one of us, should call for it; and departed for the headquarters of the army, which had halted for the night about four miles from Georgetown, and resumed its retreat early the next morning."

DePeyster's version began with a description of the drama he encountered at the navy yard before going to the White House where he meet Barker, a shipping tycoon, who was in Washington on business. DePeyster agreed with Barker's account of the events relating to the painting and concluded his narrative by declaring that it was Dolley who saved the portrait, and he insisted that all accolades should go to her:

"The patriotism of Mr. Barker who was a warm supporter of the war of '14, was exhibited in his zealous efforts to sustain the finances of the government, and to meet a large loan he had effected, for it was the occasion of his visit at that period at Washington....

After the President left for the field of battle, Mr. Barker returned to his lodgings, and I repaired to the navy yard. It may not be uninteresting to detail what occurred there during my brief visit. I had been but a few minutes in the yard, when an order came directing Commodore Fingey to despatch the marines and sailors to join the army. The sloop-of-war 'Argus' was fully equipped and ready for sea, and Capt. Creighton her commander, desired to remain on board with his crew; and by breasting his vessel off, he expressed his ability to defend the yard against 10,000 men. The English had no artillery, were much fatigued by a long march, and there is no doubt that, had Capt. Creighton's advice been taken, he had the means of accomplishing all that he promised. The Commodore, in reply observed, you have your orders, sir, proceed to execute them - The sailors were landed, and with the marines left the yard. I then proceeded to the city, and on my way to my lodgings stopped at the President's house, where I met Mr. B., and what followed his narrative details.

My chief object in sending you this narrative is with the view of rendering to Mrs. Madison the credit to which she is justly entitled for the suggestion which led to the saving of this portrait; and further, also, to show who assisted in carrying her wishes into effect. The merit which has been claimed by others, virtually belongs to her, and amidst the exciting events of that day the suggestion showed her self-possession and patriotic feelings. It is gratifying to me, even at this late hour, but happily before Mrs. Madison has passed away from among us, to place the above facts before the country, and to untie in common with it in the expression of the respect and attachment entertained for this estimable lady."

After reading the *New York Herald* articles, numerous persons, including Daniel L. Carroll, a son of Bellevue's Carroll, questioned the two gentlemen concerning the accuracy of their descriptive accounts, particularly because over a third of a century had lapsed since the portrait was hidden for safekeeping. DePeyster approached the former First Lady to write an account of her recollection of the event. This was done. Dolley's reply was later published in the *New York Express*:

"Washington, February 11, 1848.
DEAR SIR: I did not receive your favor containing the newspapers, and therefore is my impatience to assure you of my gratitude for the interest you take in my defence in the little narrative of the picture rescue.

You will see by the enclosed what was said at the time. The impression that Mr. Carroll saved Stuart's portrait of Washington is erroneous. The paper which was to accompany your letter has not reached me, but I have heard that his family believed he rescued it. On the contrary, Mr. Carroll had left me to join Mr. Madison, when I directed my servants in what manner to remove it from the wall, remaining with them until it was done. I saw Mr. Barker and yourself (the two gentlemen alluded to) passing, and accepted your offer to aid me, in any way, by inviting your to help me preserve this portrait, which you kindly carried, between you, to the humble but safe roof which sheltered it awhile.

> I acted thus because of my respect for General Washington, not that I
> felt a desire to gain laurels; but, should there be a merit in remaining
> an hour in danger of life and liberty, to save the likeness of anything,
> the merit in this case belongs to me."

The full-length portrait rescued by Dolley was a duplication of an original oil of Washington in his later years, which was painted from life by Stuart in 1796. It was the third in what became a series of four. The White House portrait was started by Stuart. He painted the head and shoulders of Washington, leaving the remaining portion of the canvass for William Winstanley to complete. Colonel William Smith, son-in-law of President John Adams, was the figure who stood for the artist to depict a rendering of the First President. Congress, paying $800.00, purchased the painting for the White House in 1800 and considered it the showpiece of the young nation. The original, known as the Lansdowne Portrait, was purchased by the trustees of the Donald W. Reynolds Foundation in 2001 for $20,000,000 as a gift to the nation and is displayed at the National Portrait Gallery, Smithsonian Institution. The portrait that hangs today in the East Room of the White House is the original Stuart/Winstanley painting that Dolley rescued. The remaining two replicas are displayed at the Pennsylvania Academy of Fine Arts and the Brooklyn Museum of Arts. Dolley's grand niece, Lucia Beverly Cutts, described the White House painting:

> "The portrait was painted partly by Gilbert Stuart, and completed by
> Winstanley, with Colonel Smith, the son-in-law of President John
> Adams, as a model for the unfinished body and limbs. Half a century
> later, when the White House was being rebuilt, this picture was
> renovated and put back in its place on the wall, together with many
> others added to the collection."

Once assured that the picture was protected, Dolley was finally ready to abandon the White House. On exiting, still trying to salvage what she could, she grabbed household silverware and other small valuables, stuffed them into an old-fashioned reticule, picked up the President's copy of the Declaration of Independence and stepped into her waiting carriage. With her personal maid Sukey, her sister Anna and Anna's three children, she headed in the direction of Georgetown. Anna's husband Richard followed in the Cutts's carriage, which was obtained by Jennings who had rushed to a stable on 14th Street to fetch it. John Freeman, the butler, driving "the coachee," left with his family in the third carriage. Lashed behind it was a feather-bed, the only piece of furniture from the mansion that survived the fires. The Madisons became the objects of many sarcastic squibs. In one such example, an unknown poet, in a lengthy poem known as *The Flights of Bladensburg*, wittedly, but somewhat inaccurately, described the flights of the Madisons and the

Cabinet. One portion portrays Dolley giving directions for her family to ride in a carriage while ordering the President to follow on horseback:

> "My sister Cutts, and Cutts and I,
>
> And Cutts's children three,
>
> Shall in the coach - and you shall ride
>
> On horseback after we."

Travel was dangerously slow. The group wound its way to the Georgetown Heights residence of the Navy Secretary and picked up his family. Everyone then proceeded to Bellevue, a four and half acre estate built on the heights above Georgetown, and joined Anne Sprigg Carroll to await the arrival of their husbands. At this point the plan appeared to be for the gentlemen to join their families at Bellevue, cross the Potomac via Little Falls Bridge and spend the night in Virginia; however, this was not to be. The President left the battle scene as Barney began his counterattack. He reached the White House, accompanied by Rush, Mason, and several other aides, around 4:00 p.m. to learn that Dolley had taken his advice and headed for safety in Georgetown. Barker and De-Peyster still remained, loading the full length portrait of Washington and a few more valuables into a wagon. A dejected sixty-three year old President did not rush leaving the Executive Mansion. The rapid overrun of the militia and Winder's retreat stunned him. Along with a small group, he lingered over an hour receiving various reports and deciding the best course to take at that time. Madison told Barker that he was surprised that a professional army could so easily defeat a militia force. Like Jefferson, he held the view that an individual fighting for his home land would do better than a paid soldier fighting on foreign soil. Barker related Madison's statement:

> "I could never have believed that so great a difference existed between regular troops and a militia force, if I had not witnessed the scenes of this day."

During this time, the location of the President's rendezvous with Dolley was changed to Foxall's Foundry, a cannon factory northwest of Georgetown along the shores of the Potomac River. Word was sent to Jones, now at Bellevue, to have everyone join him there. However, the crush of humanity fleeing the city made the journey to Foxall's difficult, if not impossible, and the plan was again changed. It now was decided that the President would cross the Potomac River as soon as possible on Mason's Ferry, and Tench Ringgold was sent to Bellevue to deliver the latest information. In this second message Madison wrote that he was proceeding to cross the river, and requested that everyone meet him on the other side. Dolley's entire group then left Bellevue and arduously made its way to the ferry site, only to learn that the President had already crossed over into Virginia. Jones described the two messages:

> "I left the Navy yard at about half past three o'clock accompanied by Mr. Duval and not long after learned that our army was rapidly retreating and that of the enemy advancing rapidly. We proceeded to Georgetown where I met my family and that of the Presidents at the house of Charles Carroll Esq of Belle Vue and received a message from the President requesting that I would join him at Foxalls works. At about 5 o'clock I set out in company with the family of the President, Mr. Carrols and my own, with Mr. Duval and proceeded through Georgetown to join the President but found he had already crossed at Masons ferry."

> "I soon after received a message from the President, by Mr. Tench Ringgold, at Mr. Charles Carroll's, informing me that he had proceeded to cross the river, and requesting that I would follow and meet him on the other side."

Monroe briefly stated that Madison was in Virginia in the area of the Little Falls during the nights of Wednesday and Thursday in his "J. M.'S Notes Respecting the Burning City in 1814;" however, he did not name the location. Furthermore, the Secretary of State offered no suggestion as to where he spent the evening of August 24th. It is thought that Monroe spent that horrific night, along with Ringgold, in Virginia at Wiley's Tavern in Fairfax County. Monroe wrote:

> "The President crossed the Potomac on the evening of the 24th, accompanied by the attorney-general and General Mason, and remained on the south side of the river a few miles above the lower falls, on the 25th. On the 26th he recrossed the Potomac, and went to Brookville, in the neighborhood of Montgomery Court-House, with intention to join General Winder."

Library of Congress

The Gilbert Stuart (1755-1828) full-length painting of George Washington (1732-1799) is perhaps America's most well known Presidential portrait. Stuart is credited with painting four of the exact same picture. The first, known as the Lansdowne Portrait, is owned by the Smithsonian Institution. Stuart started the third portrait, specifically for the new President's House, by painting the head and shoulders. It was completed by William Winstanley (1775-1806). After receiving word that the American forces were routed at Bladensburg, First Lady Dolley Madison (1768-1849) courageously remained in the White House until she was certain that the painting would be removed to a place of safety.

11

FIRING THE NAVY YARD

Among the few Americans who still remained in the city were Mordicai Booth, Captain John Creighton and Captain Thomas Tingey, commandant of the Washington Navy Yard since its founding in 1800. Earlier Wednesday afternoon, Tingey had received verbal orders from Jones to torch the navy yard if the British entered the capital. The yard was not to fall into enemy hands. Once the military at Bladensburg collapsed, Tingey was compelled to prepare for the yard's destruction. In answer to a letter written by Senator Joseph Anderson, November 10, 1814, inquiring under whose authority and by what orders was the navy yard set ablaze, Jones responded:

> "I have the honor to state that the eventual order, for the burning of the public shipping and stores, was given by the Secretary of the Navy, with the approbation of the President of the United States, and in conformity with the opinions of the Secretary of War and Navy, and assent of the other Heads of Departments, upon a consultation on that subject, in front of General Winder's quarters, on the morning of the 24th of August last, and in order to prevent the said shipping and stores from falling into the hands of the enemy."

Recognizing the engagement at Bladensburg was not going well for the American forces, the Navy Secretary hastened to the navy yard and commanded Tingey to destroy the yard if the British obtained possession of Washington. Jones realized that the commandant needed some such orders from the Navy Department, otherwise Tingey could face a possible court-martial if the invaders captured the yard. Even though the orders were verbal, Jones accepted responsibility for their issuance in his report to the Investigative Committee:

> "I went to the navy yard about two o'clock, and ordered the commandant to prepare the necessary trains for the destruction of the public shipping, and of the naval and military stores, and provisions, in the navy yard, and to destroy the same, so soon as he should ascertain that the enemy had taken possession of the city; first removing such articles of most value, as might be found practicable, particularly the new barges, if possible, and then retire in his gig....
>
> The commandant of the navy yard is a captain in the navy; the vessels and property were under his charge and command; and if no special order from the Department had been issued, and he had suffered the public shipping and property to have fallen into the hands of the enemy, he would have committed a high military crime, for which he would have been amenable before a court martial."

The Secretary of War did not issue any orders for demolishing the navy yard; however, before heading for the Cabinet rendezvous point at Fredericktown, Armstrong simply informed Tingey by messenger that the battle was lost and the navy yard could no longer be protected. Armstrong reported:

> "Perceiving that no order was taken for apprising Commodore Tingey of the retreat of the army, I sent Major Bell to communicate the fact, and to say, that the Navy Yard could no longer be covered. The commodore was of course left to follow the suggestions of his own mind, or to obey the orders, if orders had been given, of the Navy Department."

Torching the Washington Navy Yard was an extremely difficult task for Tingey. As its commanding officer, he had overseen its design and development into the largest naval facility in the country. Not wanting to set fire to the establishment prematurely, Tingey felt it necessary to justify his actions and delayed the execution of the order for nearly four hours. Creighton volunteered to ride out to locate the current whereabouts of both armies on the outside chance that Winder might be taking a stand in order to save the city. Booth was later sent on a reconnoitering mission to make certain the victors intended to occupy Washington. After scouting the city, it became obvious to both men that the Redcoats were advancing into the city and Winder's forces were not going to put up any resistance. They reported back to the navy yard with their information. Booth later wrote a detailed account of the afternoon's reconnoitering activities in his *Communication to Commodore Thomas Tingey from Mordecai Booth, His Clerk*:

> "You observed that everything was ready, but as Capt Creighton had gone out to ascertain where the army was, you would wait his return. Miller had assured me they had passed through Georgetown. Desirous of knowing positively myself, I proposed to you my going as far as the President's House.... You assented and when I reached the Jersey Avenue below Mr. Carroll's, I met Mr. Walter Cox, cornet in Caldwell's troop of horse. He told me he had left the army at Tenleytown - and I informed him where the British were. He went with me as far as the President's House.
>
> But all was a silent as a church.... Then, and not until then, was my mind fully impressed that the Metropolis of our Country was abandoned to its horrid fate. We had not proceeded far on the Pennsylvania Avenue before we overtook Captain Creighton, when I learned that no further opposition was to be expected. At the Tiber Bridge we met William Smith of Caldwell's troop; Mr. Cox turned him back on telling him they would return together to the Camp; after going to the Navy Yard. Mr. Cox proposed our getting to Capitol Hill, to pass the north end of the Capitol, that we might see if anyone was there; We saw not one soul. We went on in the direction of Tomblinson's Hotel. When about midway between that and Long's, Mr. Cox, we being in front, laid himself on his horse's neck as if observing something. I thought he was looking at what I took to be cows. He observed he saw the cows, but he also saw men advancing. They were rising from the hollow direct in front of Long's....
>
> We made a report accordingly. You then determined to fire the Yard - and asked Captn. Creighton and myself if we would keep our horses, or take a seat with you in your boat. Captn Creighton determined on going with you. My horse was too good a one to be lost. I obtained your permission to rely on him, when you told me to take care of myself and horse, and bade me farewell.... I left you only to return to my children. I passed from the Yard by the 20 buildings, and Mr. Young to the Potomac Bridge. The south draw was up. I had it put down - was scarcely over, before I saw the flames of the Yard - and had but reached the level beyond the Causeway before I saw a considerable explosion, which I conceived was the ordinance store, but possibly was the one at Greenleaf's Point, and I saw very soon after the flames at the fort, at that place - and by the time I reached the Hill - which did not exceed fifteen minutes - I saw the Capitol in flames, though I had seen lights within while on the bridge. This I had no doubt, was the work of the British. A sight *so repugnant to my feelings, so dishonourable,* so degrading, to the American character, and at the same time, so awful, almost palsied my faculties."

The evidence gathered for torching the yard was compelling. Bladensburg had been a disaster, the British had entered the capital, American troops were not going to defend the city and the unprotected navy yard was in danger of capture. Tingey waited until the last possible moment before executing the demolition plan. He finally lit the powder trains to the best stocked naval facility in the country. All of the stores, most of the buildings and two ships under construction, the 44 gun frigate *Columbia* and the 22 gun sloop of war *Argus*, were destroyed. In his report to the Secretary of the Navy, written after returning to the navy yard, August 27, 1814, Tingey related that matches were used to fire the Washington Navy Yard at 8:20 p.m.:

> "After receiving your orders of the twenty-fourth, directing the public shipping, stores, &c. at this establishment to be destroyed, in case of the success of the enemy over our army, no time was lost in making the necessary arrangements for firing the whole, and preparing boats for departing from the yard, as you had suggested.
>
> About 4 P.M. I received a message by an officer, from the Secretary of War, with information that he could 'protect me no longer.' Soon after this, I was informed that the conflagration of the Eastern Branch bridge had commenced; and, in a few minutes, the explosion announced the blowing up of that part near the 'draw,' as had been arranged in the morning....
>
> At twenty minutes past eight Captain Creighton returned; he was still extremely averse to the destruction of the property, but having informed him that your orders to me were imperative, the proper disposition of the boats being made, the matches were applied, and in a few moments the whole was in a state of irretrievable conflagration. When about leaving the wharf I observed the fire had also commenced at the works at Greenleaf's point, in the way out of the Branch we observed the Capitol on fire."

12

THE TERROR

The British rested several hours before continuing into Washington, even though Gordon's warships had not yet reached the metropolitan area. The plan was never to occupy America's capital, but to destroy it. It was a bold move on the part of Ross and Cockburn. Had Winder's army counterattacked, the Redcoats certainly would not have made it back to their ships. There was an extremely high factor of risk verses reward for entering the city. The Washington Navy Yard, where ships were built, was probably the only target worth the risk. They took no booty. There was little of value. These were angry invaders whose actions were more than just spanking the Americans for the 1813 burning of public buildings at York, an event the United States never authorized, but already had offered apologies and reparations. The destructive actions of the Redcoats undoubtedly went deeper, going back to England's surrender at Yorktown in 1781. An infant city, surrounded by woods, desperately struggling to give the appearance of a national capital, was Miss. Brown's description of Washington three months before the British arrived:

"I explored in company with some young friends the intricacies of

the Capitol, often pausing to admire its many architectural beauties.
A flight of stairs commencing in the center of a rotunda and
branching off to reach a gallery that surrounded this room excited my
admiration. While gazing on these and other beauties, among them
the full-length portraits of Louis XVI, and his Queen, Marie
Antoinette, in their royal robes, I then little dreamed of the devouring
flames that were soon so ruthlessly to feed upon them....

There were the two magnificent wings of the Capitol connected by a
long, unpainted wooden shed. Passing over a mile of rough road,
bordered here and there by Congress boarding-houses, with veritable
swamps between, you came to the President's house -beautiful with
architecture, upholstery, gilding and paintings, set down in the midst
of rough, unornamented grounds. Then another stretch of compara-
tive wilderness till you came to Georgetown. Almost every one of
any distinction drove four horses, and these fine equipages on these
wretched roads, with their elegant occupants, formed no trifling part
of the contrasts."

For many who had seen some of the great courts in Europe, it
must have been difficult to understand America's fourteen year old
unfinished capital. Gleig wrote that the Capitol building had been the
only notable fixture in the newly created city. He was not impressed
with the President's House. In his opinion, it was a public building
remarkable for nothing, except for its lack of architectural taste. It was
the largest residence at that time in the United States, yet Gleig claimed
that it was small, plain and not imposing. He was not impressed with the
Federal City, but offered the opinion that it had potential to flourish
because of its location. Gleig continued:

"It was then, and is, I believe, still in its infancy, few of the streets
being finished, and many containing not more than three or four
houses, at wide intervals from each other But its situation gives to it
advantages such as few capitals either in the new or old world can
boast of, and if it continue to be the head of the American States for
another century, it will become, I doubt not, one of the most
flourishing cities in existence. America is, and always will be, a
commercial nation, nor can a single town throughout the whole of
that vast continent boast of a better harbour than Washington.
Standing upon the Potomac, one of the most navigable of all the
rivers that empty themselves into the Chesapeake, the depth of which
is sufficient to float a frigate for some way above the town, it
possesses unrivalled facilities for the carrying on of an extensive
trade; whilst its distance from the coast is such as to place it, in a
great measure, beyond reach of insult from an enemy....

Like other infant towns, Washington is but little ornamented with
fine buildings; except the Senate-house, I really know none worthy to
be noticed. This however, is, or rather was, an edifice of some

beauty. It stood, where its ruins now stand, upon a mound called the Capitol Hill, and near a trifling stream named the Tiber; from which circumstances these modern republicans are led to flatter themselves that the days are coming when it will rival in power and grandeur the Senate-house of ancient Rome herself. It was built entirely of freestone, tastefully worked and highly polished; and, besides its numerous windows, was lighted from the top by a large and handsome cupola.

Perhaps it could not be said to belong to any decided style of architecture; but its central appearance was light, airy, and elegant. After traversing a wide and spacious entrance-hall, you arrived at the foot of a handsome spiral hanging staircase; on the right of which were two spacious apartments, one above the other, which were occupied as sitting chambers by the two houses of representatives. From these branched off several smaller rooms, fitted up as offices, and probably used as such by the various officers of state.

On the right of the staircase, again, were two other apartments equal in size to those on the left, with a like number of smaller rooms branching off from them. These were furnished as a public library, the two larger being well stocked with valuable books, principally in modern languages, whilst the others, filled with archives, national statutes, acts of legislature, &c., were used as the private rooms of the librarians.

The President's house, on the other hand, though likewise a public building, was remarkable for nothing except the absence of taste exhibited in its structure. It was small, incommodious, and plain; in no respect likely to excite the jealousy of a people peculiarly averse to all pomp or parade, even in their chief magistrate. Besides these, there were also a custom-house, several banking-houses, and a school or college, all claiming to themselves the distinction of public works; but in them there was a plainness amounting almost to coarseness, and a general air of republicanism, by no means imposing.

With respect to the number of inhabitants which Washington contained, I confess that I cannot pretend to give an opinion; but if any judgment may be formed from the extent of ground covered by what is considered as the town, I should say that they amounted to somewhere about sixty thousand. George Town, the quarter where the President's house stood, is compact and regular, containing, I should conceive, at least twenty thousand souls within itself; nor can the population of the other quarters be estimated at less than double that number."

Astride horses, Ross and Cockburn led a small advanced guard of about two hundred who marched into the deserted city at dusk. The remaining forces made camp at its eastern edge. The advance party came down Maryland Avenue in the direction of the Capitol. Michael

Shiner, a literate free black man at that time who worked as a mechanic at the navy yard, was one of the few remaining Washingtonians who witnessed the arrival of the British troops. He kept a diary, but wrote literally as he heard the words pronounced. Shiner included in his diary that the British army looked like flames of fire as its troops marched towards the city:

> "…and still the British armmy continued ther march on to Washington. Jest as we saw the armmy coming above the toll gate in Washington, we heard the tread of British armmy feet…. and as soon as we got sight of the British armmy raising that hill they look like flames of fier, all red coats, and the stoks of ther guns painted with red vermilion and the iron work shined like a Spanish dollar."

Ross halted his entrance near Capitol Hill, where a drummer sounded the call for a parley. He waited for a contingent of citizens bearing a flag of truce. Everything remained silent. No one appeared. The British cautiously moved forward, stopping to discuss the situation, perhaps 200 yards from the Capitol. Musket fire erupted from Robert Sewall's brick house to their right. This was formerly Gallatin's residence. Ross's horse was shot from under him and, by some accounts, at least one British soldier was killed and several others wounded. Stories varied as to what happened next, but the general version was that a small group quickly broke down the door of Sewell's home, killing anyone found inside. This was followed by a firing of Congreve rockets into the house, quickly sending it up in flames. Sewall's dwelling was the first structure to be torched by the invaders. It was soon followed by Americans blowing up their own navy yard, the bridge over the Eastern Branch and the fort at Greenleaf's Point. Gleig, who was not part of the advance team, related an account that suggests British soldiers killed some defenders inside Sewall's house before setting it on fire. He wrote:

> "Such being the intention of General Ross, he did not march the troops immediately into the city, but halted them upon a plain in its immediate vicinity, whilst a flag of truce was sent forward with terms. But whatever his proposal might have been, it was not so much as heard; for scarcely had the party bearing the flag entered the street, when it was fired upon from the windows of one of the houses, and the horse of the General himself, who accompanied it, killed. The indignation excited by this act throughout all ranks and classes of men in the army, was such as the nature of the case could not fail to occasion.
>
> Every thought of accommodation was instantly laid aside; the troops advanced forth-with into the town, and having first put to the sword all who were found in the house from which the shots were fired, and

reduced it to ashes, they proceeded without 'a moment's delay to burn and destroy everything in the most distant degree connected with Government."

According to Shiner, who witnessed the incident, no one ever knew who fired the shots. Many felt that it was some of the flotillamen from Barney's outfit, who had remained on the Capitol grounds long after Winder's decision to take the army further back to Tenleytown. Shiner's account varied with that of Gleig's because he observed that no one was found in the house to put to death. As a bystander, he watched the lighting of the dreaded Congreve rockets that were used to torch the house. Shiner continued in his diary:

> "The British army approach the house under the command of general Ross and his aids. His horse wher shot from under him and in a twinkle of an eye, house wher surrounded by the British armmy and search all through, up stairs and down stairs, in search of the man that shot the horse from under the general. But no man were found. After they found they couldn't find the man, they put a glow match to the house and then stood off a sertin distance and fired those Congreve Rocket. Those Rocket burnt until they came to the explosion part. They made the rafters fly East and West."

The account of Scott, Cockburn's aide-de-camp, was a little more dramatic. He claimed that Ross's party was fired upon by about three hundred men from the Capitol building itself and was caught in a cross fire from Tomlinson's Hotel on the left and Sewall's house on the right. The Lieutenant later insisted that he led the small contingent of Redcoats that broke into Sewall's house. He was quite definite that there was no one inside the residence once they entered it. It was empty; thus, no one was put to death. Even though the house was private property, it was burnt because it had been used for an act of war. At Tomlinson's Hotel, weapons and ammunition were found and, it too, was set ablaze. Scott reported:

> "Ere we arrived at the immediate suburbs of Washington it was dark. General Ross had repeatedly sounded a parley, but no attention having been paid to the summons, it was concluded that the enemy had given up all further resistance, and abandoned their capital to its fate. The General, Admiral, and their staff, accompanied by a small guard, rode therefore into the city, the two former, with Lieutenant Evans, in the front, Captain Smith, Captain McDougall, and myself, close behind them, and the soldiers composing the guard on each side.
>
> We were just on the point of entering the open space where the Capitol stood, and abreast of a large house on our left (I believe an

hotel,) and Mr. Gallatin's, on our right, when we were assailed by a volley from three hundred men who had sheltered themselves in the Capitol, and a cross fire from the houses on either side of us. The General's horse was killed on the spot, and several of the guard that accompanied us....

I was the officer ordered by Rear-Admiral Cockburn to break into the houses, which were barricaded at the bottom. It was effected with some little difficulty, and I do most positively assert that not a single individual of the enemy was put to death in the houses to the right, nor am I aware of any one having suffered at the hotel; in short, I cannot offer more conclusive evidence in support of my assertion than, that we found no one to put to death....

The houses were, however, consigned to the flames; they had been appropriated to the uses of war, and it is not to be supposed that they could be allowed to become again the source of annoyance and destruction to our men."

Moving next to the undefended Capitol itself, the Redcoats broke down the doors and for nearly an hour roamed through the empty halls and chambers. Some took souvenirs. They found the building difficult to ignite because it was structurally solid. Fires were started in various rooms, but nothing really took hold. Finally, in both the Senate and House of Representatives, furnishings, such as chairs, tables and desks, were formed into a pile, rocket powder was strewn about and rockets were fired directly into the heap. Both wings of the building were quickly ablaze and the temporary wooden structure connecting them readily ignited. The Supreme Court, located downstairs in the Senate wing was destroyed. The books comprising the Supreme Court's library were saved by clerk Elias Caldwell, who had previously moved them into his home. The books in the Library of Congress, located upstairs on the Senate side, were tinder for the sparks and quickly ignited. It was totally burned. About 3000 books perished in sheets of flames. Scott wrote that he was surprised at the magnificence and beauty of the unfinished Capitol building:

"The Capitol received the fate for which its late proprietors had thoughtlessly reserved it, by converting it into a place of arms: it was an unfinished but beautifully arranged building; the interior accommodations were upon a scale of grandeur and magnificence little suited to pure republican simplicity. We might rather have been led to suspect that the nation, whose councils were held beneath its roof, was somewhat infected with an unseemly bias for monarchical splendour.

Each of the senators and representatives had a handsome desk appropriated to his use, arranged in a semicircular order around the presidential chair, over which was placed a handsome clock, surmounted by a gilt eagle with extended wings and ruffled crest, looking towards the skies, emblematical, it is to be presumed, of the rising greatness of the young nation. Its funeral pile was lighted up as the clock under it told the hour of ten.... The position of the Capitol was elevated; the fiery beacon must have shed a sadly brilliant light upon the American habitations for miles around."

An August breeze blew sparks about and soon four neighboring buildings were blazing, among them, two houses on North Capitol Street, built under the direction George Washington. For safety, some Congressional papers had been moved by House clerk Frost into one of the houses. None survived the flames. Shiner thought that a grocery store owner, named McCormack, probably led the invaders into the Capitol itself. He continued:

"They wher a Scotchman. Kept a store on east Capitol and Alexandria. McCormack, Sr. He kept a store above that in the same square, which at that time, wher a lieutenant in Captain Burches artily company. The goods wher taken out by the British and distribided among any one that would receive them. Mr. McCormack had a very large store of groceries of all kinds, dry goods and likurs of all kinds, and great many of his goods had dierpeard out of Washington. I don't believe they got many of them, but this Scotch man store weren't interfered with. It was soposed at that time he was very officious. It was soposed that he escorted general Ross and his oficers into the united states senate and house of representative. This was done before it wher set on fier. Then after they had been in the senate and house of representative they went forth that night and burnt the capitol and the presidents house and all other public building."

With Capitol Heights ablaze, a small enemy force descended the hill around 10:30 p.m. and, under orders not to speak, silently marched two abreast down the mile long Pennsylvania Avenue to the President's House. There they were surprised to find the table set for dinner earlier in the day by the young servant Jennings. After drinking much of Madison's vintage wine, consuming the meal and collecting a few souvenirs, they torched the Executive Mansion of the United States. Ross was of the opinion that the meal was planned as an American victory celebration over the British forces. He related:

"So unexpected was our entry and capture of Washington, and so confident was Madison of the defeat of our troops, that he had prepared a supper for the expected conquers; and when our advanced party entered the President's house, they found a table laid with forty covers."

Ross's aide Smith was part of the group that consumed the meal prepared earlier by Jennings, while also enjoying some of the rare wines from the President's collection. He did not mind the torching of public structures, such as the Washington Navy Yard (the Redcoats set fire the following day to what had not already burned there), but was horrified by the barbarous burning of both the Capitol and the White House. The Captain felt that the basic reason the British entered the capital of the United States was to destroy it by fire. He felt that Cockburn would have burned the entire city if given the chance, but Ross would only allow for the destruction of the public buildings. Smith related:

> "...and we entered Washington for the barbarous purpose of destroying the city. Admiral Cockburn would have burnt the whole, but Ross would only consent to the burning of the public buildings. I had no objection to burn arsenals, dockyards, frigates building, stores, barracks, etc., but well do I recollect that, fresh from the Duke's humane warfare in the south of France, we were horrified at the order to burn the elegant Houses of Parliament and the President's house. In the later, however, we found a supper all ready, which was sufficiently cooked without more fire, and which many of us speedily consumed, unaided by the fiery elements, and drank some very good wine also. I shall never forget the destructive majesty of the flames as the torches were applied to beds, curtains, etc. Our sailors were artists at their work.

> Thus was fought the Battle of Bladensburg, which wrested from the Americans their capital Washington, and burnt its Capitol and other buildings with the ruthless firebrand of the Red Savages of the woods. Neither our Admirals nor the Government at home were satisfied that we had not allowed the work of destruction to progress, as it was considered the total annihilation of Washington and would have removed the seat of government to New York, and the Northern and Federal States were adverse to the war with England."

Gleig, who was not present at the feast in the President's House, also described the celebration as he heard of it from many who were present. He entered into his diary the thought that the Americans were so confident of victory that many remained in the city until they saw the army fleeing in the direction of Georgetown. He too felt the dinner was planned as a victory celebration for the President, Cabinet and American officers:

> "So confident had they been of the success of their troops, that few of them had dreamt of quitting their houses or abandoning the city; nor was it till the fugitives from the battle began to rush in, filling every place as they came with dismay, that the President himself thought of providing for his safety....

But this much I know, that the feast was actually prepared, though, instead of being devoured by the American officers, it went to satisfy the less delicate appetites of a party of English soldiers. When the detachment sent out to destroy Mr. Madison's house, entered his dining parlour, they found a dinner-table spread, and covers laid for forty guests. Several kinds of wine in handsome cut-glass decanters were cooling on the sideboard; plate-holders stood by the fire-place, filled with dishes and plates; knives, forks, and spoons, were arranged for immediate use; everything in short was ready for the entertainment of a ceremonious party. Such were the arrangements in the dining-room, whilst in the kitchen were others answerable to them in every respect. Spits, loaded with joints of various sorts turned before the fire; pots, saucepans, and other culinary utensils stood upon the grate; and all the other requisites for an elegant and substantial repast were exactly in a state which indicated that they had been lately and precipitately abandoned.

The reader will easily believe that these preparations were beheld, by a party of hungry soldiers, with no indifferent eye. An elegant dinner, even though considerably over-dressed, was a luxury to which few of them, at least for some time back, had been accustomed; and which, after the dangers and fatigues of the day, appeared peculiarly inviting. They sat down to it, therefore, not indeed in the most orderly manner, but with countenances which would not have disgraced a party of aldermen at a civic feast; and having satisfied their appetites with fewer complaints than would have probably escaped their rival *gourmands*, and partaken pretty freely of the wines, they finished by setting fire to the house which had so liberally entertained them."

Not yet finished for the evening, the arsonists next stopped at the Treasury building, just east of the flaming President's House. There they expected to find money or other worthy items. Disappointed at finding nothing except old records, they also set that building ablaze. The soldiers had no sooner lit the fires than an iron door was discovered. Everyone present believed it led to a vault that held valuables of the United States. An officer made his way into the room by breaking a window and found several heavy chests. He passed some of them through the broken glass. Upon opening, these were found to contain nothing but old files. As the flames and heat intensified, the officer exited and the remaining chests were abandoned. Scott wrote that there was no remunerative value in the chests, so they were left to their fate:

"The Treasury was next visited, but the specie had been safely conveyed away. The building was fired before the discovery of a strong iron door, that resisted all the efforts made to break it open. It was presumed to be the stronghold and deposit of all the valuables. The window was forced in, and the first officer who descended into the apartment, gave information that it contained several weighty boxes.

After igniting the Treasury building, Ross, Cockburn and other officers returned to Mrs. Barbara Suter's boardinghouse on Pennsylvania Avenue near 15th Street, where they had previously ordered dinner. With the city in flames from one end to the other, they actually sat down and devoured a chicken supper. Poor Mrs. Suter! Even though the hour was late, Cockburn was still desirous of continuing to torch what had not yet been ignited. He headed to the office of the *National Intelligencer*, a daily newspaper published by Joseph Gales, Jr. and William Seaton, that regularly printed articles which he claimed were consistently biased against England. Arriving there he was confronted by two women, Mrs. Pontius Stelle and Mrs. Brush, who lived nearby. They pleaded with Cockburn not to set fire to the building because they believed their houses would also be consumed by the flames. The Admiral reluctantly acquiesced, but promised that he would return the following morning and destroy the newspaper establishment. The invaders then retired for the night, leaving the fires to continue burning until they were dampened by an early morning thunderstorm. Mrs. Smith, whose husband founded the newspaper, described the event from hearsay:

> "When he went to burn Mr. Gale's office, whom he called his 'dear
> Josey'; Mrs. Brush, Mrs. Stelle and a few citizens remonstrated with
> him, assuring him that it would occasion the loss of all the buildings
> in the row.... He told Mrs. Brush and several others, that no houses
> should be injur'd but such as were shut and deserted. Mr. Cutting and
> Mrs. B. saved ours, by opening the windows"

Library of Congress

This scaled down broadside cartoon by G. Thompson depicting the Burning of Washington was first published in London October 14, 1814. In small print below the picture (not shown) is the following: "On August 24 1814 when we burnt and destroyed their Dock Yard with a Frigate and a Sloop of War, Rope Walk, Arsenal, Senate House, President's Palace, War Office, Treasury, and the Great Bridge. With the Flotilla the public property destroyed amounted to thirty Million of Dollars."

Included within the engraving are letters indicating the destruction of certain places, however, their site location is not necessarily correct. A) The upper right hand corner shows General Robert Ross and the British army; B) Cannon taken from the Americans; C) The city of Washington; D) The American flotilla destroyed; E) The Dock Yard and Arsenal destroyed; F) The Rope-Walk; G) The River Potowmack; H) The Great Bridge destroyed; I) The War Office; K) The President's Palace on fire; L) The Senate House; M) The Treasury building. There does not appear to be a letter J.

The confident Rear Admiral George Cockburn (1772-1853) is shown standing victoriously in front of the flaming city of Washington. He successfully prevailed over hesitations and Cochrane's order not to invade America's capital. The mezzotint above was finished by C. Turner in 1879. It was taken from an earlier portrait by J. J. Halls.

13

THE FLIGHTS

While the British destroyed and burned, the Americans fled and hid. A weary President began Wednesday evening as a fugitive on horseback. At sunset, in the company of at least Rush, Mason, Jennings and other servants, his small party was ferried across the Potomac River, to Mason's Island (Analostan Island). The group wound its way to the causeway that connected the seventy-five acre island with the Virginia shoreline. The gentlemen then mounted horses and headed up the Georgetown Road that led from the river to the Alexandria & Leesburg Road. They proceeded about a mile before those astride horses left Jennings and the other servants, who were traveling by foot. Once the conflagration began, the President, as did everyone else, often paused to regretfully look at the lurid sight. Writing from his home "Sydenham" outside Philadelphia, in 1855, Rush told of his flight and the vivid sight of the burning capital. His account, suggested that there was not a definitive rendezvous point the evening of August 24th. He said:

> "I have, indeed, to this hour, the vivid impression upon my eye of
> columns of flame and smoke ascending throughout the night of the
> 24th of August from the Capitol, President's house, and other public

edifices, as the whole were on fire, some burning slowly, others with bursts of flame and sparks mounting high up in the dark horizon. This never can be forgotten by me....

If at intervals the dismal sight was lost to our view, we got it again from some hilltop or eminence where we paused to look at it. We were on horseback, attended by servants, proceeding on the Virginia side of the Potomac,... intending to recross at the Great Falls that night or the next morning, so as to be again on the Maryland side, and return to Washington as the movements of the enemy and our own strength might prompt."

After riding about the countryside for some time, the Presidential group came upon Jennings and his companions who were walking along the Alexandria & Leesburg Road. The hour was late. The account later related by Jennings, described a great deal of confusion, and further suggested that a prearranged rendezvous point had never been established for that night. Jennings wrote:

"About sundown I walked over to the Georgetown ferry, and found the President and all hands (the gentlemen named before, who acted as a sort of body-guard for him) waiting for the boat. It soon returned, and we all crossed over, and passed up the road about a mile; they then loft us servants to wander about. In a short time several wagons from Bladensburg, drawn by Barney's artillery horses, passed up the road, having crossed the Long Bridge before it was set on fire. As we were cutting up some pranks (planks) a white wagoner ordered us away, and told his boy Tommy to reach out his gun, and he would shoot us. I told him "he had better have used it at Bladensburg." Just then we came up with Mr. Madison and his friends, who had been wandering about for some hours, consulting what to do."

Leaving Jennings once again, the Presidential party headed west towards Falls Church, stopping at Wren's Tavern. Even though he was extremely unpopular at this moment and feared for his life, it would have been logical for the President to pause, even if only briefly, at Wren's, located on the Alexandria & Leesburg Road. This spot had become the focal point for military operations in Fairfax County. There Madison would have been able to receive relatively current information about enemy movements, strategize with Virginia militia officers and possibly encounter the First Lady. Leaving Wren's without uniting with Dolley, the small group proceeded to Minor's Hill, the home of Colonel George Minor and his second wife, Mildred. Minor's son, George, by his first wife Ann Adams, had been at the White House the previous evening seeking supplies for the 60th Virginia Militia Regiment. The Minor residence, built on one of the highest points in the county, was not large.

It was the original patent house, a log structure to which a back wing had been added. Writing in 1959, Eleanor Templeman described the house:

> "George Minor, who was born in 1753 and married Ann Adams of Church Hill lived in this house. A back wing was added in the early 1770's, probably constructed under the supervision of their friend Colonel James Wren, the architect of The Falls Church. Its unusual construction of dry masonry walls covered with wood siding identified his style. That addition was removed a few years ago when a full second story was added to the original log house and the exterior brick added.
>
> George Minor gave the ground (at Seven Corners) for Fairfax Chapel (Methodist)."

History never recorded why Madison stopped at Minor's Hill. Presumably he was looking for a place to rest, but he was out of luck because the cabin style house was already crammed with refugees, many of whom had traveled from Alexandria. For example, Mrs. George Deneale escaped Alexandria with her family, but also brought along the five children of John Roberts who lived next door. Madison's stay was brief. There was simply no available space at the Minor residence that evening. Matilda Roberts Sayrs was one of the neighbor children who had been included in Mrs. Deneale's flight to Falls Church. Mrs. Sayrs was seven at that time, but recalled in later years to her daughter, Mary Gordon, leaving Alexandria with only her tea set and being awakened in the middle of the night to be taken outside to view the conflagration. Her recollection placed Madison at Minor's Hill Wednesday night. Mrs. Sayrs stated:

> "In the War of 12 or 14, I was a motherless child of seven years, the eldest of 5 children. My first recollections are of a large 'waggon' with 4 horses, piled up with trunks and beds and on all these were seated our dear friends and neighbors Mrs. Deneale (her husband being absent on military duty) with her family of children. Soon place was made for my sisters, self and little brother, only giving us time to carry in our laps a little tea set, which to us was our future!
>
> In a short time, we arrived at 'Miss Minor's' ten miles from our house and from Washington. We found the house filled with refugees, families who like ourselves, had come there for safety from the 'English Ships of War' who having arrived in the Chesapeake Bay, were hourly expected up the Potomac to attack Washington, the Capital of the U.S. This in a few days they accomplished.
>
> At night we used to be dreadfully scared by noises like horses around our house all hours of the night, so terrified were children for fear the 'British' as we called them, would find us out. One night in

particular, the impression has never left me, _____ out of bed or rather the 'Pallet' all had to sleep on. I was carried with the others out in the yard. At first I thought the world must be on fire --- such a flame I have never since seen. We were told the 'British' had taken Washington and burning it up.... I was told not to cry. President Madison had had escaped to the house the night of the fire and left before day next morning."

Booth continued in his report to Tingey that he had reached Wren's Tavern about midnight, where he was united with his children. He was informed by a hostile citizen that the President was about a mile away. Booth made the assumption that Madison spent the night at Minor's Hill. Desperately needing Presidential or Cabinet level approval to move powder hidden at Dulaney's farm in Falls Church further inland, Booth rode to the Minor residence early Thursday morning. When arriving there, he was informed that Madison, Rush and Mason had only stopped there for a brief time the prior evening:

> "... and about midnight I reached Wren's - where I found my children - all were up; and people constantly passing - most of the baggage and other waggons had passed - and I had been but a short time at the home, when a man who stopped, stated - the President was then within a mile of the place - and threw out in my opinion, very improper threats - However, on my making some observations, he seemed to be very quiet.

> Thursday 25th. I was up at the dawn of day, and as soon as I could get my horse, I took young Wren with me, to show me the way to Mr. Minor's, where, it was said, the President was - he had been there the evening before with Genl. John Mason and Mr. R. Rush, but stay'd only a short time. I returned to Wren's."

There is only circumstantial evidence as to where the President ended what well may have been the most arduous day of his life. Reputedly, it was at the Salona mansion, the residence of the Reverend William and Ann Carter Maffitt, located in what is now McLean. The stately brick house was about two miles west of Minor's Hill, on the opposite side of a local tributary that flowed into the Potomac, called Pimmit Run. The house set back but fronted the Falls Road, a major thoroughfare in Fairfax County that connected with the bridge at the Little Falls. Madison and his companions certainly had a guide as they rode from Minor's Hill to Salona, because they reportedly used the back lanes; a shorter, more direct route. Jennings eventually walked to the log house of a Methodist minister and received shelter there. This would have been the home of the Reverend William and Sarah Adams Watters. The Reverend Watters was the first native born itinerant Methodist minister in the United States. Sarah was the sister of the Colonel Minor in charge of the 60th Virginia Militia. Their log cabin home, named El Nido, was located about half way between Minor's Hill and Salona in an area that later became known as Chesterbrook. The President would have ridden past, or very near, El Nido on his way to Salona. Jennings continued:

> "I walked on to a Methodist minister's, and in the evening, while he
> was prayer, I heard a tremendous explosion, and, rushing out, saw
> that the public buildings navy yard, ropewalks, &c., were on fire."

Meantime, Dolley and her entourage struggled towards safety in Virginia through Georgetown's clogged roads heavily encumbered with a panicked populace, stuffed carriages, over loaded wagons and fleeing militia. She escaped in the female company of at least her maid Sukey, her sister Anna, Mrs. Jones and Mrs. Carroll, plus their children and servants. At least two gentlemen, Edward Duvall, a clerk at the Navy Department, and Jones traveled with them, with the Navy Secretary more or less in charge of the group. Cutts may have continued into Virginia with the group, but he was back in the city the following morning. Carroll remained in the city to protect his home, according to a statement made by his son Daniel in 1848. Even though the women had carriages in which to ride, they often walked because it became the least dangerous mode of travel. The group crossed the Potomac via the Little Falls Bridge, headed west on the Falls Road, and climbed the long steep hill adjacent to Pimmit Run eventually arriving at Rokeby, the newly built farmhouse of Dolley's friends Richard Henry and Matilda Lee Love. Here they wearily stopped for the night, just missing Monroe and Ringgold who had reached Rokeby earlier looking for Madison. Jennings included in his *Reminiscences* that Dolley spent Wednesday night at the Love residence by simply stating:

> "Mrs. Madison slept that night at Mrs. Love's, two or three miles
> over the river."

In her *Reminiscences*, written years later, Mrs. Love confirmed that the First Lady spent the night Washington burned at Rokeby, and that Monroe stopped by before her arrival, looking for the President. She went on to say that Madison had fled further into the country, but did not indicate where or how far; however, Salona, located about a mile and a half further inland, would fit her description. Mrs. Love recalled:

> "Mrs. Madison and a number of city people took refuge at my house
> the night the British took Washington; Mr. Madison had gone farther

up the country. Early in the evening Mr. Monroe came to my house to look for Mr. Madison; as Mr. Monroe was weary I gave him his supper, and asked him if he thought I was safe where I was for the night, 'Madam,' he said, 'as safe as if you were in the Allegheny Mountains.' Oh, it was a trying time, for Mr. Love's Company, with all the militia of the State of Virginia, was called out, and I was in a peck of trouble."

Anne Hollingsworth Wharton also related that Dolley spent the night at Rokeby in her book *Social Life in the Early Republic*. She included that Dolley was welcomed by the mistress of the house, but grudgingly waited upon by the servants. She wrote:

"When Mrs. Love told the old colored cook to hurry and make a cup of coffee for Mrs. Madison, who was suffering from the excitement and fatigue of the day, the cook replied, 'I make a cup of coffee for you, Mis' Matilda, but I'm not gwine to hurry for Mis' Madison, for I done heerd Mr. Madison and Mr. Armstrong done sold the country to the British.'"

Mixed with the fleeing populace, Winder's shattered army fled through the city, then through Georgetown, finally halting two miles past on the heights at Tenleytown. Here, the General tried to collect his dispersed troops, but had little luck in putting anything together. The men simply vanished and returned to their homes. He did not stay long at Tenleytown. By midnight the General had moved a small force that he had been able to gather five miles further inland, and by dawn his meager army was at Montgomery Court House, Maryland, sixteen miles from Washington. He continued in his report to the Investigative Committee:

"...it was wise and proper to retire through Georgetown, and take post in the rear of it, on the heights, to collect my force. I accordingly pursued this course, and halted at Tenely town two miles north of Georgetown, on the Frederick road. Here was evinced one of the great defect of all undisciplined and unorganized troops; no effort could rouse officers and men to the exertion necessary to place themselves in such a state of comfort and security as is attainable, even under very disadvantageous circumstances.

Such of them as could be halted, instead of making those efforts, gave themselves up to the uncontrolled feelings which fatigue, exhaustion, and privation produced, and many hundreds, in spite of all precautions and efforts, passed on and pursued their way, either towards home or in search of refreshments and quarters. After waiting in this position until I supposed I collected all the force that could be gathered, I proceeded about five miles further on the river road, which leads a little wide to the left of Montgomery court house, and in the morning gave orders for the whole to assemble at

Montgomery court house.

"This position promised us shelter from the rain that began to fall an hour before day; was the most probable place for the supply of provisions, which the troops very much needed; and was a position from which we could best interpose between the enemy and Baltimore, and to which place, at that time, nobody doubted he intended to go land from Washington."

Clearly, August 24, 1814, was a night of terror and anguish for inhabitants who remained in the city and those who watched the conflagration from afar. The flames or glow of the burning capital could be seen from distances such as Annapolis, Baltimore and Leesburg. In the August heat the threat of flames or sparks spreading and destroying the entire city was quite real. Many were certain that they had lost everything; many did. Unexpected relief came from the heavens before sunrise, as a heavy thunderstorm rumbled through the area extinguishing many of the fires. This fortunate storm probably saved the nation's capital from complete destruction. Gleig wrote that he was asleep upon the ground when the thunder and rain awoke everyone around him:

"But the night was not even now destined to be passed in quiet. It might be about twelve or one o'clock, when a tremendous peal of thunder, so loud as to drown, for an instant, every noise, awoke us. The rain was falling in torrents, and flash after flash of vivid lightning displayed not only the bivouac, but the streets, the houses, nay the very windows in the town, with a degree of minuteness far greater than the beams of a noon-day sun would have produced.

The effect was magnificent beyond the power of language to describe. Not even the drenching, against which cloaks and blankets failed to afford protection, could lead me to neglect the occurrence; for I really do not recollect, at any period of my life, to have been witness to a spectacle so imposing."

James Madison (1751-1836), the fourth President of the United States, is best remembered as "The Father of the Constitution." Inheriting uneasy relations with England from the Jefferson administration, Madison was forced to ask Congress to declare war against Great Britain in 1812. The public quickly turned against him and he became the object of much criticism. With the ratification of the peace treaty in 1815, his popularity was elevated to that of a national hero. This was not so much because the war was over, but because he brought it to a conclusion operating within the framework of the Constitution and militia forces won a decisive battle at New Orleans.

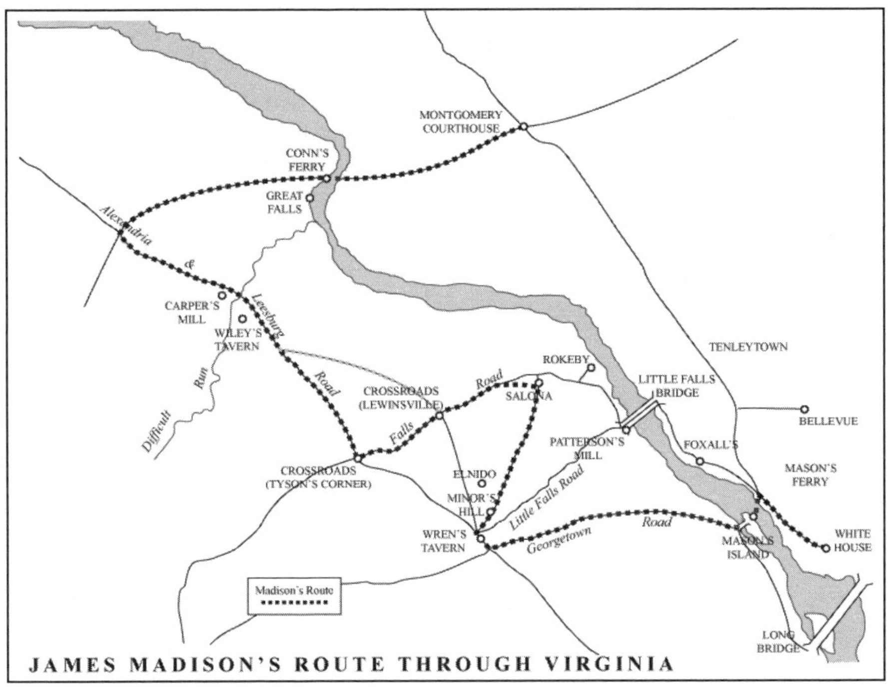

Map by Charles Herrick

The President's flight through Virginia is not exact, but a fairly clear picture of his route can be pieced together. After exiting the White House, his first stop was at Mason's Ferry (Georgetown Ferry). He was ferried across to Mason's Island, where he took the causeway to Virginia and traveled the Georgetown Road to the Alexandria & Leesburg Road. He headed west and stopped at Wren's Tavern before continuing to Minor's Hill. It is thought that Madison spent the night of August 24, 1814 at Salona and used the back roads/lanes to get there. The following day he rode back to Wren's and then returned to Salona, leaving there shortly before the violent thunderstorm broke. Madison waited out the storm near a place known only as the Crossroads. Later, while headed towards Wiley's Tavern, he encountered Booth along the Alexandria & Leesburg Road. The President remained at Wiley's several hours and then set out during the darkness for Conn's Ferry, intending to join Winder's forces at Montgomery Court House. Unable to cross the Potomac at that time, he waited above the Great Falls until Friday afternoon until the river was passable. He was then ferried over to Maryland.

Fairfax County Library Archives

Salona, a federal style brick house, probably sheltered President James Madison the night of August 24, 1814 and offered hospitality to his wife Dolley the next day.

Courtesy Sheila Heath

Shown is a log attachment to the original log cabin built by William Watters in 1783 on land bought from his father-in-law Colonel William Adams. A framed structure was later built over the original log house.

14

WILEY'S TAVERN

At separate homes in Virginia, the President and First Lady awoke on Thursday morning to the view of fresh flames and smoke as the arsonists continued their handiwork. Madison arose early, mounted his horse, and retraced his route of the prior evening back to Falls Church. He was hoping to receive word concerning the whereabouts of Dolley and updates, if any, about the location of the American forces and the probability of Winder initiating a counterattack. He stopped at Wren's Tavern. While there he met with Captain George Graham, commander of a troop of Fairfax Dragoons, who provided him with a much needed small guard of two armed cavalrymen. Before leaving, Madison told Graham that he hoped to fine Dolley at Mr. Maffitt's and set off in that direction. Booth, who had failed to find Madison earlier that morning at Minor's Hill, had proceeded to Dulany's farm to organize the removal of barrels of powder hidden there because residents in the area were uneasy about such a large quantity of explosives stored in a non military facility. When finished with this task he returned to Wren's, continuing to inquire about the whereabouts of the President. He was informed that Madison had headed for Salona. Booth included in his report:

> "I then went to the farm of Mr. Dulany to see Sergeant Major Forrest, and to give him orders.... After giving the necessary order, I returned to Wren's - Captn. Smallwood was just leaving it, with his family and my children for my relations, L. Lee's, in Loudoun County. He informed me that the President had been there, and had just gone off. Captn. Graham informed me, he had gone to Mr. Maffitt's, where he

expected to find Mrs. Madison - and if I wished to see him, if I would lose no time, perhaps overtake him."

Madison returned to the Maffitts', but he did not encounter the First Lady. She had already departed. Leaving Rokeby, Dolley briefly stopped at Salona to visit another friend Mrs. Maffitt. The stately brick house, circa 1800, was built on property owned at the turn of the century by "Light Horse Harry" Lee, a Revolutionary War hero and founder of Matildaville at the Great Falls. Salona was the grandest residence in the still primitive wooded area. The Maffitts purchased the estate in 1812. The refugees waited and rested while receiving intelligence reports, viewing the rekindled fires that were destroying the city, and eating a quickly prepared meal (Mrs. Love's larder must have been empty by Thursday morning). Jones, leaving word of their destination, decided to push everyone further inland to Wiley's before the President returned. The group reached the tavern about the time a violent afternoon thunderstorm, with winds reaching hurricane strength, struck the entire Washington metropolitan area. A tornado ripped through the city itself. The weary First Lady went upstairs. When learning who her latest refuge was, the furious wife of the innkeeper went to the bottom of the stairs and announced that the First Lady should get out. Jennings gave the following account in his *Reminiscences*, as later described to him by Dolley's maid Sukey:

> "After leaving that place (Rokeby) she called in at a house, and went up stairs. The lady of the house learning who she was, became furious, and went to the stairs and screamed out, 'Miss Madison! if that's you, come down and go out! Your husband has got mine out fighting, and d____ you, you shan't stay in my house; so get out!'"

Dolley steadfastly remained at Wiley's waiting the arrival of her husband. The tavern was located along the south side of the Alexandria & Leesburg Road east of a stream appropriately named Difficult Run, roughly sixteen miles from Georgetown. Charles Ingersoll, acquainted with both of the Madisons, described in 1849 the deplorable lack of hospitality the First Lady received when her party reached Wiley's:

> "The tavern in which Mrs. Madison was seeking shelter, and her vagrant husband, was filled with ladies, also fugitives from dreaded hostilities, who insisted that the wife of him who caused them, by his abominable war, should not be received under the same roof with its innocent victims; the wife of a President who had brought such calamities on the country had no claim to admission under the same roof with ladies driven from their own, but deserved to be expelled from all doors. Ladies who had partaken, at Mrs. Madison's

drawing-room, the welcome of the President's mansion, and who lived to become sensible of their error, prejudiced by party, embittered by hostilities, and maddened by expulsion from their homes, to seek shelter in a country inn, combined to refuse her admission there.

The tavern-keeper and his wife were of opposite politics; he for the war, and she vehement against it and its abominable author. While the storm of passion raged with the tornado beginning its desolations, the men of Mrs. Madison's escort were obliged to overcome the ungracious and unladylike resistance to her shelter in an inn, which stood in the midst of an apple orchard, heavily laden with ripe fruit, torn by the tempest from the trees, and dashed with noisy force against the windows and doors of the house. At length admitted only just in time to escape the hail of apples, tongues and tempest, the ladies were allowed the comfort of a plain meal, of which Mrs. Madison saved enough for the President whenever he might arrive."

Not encountering Dolley at Salona, Madison left in the company of Rush and the two dragoons, and set out for Wiley's, traveling along the Falls Road. Mason had gone elsewhere, but rejoined the President later at the tavern. The small group had not ridden far before the skies darkened and the violent thunderstorm struck. According to Booth, shelter was found by the President at a crossroads about five miles from the bridge near Little Falls. There, Madison was informed that the First Lady had passed by earlier. It was never made clear at which crossroads the President waited out the storm: there were two possible locations between Salona and Wiley's. The most likely place would have been the junction of the Falls Road and the Alexandria & Leesburg Road, on the edge of an area in Fairfax County that became known as Tyson's Corner. This was the location of the county's first courthouse. It was settled and offered many houses; however, it was approximately seven miles from the bridge. The other prospect was the intersection of the Falls Road and the Great Falls Road in an area that was later named Lewinsville, but at that time was not settled. This area was five miles from the bridge, but offered very little in the form of shelter. Booth wrote in his narrative to Tingley:

"I had not gone more than a mile, before I was overtaken by the most tremendous storm, I had ever witnessed. I was compel'd to take shelter and found myself under the hospitable roof of Mr. Wm. McLain - as soon as the storm was over, I was on my horse; but before I had proceeded far, I met a man who told me the President had sheltered himself from the storm at a place known by the name of the Cross roads, five miles from the little falls Bridge - that there he had learned that Mrs. Madison had passed on her way to Wilie Tavern - and the President had gone on there."

The horrific storm lasted well over two hours. When it subsided, Madison and Rush were back in the saddle, headed for the tavern. They were now riding over sloppy roads, covered with debris. Booth finally caught up with the President along the Alexandria & Leesburg Road. He now received the official confirmation he was seeking about moving the powder further inland, although he had already begun its relocation. Booth rode with the small group until they came upon three wagons moving some of the explosives that were under his charge. He stopped and gave further instructions to the drivers where to deliver the wagons. Madison, Rush and the dragoons continued, arriving at the tavern just before sunset. Booth arrived shortly thereafter. In his continuing report to Tingey, Booth related that he saw Dolley and others when he briefly stopped at Wiley's on his way to Leesburg. Booth wrote:

> "I followed as I expected my family would pass Wilies - I very soon overtook the President, accompanied by Mr. R. Rush and two of Graham's troopers as a guard. I continued with them until within a short distance of Wilies - and meeting with three of the waggons that had been engaged in removing powder, and had run the day before, I stopped to order them to Mr. Bennett - (bye the bye they did not go) and I soon reached Wilies. There I found the Secretary of the Navy, Mr. John Graham, and several other gentlemen; Mrs. Madison, Mrs. Jones, and other ladies."

The exhausted President rested at Wiley's until midnight. He then set out to cross the Potomac from the Conn's Ferry landing above the Great Falls, planning to link with Winder and the American forces at Montgomery Court House. With him were at least the two dragoons, servants, Jones, Rush, Mason and John Graham, a clerk at the state department. Monroe and Ringgold, who reportedly spent the previous evening at Wiley's, had been ferried across earlier in the day before the storm. Once reaching the ferry site, everyone recognized that a crossing was impossible, particularly in the dark. The Potomac was raging due to the afternoon thunderstorm. Jones returned to Wiley's. Everyone else remained and crossed the still dangerously turbulent river early Friday afternoon. An accurate account has never surfaced to indicate where Madison and his friends spent the remainder of that morning, Friday, August 26. Some accounts have suggested that the President received shelter in the small home of the ferryman until the crossing was possible. Booth continued:

> "At a late hour, perhaps twelve o'clock at night, The President, Secretary of the Navy, Genl. Mason, who I met as I was in search of my family, Mr. Graham, and other gentlemen, with an escort of Grahams Dragoons (this was Captain George Graham), left Wilies

with an intention of passing the Potowmack river above the Big Falls, and joining the Army. This the Secretary of the Navy informed me of, himself. The party were disappointed in crossing the river as they had intended.

Friday 26th - That evening I met the Secretary of the Navy as he had been disappointed in crossing the Potowmack, had returned to carry his Lady and some others in company to Fredericktown - after which he intended joining the army.   I requested to know this commands to you. He observed he had no others {than} that should the enemy evacuate the City, you would use all diligence in collecting the public stores.

This evening I learned that from one hundred and thirty to one hundred and fifty wagons belonging to the army had crossed the Potowmack just above the mouth of Goose Creek; this is a distance of at least forty miles from the City of Washington, & perhaps twenty to Montgomery Court House, where they expected to join the army - Montgomery Court House is twenty-four miles from Bladensburg, by way of Georgetown.

I passed General Young's brigade that night, one mile above Wilie's, and reached that place about eight o'clock at night."

Dorothy Payne Todd Madison, or Dolley (1768-1849), was raised a Quaker, but discarded this image when she married James Madison an Episcopalian. As the wife of the Secretary of State during the Jefferson administration, Mrs. Madison became the central figure of Washington society. As the First Lady, Dolley brought culture and fashion to the capital and President's House. She kept up a brave front after the British landed at Benedict. Being warned that Bladensburg had fallen and, thus her life was in danger, Dolley showed more courage than most of Winder's army by bravely remaining in the White House until she knew the full–length portrait of the First President was secured.

Photo Carole Herrick

Minor's Hill, located in Fairfax County, was built on top the highest elevation in the area, adjacent to the District of Columbia boundary line. President James Madison stopped here the night the British burned Washington. The First Lady received refuge from the Minor family August 26 and 27, before returning to the charred capital Sunday, August 28, 1814.

Fairfax County Public Library Archives

Colvin Run Mill, formerly known as Carper's Mill, as shown in this 1930's photograph, was located near Wiley's tavern, but on the opposite side of a tributary called Difficult Run. While marching to Conn's Ferry Landing, Brigadier General Robert Young's Alexandria brigade made camp here, while checking out citizen concerns about a British inspired slave rebellion.

119

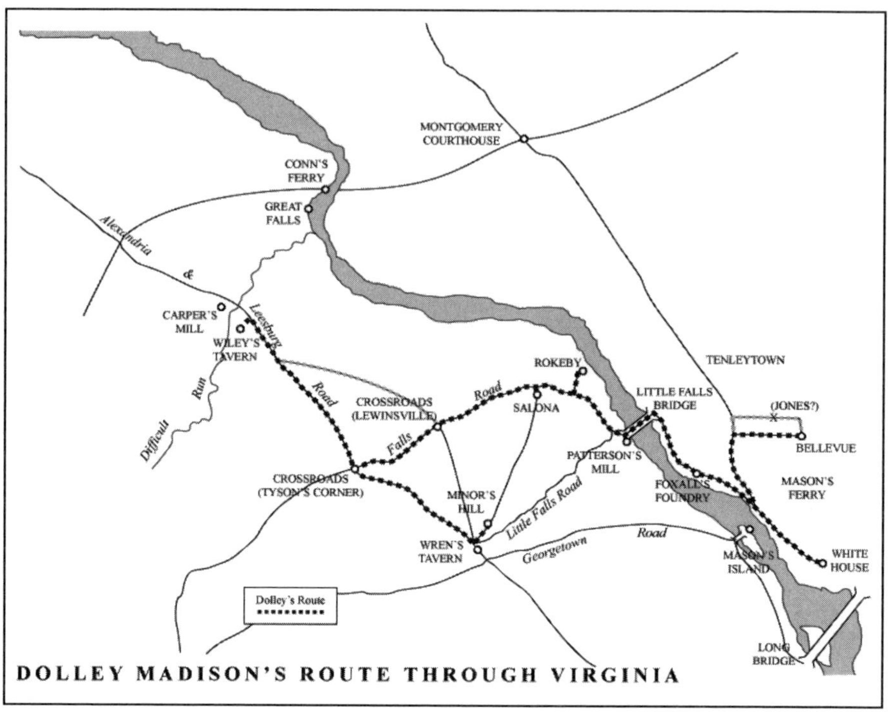

DOLLEY MADISON'S ROUTE THROUGH VIRGINIA

Map by Charles Herrick

The above is the most likely route that Dolley used when escaping the British. Leaving the White House, the First Lady headed west on Pennsylvania Avenue turning onto High Street and traveled through Georgetown. Her first stop was at the Jones' residence in Georgetown Heights. Because no record is available of this exact location, an X has been placed on the map indicating a general location. Dolley next stopped at Bellevue to await the arrival of the President. Receiving word that he was not coming, she traveled back down High Street to Mason's Ferry (Georgetown Ferry) only to learn that the Presidential party had already crossed the Potomac. Her carriage then turned west on Water Street for Virginia. Using the Little Falls Bridge, she crossed the Potomac, traveling the Falls Road until she turned off for Rokeby. There she spent the night of August 24, 1814. Thursday morning it is thought that Dolley stopped briefly at Salona. She then continued along the Falls Road to its junction with the Alexandria & Leesburg Road, where her carriage turned west, halting at Wiley's Tavern. Dolley remained at Wiley's until early Friday when she went to Minor's Hill, taking the Alexandria & Leesburg Road. She remained at the Minors' residence until Sunday morning, when she returned to the nation's capital. The route the First Lady traveled from Minor's Hill to the Cutts' residence on F Street in Washington is unclear.

15

THE RUSSE DE GUERRE

The President and First Lady were safely in Virginia by the time the arsonists resumed further destruction by Thursdays sunrise. They rekindled fires dampened by the early morning thunderstorm and ignited other public buildings that had not yet been torched. A detachment, under Colonel Timothy Jones, marched back down Pennsylvania Avenue and set fire to the brick building west of the President's House that jointly housed the Departments of State, War and Navy. Three ropewalks, owned by Ringgold, were set on fire. The Long Bridge, one of two bridges that connected Washington with Virginia, was set ablaze at each end. This action was unusual because British soldiers set fire to the eastern end, believing that Americans were attempting to cross, and the Americans set fire to the western side, thinking the Redcoats were planning to cross. A detachment, led by Captain John Wainwright, tramped to the navy yard to finish destroying everything that escaped the fires set by Tingey. There they found the yard swarming with American looters. Shortly, Wainwright had everything ablaze. Before leaving, enemy soldiers vandalized the Naval Monument, dedicated to Captain Richard Somers and his men who were killed in 1804 when the gunboat

Intrepid, outfitted as a floating mine, exploded in the Harbor of Tripoli during the Barbary Coast Wars. Later known as the Tripoli Monument, it was the first military monument in the United States and a source of great national pride for a young nation without much history. Many considered its mutilation one of the more despicable acts of the invasion. John Williams, an American officer during the War of 1812, wrote:

> "One of the least credible acts committed by the enemy was the mutilation of the monument which now stands opposite the west front of the Capitol, which had been erected at the navy yard by private subscriptions of the officers of the navy, to commemorate their comrades who were killed in the war with Tripoli."

Learning over breakfast, that Jones was setting fire to the Departments of State, War and Navy, to be followed by igniting the Patent and Post Offices, Thornton, along with Carroll, sought out the British Colonel to request that a musical instrument recently designed by Thornton be retrieved before the Patent Office was set ablaze. Jones agreed, and then went to the *National Intelligencer* to oversee the demolition of that place, after sending a contingent to Blodgett's Hotel, which housed the Patent and Post Offices. As the troops were preparing to burn the Patent Office they encountered Thornton who, as the Superintendent of Patents, now argued that everything in the building was private property and, thus, should not be destroyed. He further declared that "to burn what would be useful to all mankind would be as barbarous as to burn the Alexandria Library, for which the Turks have been condemned by all enlightened nations." Major Waters, the officer in charge, suggested that Thornton should talk again with Jones, and he would await the decision. Thornton found the Colonel at the newspaper office and argued his case. Jones accepted Thornton's position and the Patent Office was not set ablaze. In a "Letter to the Editor" printed in the *National Intelligencer*, September 7, 1814, Thornton related his experience concerning saving the Patent Office:

> "Hearing next morning, while at breakfast in Georgetown, that the British were preparing to burn the War Office and the public building containing the models of the arts, I was desirous not only of saving an instrument that had cost me great labor, but of preserving if possible the building and all the models --- I therefore left my breakfast and hastened forward, determining to request the first known democrat I should meet to accompany me, lest the malevolent should insinuate that I had in any manner held an improper communication with the invaders of the country.
>
> I met with Charles Carroll, Esq, one of the most respectable

gentlemen in the District. I begged him to accompany me for the reasons given; he very politely attended me. We arrived at the very moment when the English Col. Jones and his men were proceeding to burn the War Office;   Mr. Carroll had already accompanied the Mayor of Georgetown in a peace deputation and was therefore known to some of the officers; he informed Col. Jones that I had waited on him to request permission to take out of the Patent Office a musical instrument; the Colonel immediately replied, that as it was not their intention to destroy any private property. I was perfectly at liberty to take it....

I next called on Mr. Nicholson, my model maker and messenger, and desired him to attend me, he did and the British soldiers were then marching in two columns to burn the building. When we arrived there we found the Revd. Mr. Browne, Mr. Lyon and Mr. Hatfield near the Patent Office. Major Waters, who was then on guard and waiting the command of Colonel Jones, informed me that the private property might be taken out. I told him that there was nothing but private property of any consequence, and that any public property to which he objected might be burnt in the street, provided the building might be preserved, which contained hundreds of models of the arts, and that it would be impossible to remove them, and to burn what would be useful to all mankind, would be as barbarous as formerly to burn the Alexandrian Library, for which the Turks have been ever since condemned by all enlightened nations.

The Major desired me to go again with him to Col. Jones, who was attending some of his men engaged in destroying Mr. Gale's types and printing apparatus. I went to the Avenue and was kindly received by the Colonel; they took their men away and promised to spare the building."

Even though private property was generally respected, Cockburn disregarded this principle when it came to the office of the *National Intelligencer*, the country's first national newspaper. He personally was on hand to supervise the destruction that was carried out by Jones and his wrecking crew. This act to private property was based on the Admiral's personal vendetta against Gales, the senior editor, who, he claimed, wrote unflattering articles about him. Reportedly, the Admiral ordered that all the C's in the type cases be destroyed so that the editors could no longer vilify his name. In deference to concerns that the entire neighborhood would go up in flames if the building were torched, the presses were smashed and the broken up type tossed out the windows. Everything else was taken outside and thrown onto a bonfire. The building was then torn down. Mrs. Smith, whose husband founded the newspaper in 1800, did not witness the event. She related a remark made by Cockburn to a bystander in her continuing letter to her sister:

> "'Well,' said he, 'good people I do not wish to injure you, but I am
> really afraid my friend Josey will be affronted with me, if after
> burning Jemmy's palace, I do not pay him the same compliment, ---
> so my lads, take your axes, pull down the house, and burn the papers
> in the street.' This was accordingly done."

The confidence of the invaders began to wane, however, during the afternoon because two unforeseen disasters rattled their nerves, forcing Ross to rethink their length of stay. Around noon the General sent a detachment of four officers and about 200 soldiers to Greenleaf's Point, with orders to finish the destruction of the magazine there. The contents of the arsenal had been partially destroyed by the Americans before abandoning it, but they did not have time to remove about one hundred and fifty barrels of powder to a place of concealment. The British found the kegs and began dropping them into a well located near the barracks. It turned out to be a dry well. The well exploded. Numerous British soldiers were immediately killed; many never identified. Forty-four badly wounded Redcoats were carried back to the city for care in a makeshift hospital that was hastily put together along Carroll Row. Reports varied as to what triggered the explosion. The following accounts offered three different versions of the horrific event. The first was written by Scott in *Recollections of a Naval Life,* the second was printed in the *National Intelligencer,* and the last was an entry in the diary of Mrs. Thornton:

> "A serious accident occurred on the morning of the 25th to a party
> employed at Greenleaf Point, in destroying the arms and ammunition
> in the fort. A large quantity of powder was found, and, in order to
> effect its destruction with safety, it was thrown down a well of
> tolerable depth, though not full of water, near the magazine. So
> many barrels of powder had been deposited in it, that the casks and
> loose powder soon rested above the water line; it was unfortunately
> not reported by the workmen to the officer superintending the duty,
> and they contained rolling cask after cask down the abyss.
>
> An awful explosion took place, caused, it is supposed, by the sparks
> of fire emitted by the striking of the barrels in their descent against
> the stony sides of the well. This melancholy catastrophe killed
> twelve and wounded upwards of thirty men: many of the latter were
> so dreadfully mutilated that instant death would have a blessing to
> them."

> "The magazine at Greenleaf's Point was destroyed (partially only)
> and the guns spiked on Thursday. In a dry well belonging to the
> barracks our soldiers had thrown many barrels of powder for

concealment. After exploding the magazine, the British soldiers
threw casually into this well one or two of their matches, which
communicated to the powder deposited there. The effect was terrific.
Every one of his soldiers near was blown into eternity, many at a
greater distance wounded, and the excavation remains as evidence of
the great force of this explosion."

"We went to see the effect of the explosion of the well that had
gunpowder put in it by our people to hide it as supposed. --- We burnt
the buildings at the point to prevent the Enemy getting the arms -
which certainly might have been secured & they might have given
the buildings a chance of being preserved. --- The Enemy spiked a
few of the cannon but left them generally standing of their carriages
as they found them --- they lost a great many men by this accidental
explosion which has made a monstrous cavity at least (doesn't say)
feet diameter. --- The magazine of powder blew up by this explosion
but all the powder was not destroyed. It is generally thought that the
navy yd & the point both might easily have been defended if
preparation had been made in time. --- But they did not think they
would come."

The unexpected explosion at Greenleaf's Point was shortly
followed by the horrific afternoon thunderstorm that rumbled through the
Washington area and forced Madison to take shelter at the crossroads. A
damaging tornado swirled through the capitol city. Hurricane force
winds, heavy rain and bolts of lightening, forced British troops who were
all in the open to lay flat on the ground and cling to anything possible
until it was over. Trees were uprooted. Gleig was blown off his horse.
Thirty British soldiers were killed when a building fell on them. The
roof was blown off Blodget's Hotel, just saved from the flames by
Thornton a few hours earlier. By the time it was over, the occupying
army was in shambles. Gleig vividly described this event in his diary.
His account became the basis for Washington's first recorded
tornado/hurricane:

"... the sky grew suddenly dark, and the most tremendous hurricane
ever remembered by the oldest inhabitant in the place came on. Of
the prodigious force of the wind it is impossible for one who was not
an eye-witness to its effects to form a conception. Roofs of houses
were torn off by it, and whirled into the air like sheets of paper;
whilst the rain which accompanied it resembled the rushing of a
mighty cataract rather than the dropping of a shower.

The darkness was as great as if the sun had long set, and the last
remains of twilight had come on, occasionally relieved by flashes of
vivid lightning streaming through it; which, together with the noise of
the wind and the thunder, the crash of falling buildings, and the

tearing of roofs as they were stript from the walls, produced the most appalling effect I ever have, and probably ever shall, witness. The storm lasted for nearly two hours without intermission, during which time many of the houses spared by us were blown down, and thirty of our men, besides several of the inhabitants, buried beneath the ruins.

Our column was as completely dispersed as if it had received a total defeat; some of the men flying for shelter behind walls and buildings, and others falling flat upon the ground, to prevent themselves from being carried away by the tempest; nay, such was the violence of the wind, that two pieces of light cannon, which stood upon the eminence, were fairly lifted from the ground, and borne several yards to the rear."

Gales did not let Cockburn's determined demolition of the *National Intelligencer* deter him. He quickly put together a newspaper of sorts and a week later his paper was again in operation, although in an abbreviated form. On that date, September 1, 1814, his paper described the tornado/hurricane. In a separate article Gales apologized for the condition of the paper, while, at the same time, seeking funds from its readers, many of whom incurred financial ruin due to the invasion:

"On Thursday evening last, while our devoted city was in possession of the Enemy, it was visited by a tremendous hurricane, which did great damage to the houses, blowing off the roofs of many, destroying chimnies, fences, &c. In some parts of the city every house was more or less injured. Much injury was doubtless done higher up the country, where indeed it levelled an immense number of trees, uprooting them here and there, but more frequently twisting them off their roots."

"To Subscribers. - Having purchased from one of our brother printers one small fount of type, we have issued the paper a day or two in its present shape, which it must retain until we are enabled to replace the type so meanly and malignantly destroyed by the enemy. For any deficiency of matter, or irregularity of transmission, an apology must be found in the absence of many of our hands in the different military corps, and the disadvantages under which others are employed. We shall do the best we can.

We should suppose we need only state that our recent loss will require the use of every cent of money we can command, to induce those who know themselves to be indebted to the establishment forthwith to pay their respective dues, and in addition to elicit payment in advance from all who can afford it. The Editors are happy to say that their account books and subscription lists were saved from the general destruction of their books and papers."

Between the explosion, the storm, and conflicting reports that the American forces were regrouping en masse on the heights above Georgetown, Ross and Cockburn determined that it was time to leave. While the President and his group patiently waited out the darkness above Great Falls, the British army began quietly retreating back to their fleet. They left shortly after sunset, leaving their wounded behind and many of their fallen comrades unburied. The British forces had been sizably reduced due to deaths and injuries incurred by the battle, deserters, heat stroke, the explosion and the storm. Their mission was accomplished. Barney's flotilla was destroyed and America's capital was reduced to ashes. The occupying army imposed an 8:00 p.m. curfew upon the residents. Then it noiselessly evacuated, leaving a rear guard consisting of a few soldiers who presented a pseudo scene (*ruses de guerre*), by keeping campfires burning and moving about in front of them, giving the impression that the entire army remained encamped on the hillsides. The invading forces occupied the nation's capitol about twenty-four hours. Smith was concerned with the practicality of a night retreat and spoke to Ross about the matter. He wrote:

> "I had been out in the camp, and when I returned after dark, General Ross says, 'I have ordered the army to march at night.' To-night?' I said. 'I hope not, sir. The road you well know, for four miles to Bladensburg, is excellent, and wide enough to march with a front of subdivisions. After that we have to move through woods by a track, not a road. Let us move so as to reach Bladensburg by daylight. Our men will have a night's rest, and be refreshed after the battle. I have also to load all the wounded, and to issue flour, which I have also caused to be collected.' (I had seized in Washington everything in the shape of transport, and Baxter, the Surgeon, brought away every wounded man who could travel.) General Ross said, 'I have made the arrangement with Evans, and we must march.' I muttered to myself, 'Oh, for dear John Colborne!'"

This drawing by George Munger c1814 shows the remains of the Capitol building after it was set ablaze by the British. The picture shows the missing roof of both wings and the side of the House of Representatives braced with firewood to prevent its collapse.

16

BRITISH WITHDRAWAL

The retreat back to the ships followed the same route taken by the advance a few days earlier, but this time it was an exhausting and disorderly march. The Redcoats reached Bladensburg around midnight and stopped for about an hour to regroup. They viewed the gruesome corpses of their fallen comrades who still remained unburied on the field. Ross did not take time to honor these men by placing them in the ground; this task was left to the Americans. Knapsacks were filled with flour, while Ross had the casualties who could travel loaded into carts or wagons. Many wounded were left behind. Their care was entrusted to British surgeons, the English agent for the exchange of prisoners, and Barney, who was still at Bladensburg recovering from his injury. The enemy then again moved forward in continued silence in the direction of Upper Marlboro. All during the night stragglers lagged behind and exhausted men left the ranks to plunder the countryside, forcing the General to call a halt at 7:00 a.m. in order to rest his men. Smith described the nighttime march:

> "We started at nine, and marched rapidly and in good order to
> Bladensburg, where we halted for about an hour to load the wounded.

The barrels of flour were arranged in the streets, the heads knocked in, and every soldier told to take some. Soldiers are greedy fellows, and many filled their haversacks. During a tedious night's march through woods as dark as chaos, they found the flour far from agreeable to carry and threw it away by degrees. If it had not been for the flour thus marking the track, the whole column would have lost its road. Such a scene of intolerable and unnecessary confusion I never witnessed. At daylight we were still not three miles from Bladensburg. Our soldiers were dead done, and so fatigued, there was nothing for it but to halt and bring into play the flour, which was soon set about, while we Staff were looking out like a Lieutenant of the Navy in chase, to see the Yankees come down upon us with showers of sharpshooters. Thanks to their kind consideration they abstained from doing so, but we were very much in their power.

…I recommend every officer in command to avoid a night march as he would the devil, unless on a good road, and even thus every precaution must be taken by all staff officers to keep up the communications, or regularity cannot be ensured. I have seen many night marches, but I never yet saw time gained, or anything beyond the evil of fatiguing your men and defeating your own object. You may move before daylight, *i.e.* an hour or two, if the nights are light. By this means, about the time the column requires collection, daylight enables you to do it. You have got a start of your enemy, your men are in full vigor either to march rapidly or, in case of difficulty, to fight. But avoid night marches. However, owing to their want of knowledge of the art of war, the enemy on this occasion allowed us to get to our boats perfectly unmolested."

There were no official figures from the opposing sides giving an accurate count of men killed or injured at Bladensburg, or the number of British who reboarded the ships waiting in the Patuxent. As stated earlier, Winder in writing to Armstrong three days after the battle assessed the damage to the enemy at 400 either killed or wounded and 30 to 40 Americans killed, with 50 to 60 wounded. Smith thought that the British took a loss of at least 300 men. Gleig recorded that upwards of 500 British soldiers were either killed or wounded. Ross wrote his "Official Account of the Capture of Washington" to Great Britain's Secretary of War, Lord Bathurst, from the *Tonnant*, August 30. This was two weeks before his sudden death at the Battle of North Point, outside Baltimore, after receiving a ball from a sniper's musket. Ross assigned Smith the duty of taking his report to England. Smith arrived in London on September 27, and delivered the dispatch to Bathurst. The General's report did not include figures for his loss of men, which was considered unnecessarily high. He was aware of circulating rumors that many were concerned he had been reckless with the lives of the British forces, not only at Bladensburg, but also during the marches to and from Benedict.

Rumored estimates of English troops left behind, whether deserters, prisoners, wounded or dead, varied within a range of between 15 and 20 percent. Furthermore, his account of the destruction to Washington was somewhat misleading. He itemized the arson that took place, giving the appearance that his forces put the torch to everything. London received the following:

> "My Lord - I have the honor to communicate to your Lordship, that on the night of the 24th inst. after defeating the army of the United States on that day, the troops under my command entered and took possession of the City of Washington....
>
> Having halted the army for a short time, I determined to march upon Washington, and reached that city at 8 o'clock that night. Judging it of consequence to complete the destruction of the public buildings with the least possible delay, so that the army might retire without loss of time, the following buildings were set fire to and consumed - the Capitol, including the Senate house and House of representation, the arsenal, the dock-yard, treasury, war office, President's palace, rope-walk, and the great bridge across the Potowmac: In the dock-yard a frigate nearly ready to be launched, and a slope of war, were consumed. The two bridges leading to Washington over the eastern branch, had been destroyed by the enemy, who apprehended an attack from that quarter.
>
> An attack upon an enemy so strongly posted could not be effected without loss. I have to lament that the wounds received by Col. Thornton, and the other Officers and soldiers left at Bladensburg, were such as prevented their removal. As many of the wounded as could be brought off were removed, the others being left with medical care and attendants. The arrangements made by Staff Sergeant Baxter for their accommodation have been as satisfactory as circumstances would admit of. The Agent for British prisoners of war very fortunately residing at Bladensburg, I have recommended the wounded officers and men to his particular attention, and trust to his being able to effect their exchange when sufficiently recovered."

Before the enemy retired, Dr. Hanson Catlett, a staff surgeon in Winder's army, displaying a white flag, was allowed into Bladensburg to attend the American wounded. He was probably in the best position to offer a reliable estimate as to the number of those killed or injured during the invasion. Catlett thought the loss to the American forces was 10 to 12 killed and 30 wounded, totaling 42. His loss estimate for the enemy troops was about 400 wounded and 150 killed, totaling 550. This would have been over twelve percent of Ross's army, not including bodies buried after the British retreat, victims of the hurricane, the explosion, deserters, or those who simply dropped dead from the heat or fatigue during the march to and from Washington. Interestingly the Americans either killed or wounded, consisted mainly of Barney and his flotillamen who stood their ground while Winder's citizen forces excitedly fled the field. Catlett reported:

> "...and the next day, when I came in with a flag, to attend our wounded, I learned from some of their officers that they suspected our troops were still on the heights above Georgetown, though they were at Montgomery Court House, from which place General Winder had ordered me back to Bladensburg, with permission of the British commander, for the purpose mentioned. I met the advance of the British army on Capitol Hill, supposed to be about seven hundred, and passed their main body, supposed about two thousand, on the hill this side of the turnpike. They appeared to be preparing to move; had about forty miserable horses haltered up, ten or twelve carts or wagons, one ox cart, one coachee, and several gigs, which the officers were industriously assisting to tackle up, and were immediately sent on the Bladensburg, to move off their wounded. A drove of sixty or seventy cattle preceded this cavalcade.

> On our arrival at Bladensburg, the surgeons were ordered to select all the wounded who could walk, (those with broken arms and the like) and send them off immediately. The forty horses were mounted with such that could ride, the carts and wagons loaded, and ninety odd wounded left behind. I estimated their wounded at three to four hundred, besides forty or fifty left in this city. One of the British surgeons informed me they had buried that day about one hundred on the field; and the men who were sent out next day after retreat of the enemy, to bury three or four Americans, reported that they also buried fifty or sixty red-coats, or British.

> I found at Bladensburg Commodore Barney, Captain Miller, of marines, and seventeen other Americans, badly wounded. I estimate our whole loss at ten or twelve killed on the field, and thirty odd wounded; though others, who had less opportunity of judging, estimate it at more than double.

> About midnight (being up all night) I heard the sound of a bugle, and was informed that the whole British army were passing through the lower end of the village. In the morning, early, I saw them still going off in small squads, and some stragglers were moving off till noon, about which time we learned that their main body were halted about eight miles on the road to Marlborough."

The retreating march resumed Friday around noon, arriving at Upper Marlboro that evening where the British again made camp. The weary soldiers continued to leave the ranks, with many plundering the surrounding countryside. A group of locals, including Beanes, who had been more than graciously hospitable to the invading forces on their march to Washington, captured a few marauding stragglers and placed them in jail. British horsemen who were on patrol scouting for signs of American troops moving in their direction, learned about the incident. They immediately rode to Beanes' manor house, arriving there after midnight, and seized him while he was still in bed. Mrs. Thornton thought that an American informant was the cause behind the arrest of Beanes. She included in her diary:

> "Dr. Beans taken a prisoner in consequence of some busy informant following the English and telling them that Dr. Beans was engaged in taking up some straggling soldiers. This they considered a breach of his promise of neutrality. They sent back some men who carried him off in the night, hardly permitting him to put on his clothes."

The scouting party took Beanes, along with at least two other captives, Dr. William Hill and Philip Weems, (Robert Bowie, a former Maryland governor, may have been part of the group) back to enemy headquarters. Ross ordered that they be held as prisoners for violating a pledge of good conduct, or rather, neutrality. Gleig suggested that it was an escaped Redcoat, rather than an American informant, who presented the patrolling infantry with the knowledge that a few British soldiers were jailed at Upper Marlboro. He also implied that residents at Upper Marlboro put to death some of the looting Redcoats who strayed from the column. He wrote:

> "Whilst the infantry were thus employed, the cavalry was sent back as far as Marlborough, to discover whether there were any American forces in pursuit; and it was well for the few stragglers who had been left behind that this recognizance was made. Thought there appeared to be no disposition on the part of the American General to follow our steps and to harass the retreat, the inhabitants of that village, at the instigation of a medical practitioner called Bain, had risen in arms as soon as we departed; and falling upon such individuals as strayed from the column, put some of them to death, and made others prisoners.
>
> A soldier whom they had taken, and who had escaped, gave information of these proceedings to the troopers, just as they were about to return to head-quarters; upon which they immediately wheeled about, and galloping into the village, pulled the doctor out of his bed (for it was early in the morning), compelled him, by a threat of instant death, to liberate his prisoners; and mounting him before one of the party, brought him in triumph to the camp."

At sunrise Saturday the invaders continued retracing their steps in the direction of Nottingham, taking with them their seized captives. The army remained at Nottingham throughout the night, resting there until late the following afternoon when it set out for Benedict, the last leg

of their march. The British forces reached their destination early
Monday morning without any resistance or preventative measures on the
part of the Americans and leisurely re-embarked their ships the following
day, Tuesday, August 30. The unfortunate prisoners were transferred to
Cochrane's flagship the *Tonnant*, where they remained in captivity while
enraged Marylanders scrambled about seeking solutions for their release.
Smith described a very uneventful re-embarkation:

> "We reached our landing-place unmolested, and at our leisure
> embarked our army, which began to suffer very much from
> dysentery. A long sea voyage is the worst possible preparation for
> long and fatiguing marches. The men are fat, in no exercise, have
> lost the habit of wearing their accoutrements, packs, etc. --- in short,
> they are not the same army they were on embarcation. Before our
> men left the Gironde, thirty miles a day would have nothing to them."

The enemy troops wasted everything in their path. Arresting the
plundering British soldiers was one of the few resources residents had to
protect their property. Monroe, in his first dispatch to Madison from
Horse Road, August 21, pointed out that the land was being destroyed
three to four miles inland all along the Patuxent River. Mrs. Smith, in
writing to her sister from Sidney, the Smiths country farm, a portion of
which the Catholic University later built upon, vividly described the
destruction to the people and the countryside by the British advance and
retreat. Mrs. Smith put a female perspective to the invasion as she
related the horrors of war and the suffering to the people. Her last
sentence was particularly poignant as she observed a basic fact of war ---
that there are those who are left behind who grieve:

> "At Bladensburgh which was inhabited chiefly by poor persons, the
> gentlemen having large houses and farms around the houses are much
> damaged by cannon ball &c --- many of them occupied by the British
> wounded and our wounded men. (The army left all of their wounded
> for us to take care of) --- The poor owners thus excluded, their
> gardens, corn fields and enclosures laid waste; their horses all taken.
> In the army's march from Benedict they made tents and beds of all
> the green corn, for which purpose they cut down whole fields. I am
> told this country (from Benedict to Washington) is totally laid waste;
> you can scarcely get anything for man or horse to eat. They strip'd
> the people of their clothing, taking women's and even children's
> clothes. All this was done by the straggling parties of soldiers who
> robb'd only the poor.

> At Bladensburg, Marlboro' and Wood Yard, the officers had guards
> placed around the houses of many considerable and wealthy persons
> and obtruded no further than to go to lodge, breakfast or dine with the
> gentlemen, except where they found houses empty and deserted, in

134

which case they generally destroyed them. We ran a great risque in
deserting ours. We are again establish'd and I now think nothing
(excepting an army of Cossacks) shall induce me again to leave it.

The battle was very near to us. In the next farm, there was
skirmishing, and 10 dead bodies were found (of the enemy) some
only 4 or 5 days ago.... Several hundred of our flying troops were at
her house (Mrs. Bradley), she dress'd their wounds and gave them
meat and drink. I am persuaded the enemy lost many more than was
first supposed, as bodies are daily found, unburied, under bushes, in
gulleys. Alas poor wretches, how many anxious hearts in England
may be looking for your return!"

After landing his forces at North Point near Baltimore, Major General Robert Ross (1766-1814) was leading his men toward the city when a skirmish broke out at Godly Wood. He was shot through his right arm and chest by an American sharpshooter. Ross fell into the arms of his aid-de-camp, Captain Duncan McDougall, and died shortly thereafter.

17

RETURN TO THE CAPITAL

Unaware that the British army had evacuated Washington, the Presidential party crossed the Potomac into Maryland on Friday afternoon, August 26. They rode to Montgomery Court House, hoping to connect with Winder's army and learn from Monroe, or his scouts, the latest news about the blackened capital. They arrived late in the day (around 6:00 p.m.) to be informed that the army left about noon marching towards Baltimore, where Winder believed the British were headed. Madison, intent on catching up with Winder, continued chasing the army. The group rode another eight miles and, around 9:00 p.m., arrived at the Quaker community of Brookville. Here they stopped for the evening and were provided shelter in the home of the village postmaster Caleb Bentley and his wife Henrietta, friends of Dolley's. By 10:00 p.m. the President sent a message to Monroe inquiring if he should remain in Brookville or continue onward to meet the army:

> "Brookville, Aug. 26, 1814, 10 o'clock p.m.
> Dear Sir ____ I expected this morning to have reached General W.
> and yourself before your departure from Montgomery C. H., but was
> delayed so that I did not arrive there till six o'clock, partly to obtain

quarters, partly to be within communication with you. I have proceeded thus far, in company with Mr. Rush, General Mason, &c., and avail myself of the bearer to inform you, that I will either wait here for you to join me, or follow and join you, as you may think best. Let me know your idea on the subject by the bearer. If you decide on coming hither, the sooner the better. Mr. Rush will remain here also. Mr. Jones is with my family and his own on the other side of the Potomac, but will come to the city the moment he hears of its evacuation. General Armstrong and Mr. Campbell are, I understand, at Fredericktown. I shall give them immediate notice of the change in the state of things, and desire them to conform to it."

Meanwhile, there were serious rumors that the British had instigated a slave insurrection. Additional reports were also circulating that looting had become wide spread in the abandoned capital. The terror of a slave uprising was quite real. It was something dreaded far more by the Americans than the invading army. This new fear was not confined just to the Federal City. It spilled over into Virginia as evidenced by Mrs. Love, who after seeing Dolley off Thursday morning, fled Rokeby with her sister for safety further inland to be a good distance from the British. While in route, she heard and listened to various rumors wildly circulating that a massive slave revolt had broken out. She panicked and forced her carriage driver at gun point to turn around and return to Rokeby. She felt safer nearer the British troops. This experience was related many years later in her *Recollections*:

> "As everything was so unsettled, we concluded to go into the interior of the country, and for that purpose set out, but were turned back by the alarm of a servile insurrection. So, thinking we would be safer near the army, we retraced our steps. I can't say I was ever afraid of any such thing. The man who was driving us kept saying he did not think his horses would get us back by night, and I, thinking he was in the plot, told my sister that if he did not go on, I would cock the gun we had in the carriage with us and threaten to shoot him, though I had never shot a gun in my life. I met a neighbor in the evening and told him what we had heard, and he was pleased to say that I was one of the most fearless women he had ever seen. When I got home I found everybody gone to town, having heard the same report.
>
> I will here record an anecdote to show how little things keep up excitement. Soon after we got home a drum was heard; the time was come, and all were waiting the result in horror, when the gentleman, who had gone out to see who was coming, found an old man who lived at a mill nearby, beating a drum to scare away the rats! The gentlemen made him keep watch at my gate all night."

Also in Virginia, Brigadier General Robert Young was leading his troops to Conn's Ferry on Friday, August 26, intending to cross the

Potomac and join Winder's army, when local inhabitants approached him requesting protection from the rumored slave insurrection. Young halted his brigade at Carper's Mill, just west of Wiley's Tavern, and sent out scouts to ascertain the correctness of the situation. The rebellion proved to be false, but it was not until late the following day that his militia troops were able to be ferried across the river to Maryland. Young spoke of the event in his statement to the Investigative Committee on October 3, 1814:

> "I had sent a vidette into the city of Washington, and learnt that the enemy were in possession and were firing the public buildings. I took up my line of march for Conns' ferry, a small distance above the Great Falls of the Potomac, and immediately opposite Montgomery Court House, where I was informed General Winder's army then were. The troops were, on the twenty-sixth, delayed on their march, near Carper's mills, opposite the Great Falls of the Potomac, by an alarm of domestic nature, which I was credulous enough to give credence to, from the respectability of the country people who came to me for protection, and I accordingly halted my brigade and sent out my light troops, and one troop of cavalry, which had joined me from Fauquier, to ascertain the facts, which finally proved erroneous....
>
> On the evening of the twenty-seventh of August I crossed my troops over the Potomac, at Conns' ferry, and the river being rocky, and but one boat, and owing to high winds, I was unable to pass the artillery and baggage across until late in the evening of the twenty-eighth of August."

As it turned out, there was no slave insurrection. They were far more fearful of the British than their own countrymen and did their best to remain in hiding. But this was not the case with the looters. Once the enemy had deserted the city the plundering began in earnest. Much that survived the British did not survive the American vandals. Thornton, who was constantly riding in and out of Washington to keep abreast of things, returned to the city again on Friday to make certain the British did not break their promise of not burning the Patent Office. He found the enemy had left during the night, but that vandalism had become just as great, if not a greater, problem. Since Mayor Blake had not yet returned to the city, Thornton appointed himself as a sort of unofficial mayor and set about doing mayoral duties. He busied himself doing such things as visiting the wounded British at Carroll Row, closing the gates of the navy yard, establishing guards at the ruins of government buildings and appointing citizen guards, which included captured British soldiers, to patrol the streets at night. Thornton's defensive description of his activities was printed in the *National Intelligencer*, September 7, 1814:

"Finding the Mayor not yet in the city, I as the only Justice of the Peace, appointed a guard at the President's House and Offices, another at the Capitol to prevent plunderers who carrying off articles to the amount of thousand of dollars. When at the Capitol, I was informed that a dreadful scene of plunder was exhibited at the Navy Yard. I went and ordered the gates to be shut, and stopped every plunderer. While placing a guard there, Commodore Tingey arrived. I delivered every thing to him; and in returning was told the English sick and wounded were in want, and had no provision.

I visited them, and was informed by Sergeant Sinclair of the British 21st regt. who had the command of these men, that Dr. James Ewell had in the most humane manner attended them as a physician, and, as far as he could, he had supplied them with necessaries. Major L'Enfant, with great humanity, besides being useful in some precautionary measures, desired I would have carts sent in for some of our wounded men on the commons. I understood he had engaged one, and I desired he would send as many as he thought necessary, for which I would be answerable. I have heard since they had been removed.

I then waited on Dr. James Ewell, to thank him in the name of the city for his goodness towards the distressed, who, being in our power, and especially in misery, were no longer enemies. He told me there was no provision for them of any kind. I appointed a Commissary, and ordered every thing that the Doctor thought requisite, for which I would be responsible.

The sergeant requested my protection for all his men. I told him they would be protected; and as I had seen several stragglers, and as our people would patrole the streets in squads of six at least in every ward, and might meet some of them, it would be well to send a man with each of our patroles as a guard to challenge them, and thereby prevent our people from firing on them; and if any should be found, to take them to the Sergeant, who would put them under guard for further orders. He promised to obey every order. I gave orders and he fulfilled them. Some stragglers, I understand, were taken up, and perfect order kept throughout the city.

After I had made all the arrangements, the Mayor arrived. I informed him of all I had done, and stated, that I then delivered over to him all the authority I had from the duty of office assumed. He, I believe, and my fellow-citizens, approved of my conduct. I returned late to my family in the country."

Blake returned at 3:00 p.m that same afternoon and was not pleased with Thornton and his self appointed "borrowed authority." The Mayor rejected Thornton's idea of using enemy troops as guards, and formed a committee that established a system of citizen patrols, that even included himself, to guard the streets at night. Captain Elias Caldwell's cavalry arrived around sunset, giving some semblance of authority to the District. The looting stopped and, by the time Madison and his cabinet arrived the next evening, order had been restored. Blake responded to Thornton's letter in the *National Intelligencer* by writing:

> "On Friday about noon, I heard the enemy had evacuated the City the night before. The Potomac Bridge being burnt, I immediately proceeded to Mason's ferry and was among the first that returned --- it was about 3 o'clock, P.M. I found it not only left by the enemy, but also by probably nine tenths of its inhabitants. I was told that great agitation and alarm prevailed, on account of a number of arms and a quantity of ammunition having fallen into the hands of a *certain population* which was then most numerous. Measures were immediately taken to convene as many of the citizens as practicable at McKeowen's Hotel, in order to adopt measures for our security for that night.

> On my way to the meeting, I met Dr. Thornton in the street, he told me his story about the saving of the General Post Office, and the arrangement he had made about a Patrole, composed in part of some of our citizens and the British soldiers left with their sick and wounded. I replied that a meeting would be held at McKeowen's at 5 o'clock and requested him to attend; but never gave my assent to the British soldiery or any part of them patroling our streets --- on the contrary, it is well known that I contended they were our prisoners and reprobated the idea of placing ourselves under British protection --- in this opinion the meeting thought with me, and Dr. Thornton's arrangement was rejected.

> The first object that engaged their attention was our own personal safety, and a resolution was adopted that every white male citizen should continue up the whole night and patrole the streets, and a Captain was appointed to each ward. I patroled the streets with my musket through the night, but at this moment of the greatest peril, when the services of every one were so peculiarly desirable, I had not the pleasure of seeing Dr. Thornton; he sought safety by retiring to the country....

> About dusk, Captain Caldwell and his troop came into the city and stopped at McKeowen's, where I then was --- I mentioned to him, as the highest military officer in the city at the time, the arrangement of Dr. T. --- he agreed with me as to its impropriety --- observing that we would disarm the British Guard in the morning --- he also agreed to act with me in a military capacity in all manners necessary for restoring tranquility, until a superior military officer arrived. The police officers were nearly all absent on military duty.

> The night passed without any disturbance and without meeting with any British stragglers."

By Saturday Madison and his Cabinet were scattered at four different locations. Armstrong and Campbell were patiently waiting at the appointed rendezvous in Fredericktown, Jones was probably still at Wiley's, Monroe was with the army, and the President and Rush were at Brookville. Monroe did not receive Madison's Friday night inquiry as to whether he should join the army until early Saturday. By this time, he had already sent word to the President, updating him that the enemy had vacated the city and appeared to be retreating towards Benedict. Because the fragmented government needed to show immediate strength and restore the confidence of the people in its leadership, he urged Madison to quickly return to the capital; however, Monroe became restless, and rode to Brookville and joined the President and Rush in their return to Washington. Monroe continued in his "Notes Respecting the Burning City:"

> "On the 27th the secretary of state, having heard that the enemy had evacuated the city, notified it, by express, to the President, and advised immediate return to the city for the purpose of reestablishing. He joined the President on the same day at Brookville, and he, accompanied by the secretary of state and attorney-general, set out immediately for Washington, where they arrived at five in the afternoon."

Madison wasted no time in summoning his Cabinet back to Washington. Before exiting Brookville at noon on Saturday, he sent a courier to Fredericktown with messages for both Armstrong and Campbell. The President also wrote to the Secretary of Navy at Wiley's Tavern, alerting him of the British evacuation and urging him to hurry back to Washington. This note, and the one to Monroe at 10:00 the previous evening, indicated that he thought Dolley, the Jones' family and others had remained at the inn; or, at least, he was hopeful that this was the case. Madison wrote to Jones:

> "Brookville Aug. 27, 10 OC
> On our arrival at Montgomery Ct. House found, according to report, that the army had left it about noon, in full march toward Baltimore, where the Enemy were supposed to be landing their troops. We came to this place last evening with a view of joining the Secy. of State with the army, or of going with him to Washington as he might think best. I have just recd. a note from him saying that the Enemy were on their way to Marlbo, and recommending that we repair to the city as soon as possible. Mr. Rush and myself will set out immediately and I send notice by express to Genl. A & W.C, who I understand are at Frederick Town. I hope you will, with the party attached to your care, have remained at Wiley's and be so much the more quick in your return to the city."

Unaware that Dolley had departed the tavern early Friday, for friendlier shelter at the Minor residence in Falls Church, the President also included a message to her with the one to Jones. He updated her about the turn of events, relating that he was returning to the city. He suggested that she also return as soon as possible. Madison wrote:

"Brookville Aug 27th 10 oclock

My Dearest,

Finding that our army had left Montgomery C. H. we pushed on to this place, with a view to join it, or proceed to the City, as further information might prescribe. I have just recd. a line from Col. Monroe saying that the enemy were out of Washington & on the retreat to their ships, & advising our immediate return to Washington. We shall accordingly set out thither immediately, you will of course take the same resolution. I know not where we are in the first instance, to hide our heads; but shall look for a place on my arrival. Mr. Rush offers his house in the six buildings & the offer claims attention. Perhaps I may fall in with Mr. Cutts & have the aid of his advice. I saw Mr. Bradley at Montgomery C. H. who told me that Mrs. Cutts was well. Jamey will give you some particulars.

P. S. I have not time to write, since the above it is found necessary to detain Jamey & send a trooper."

Mrs. Smith was absent from Brookville during Madison's brief stay. She was at a farm house about four miles away, taking care of Mason's wife who was dangerously ill with a highly inflammatory bilious fever. When Mason eventually arrived on Saturday to take care of his wife, Mrs. Smith returned to the Quaker village. The President had already left for Washington, but she was told about his visit and described what was related in a continuing letter to her sister:

"Just at bed time the Presd. had arrived and all hands went to work to prepare supper and lodgings for him, his companions and guards, --- beds were spread in the parlour, the house was filled and guards placed round the house during the night. A large troop of horse likewise arrived and encamp'd for the night, beside the mill-wall in a beautiful little plain, so embosom'd in woods and hills. The tents were scatter'd along the riverlet and the fires they kindled on the ground and the lights within the tents had a beautiful appearance. All the villagers, gentlemen and ladies, young and old, throng'd to see the President. He was tranquil as usual, and tho' much distressed by the dreadful event, which had taken place not dispirited. He advised Mr. Smith to return to the city, wither he was himself going. Mr. Monroe and some other gentlemen join'd him and about noon he set off for our suffering city."

In spite of the hostilities that took place upon her arrival, Dolley

143

and those traveling with her remained at Wiley's Thursday night after the Presidential party headed for Conn's Ferry. Leaving the security of the Jones' family and others, she left the tavern the following day in the company of at least Sukey, Anna and Anna's children. Rather than traveling further inland, she headed back towards Washington and stayed at Minor's Hill in Falls Church. Jennings further elaborated:

> "... and went to Mrs. Minor's, a few miles further, where she stayed a day or two, and then returned to Washington, where she found Mr. Madison at her brother-in-law's, Richard Cutts, on F Street. All the facts about Mrs. M. I learned from her servant Sukey."

Seven year old Matilda Roberts Sayrs was still a refugee at the Minor home when the First Lady arrived. In relating her experiences in *Childhood in 1812 - A True Story*, she painted a charming picture of the times and happenings, confirming that Dolley found shelter at Minor's Hill. The gorgeously attired Dolley made a lasting impression upon her. The children's dress-up party described below took place after everyone was back home in Alexandria. At Minor's Hill, Mrs. Sayrs observed Dolley's elegant wardrobe and, in portraying the First Lady, she included Dolley's trademarks - a covered throat and something worn on her head. Mrs. Sayrs recalled:

> "To us little ones in our country refuge all was a mystery, but we understood enough to be very much afraid the British would capture us. But we had some very good company in our trouble. There were in the house two ladies who always came out of their rooms elegantly dressed and who one day mysteriously disappeared. We afterward learned that they were Mrs. Madison, the wife of the President, and her sister.

> ... for we had resolved upon having a masquerade, and each of us had decided upon some character which she intended to personate. After my war episode Mrs. Madison had become my ideal of elegance, and hers was the character which I had selected. A trunk of old clothes in the garret was a mine of wealth to us. My dress was of white satin, sleeves and a lace frill around the throat. A white veil was twisted into a massive head dress and a pair of white slippers made me feel that nothing more was to be desired."

18

ALEXANDRIA SURRENDERS

The Presidential party arrived back in the smoldering capital by 5:00 p.m. Saturday and immediately set about to repair the shattered government. Madison was able to stay at his brother-in-law's residence on F Street. But all was not calm! About an hour after his arrival, everyone heard the rumble of distant cannon fire as it drifted up the Potomac. The British soldiers may have vacated the city, but the Royal Navy had finally worked its way up the river, and Gordon's squadron of seven vessels was approaching Alexandria intending to capture that port. However, the ships had to pass Fort Warburton, the only obstacle left in their way. For over two hours that evening the roar of cannonading could be heard throughout the area as Gordon's sailors bombarded the fort, not realizing it had been vacated earlier by the Americans. Captain Samuel Dyson, believing that enemy soldiers were threatening his rear by land, acted on verbal orders from Winder that the fort should be destroyed if it could not be defended. He ordered the placement of a trail of gunpowder leading to over three thousand pounds of explosives in the magazine. Once in place, Dyson and his men simply left the fort. Not a single shot was fired! Gordon's constant bombardment lasted a little over two hours, until the magazine ignited and blew up at about 8:30. The explosion reverberated throughout the entire greater Washington area. Gordon's Log Book contained the following:

<u>"Log of Proceedings, HMS Seahorse</u>

P. M. Saturday 27 August 1814.
12 - 4 ... Squadron in company running up the Potomac under easy sail over the flat channel between Stump Neck and Indian Pt. Shore steep until past the split of Crane Is.

4 – 8 5.30 Anchored abreast Fort Washington. .6.30 Anchored with the squadron a little below it in 6 frms. Bomb Vessels taking their range and throwing a few shells.

8 – 12 8:30 Explosion took place in the Fort supposed to be the magazine. Sent Boats to buoy the channel abreast. Grand Boats found the garrison to have quitted."

Once the enemy guns fell silent, area residents recognized that the river was now completely undefended and Gordon's squadron would easily advance further towards Alexandria, Georgetown and, once again, the capital. The terror was not yet over! From his camp at Mason's Island two days later, Dyson responded to Armstrong's order demanding a report explaining why the fort was set to be blown up, evacuated, and under whose orders Dyson had acted. The Captain wrote:

"Sir: I had the honor to receive your communication of the 29th instant. The orders received from Brigadier General Winder, through Major Hite, verbally, on the 24th instant, were, in case I was oppressed by, or heard of, an enemy in my rear, to spike our guns and make my escape over the river. The enemy approached by water on the 27th, and we had learned that day, through several channels, that the enemy had been reinforced at Benedict two thousand strong, and that they were on their march to co-operate with the fleet, in addition to the force which left the city. Under all these circumstances the officers under my command were consulted, and agreed it was best to abandon the fort and effect a retreat. The force under my command was thought not equal to a defence of the place."

The small British fleet had not yet reached Alexandria when a delegation of three citizens rowed down river Sunday morning, August 28, carrying a flag of truce to meet the advancing foe. Flag bearers Charles Simms, Jonathan Swift and Edmund Lee, acted under the authority of the Common Council. They boarded Gordon's ship, the *Seahorse,* to inquire about the fate of their city. The Captain did not offer any terms at that time, but assured them that if the squadron were not molested, no harm would come to Alexandria and its inhabitants. Lee described the event through a "Letter to the Editor," printed in the *Alexandria Gazette*, September 3, 1814:

> "The Alexandrians made no offer to surrender before the *squadron passed the fort*. There was no attempt at a communication with the fleet until after the fort had been abandoned by the troops of the United States and the magazine was blown up. This was done on Saturday evening. On Sunday morning about ten o'clock the whole of the fleet were considerably above the fort, and the barges a long distance above it. At this moment, not before, did the flag set out to meet the fleet, which was done above the fort."

Obviously alarmed by the changed situation, the President sent another message early Sunday to Dolley, who he thought still remained in Virginia, warning her to hold off returning to the city as it was not safe. However, the First Lady was already on her way back to the capital. Dolley was not aware of her husband's message of concern suggesting that she "stay put," until after she was safely back in Washington later that afternoon, resting at her sister Anna's home. In this note, the President recognized that she was no longer traveling in the company of the Jones' family. Madison wrote:

> "I cannot yet learn what has been the result. Should the port have been taken, the British ships with their barges will be able to throw the city again into alarm, and you may be again compelled to retire from it, which I find would have a disagreeable effect. Should the ships have failed in their attack, you can not return too soon. (I shall) keep Freeman till the question is decided, and then lose no time in sending him to you. In the meantime it will be best for you to remain at your present quarters. I wrote you yesterday morning by express, from Brookville, and at the same time to the Secy of the Navy, supposing you all to be together. It is possible the separation may have prevented your receiving the letter. I returned to the city yesterday, in company with Mr. Monroe, Mr. Rush &c., and have summoned the Heads of Dept. to meet here without delay. Enclosed is a letter from Mr. Cutts. My next will be by Freeman, & as soon as I can decide the points of your coming on."

When the unprotected inhabitants of Alexandria surrendered their town, many in Georgetown and the District were prepared to follow their example. The President desperately needed to show strength of leadership, fearing that the government might collapse. There was no force organized for any defense of the entire metropolitan area. In view of the fact that the Secretary of War had not yet returned to the city, and Winder's army was marching for Baltimore, Madison asked Monroe to assume command for the defense of the city on an interim basis. In

December, 1814, Monroe stated to Jefferson:

> "The President, Mr. Rush & I return'd on the 27th. The squadron of the enemy was then before fort Washington. Alex. had capitulated; this city was prepar'd to surrender a second time, & Georgetown, was ready to capitulate. The infection ran along the coast. Baltimore totter'd, as did other places, all of which were unprepar'd to resist an immediate attack. Armstrong was at Frederick town & Winder at Baltimore. No time could be spar'd. The President requested me to act in their stead, which I did as well as I could. The citizens cooperated with me."

Together, Madison, Monroe and Rush toured the charred city Sunday morning inspecting the damage, while arranging for its defense in case the enemy ships moved further up the Potomac. Returning from the navy yard, they encountered Thornton who headed a delegation that wanted to raise a flag of truce for the nation's capital. He demanded that the President send a committee of citizens to the commander of the British squadron with permission to surrender Washington. Appalled, Madison refused, responding that such an act would be dishonorable! He insisted there were enough troops if called together, and the city would be defended. Thornton's description of this exchange was printed later in the *National Intelligencer*:

> "On the 28th, I learnt that the people, being afraid of the landing of the British seamen, who they thought were immediately bound for the city, I had desired the Mayor to wait on the President, and request permission to send a deputation – not to enter into a capitulation of any kind, but to represent to the commander of the British squadron, that it was understood when their army destroyed the public buildings and property no other would be molested, and to request therefore they would not permit their sailors to land; but learning at the same time that the President had refused to hear of a deputation, and understanding that the people on all sides deprecated a mere shew of resistance; for it was supposed our men had not generally returned, and that the few who had returned were all dispersed, I rode immediately to the President, who was attended by the Secretary of State and the Attorney General.
>
> I represented the general feelings of the people on the above supposition, but was answered that it would be dishonorable to send any deputation, and that we would defend the city to the very last; that our men had returned, and we should have sufficient force if called together, and I was desired to aid in rousing them to arms. I obeyed the call - returned, rode in all directions, and called to arms. I sent for the troops from Bladensburg, and urged them from various places. I went to the different quarters, and gave, as far as I could, every assistance in my power to fulfill the wishes of the

government."

In his letter to the newspaper, the Superintendent of Patents left out his hostile encounter with Monroe, who backed up the President with a very forceful show of strength. Madison was adamant that under no circumstances would he surrender the nation's capital to the British; but Thornton persisted, arguing that Washington had little time to prepare for an adequate defense. Monroe, as acting Secretary of War, had finally heard enough, and, taking charge of the situation, informed Thornton that any deputation that met with the enemy would meet the bayonet. Monroe described the encounter:

> "On the 28th in the morning, the President, with Mr. Monroe and the attorney-general, visited the navy yard, the arsenal at Greenleaf's Point, and passing along the shore of the Potomac, up towards Georgetown, Mr. Monroe, as secretary of war and military commander, adopted measures, under sanction of the President, for the defense of the city and of Georgetown. As they passed near the capitol he was informed that the citizens of Washington were preparing to send a deputation to the British commander for the purpose of capitulating.
>
> He forbid the measure. It was then remarked that the situation of the inhabitants was deplorable; there being no force prepared for their defense, their house might be burnt down. Mr. Monroe then observed that he had been charged by the President with authority to take measures for the defense of the city, and that it should be defended; that if any deputation moved toward the enemy it should be repelled by the bayonet."

Everyone firmly believed that the British were going to make another assault on the Federal City, and terror again clouded the entire area. Madison's quick return to the capital and his visible presence within hours of the British withdrawal restored public confidence. Monroe, a man of action, was the galvanizing force needed to put new heart into his country men. Together they created a new positive spirit. Batteries were quickly mounted for the defense of Washington at Greenleaf's Point, Windmill Point and near the burnt Long Bridge. A three point plan was implemented with the purpose of impeding or stopping the raiders from sailing back down the river to the Chesapeake Bay. 1) Captain David Porter, General John Hungerford, and Young were to proceed to the White House cliffs, also known as the Heights of Belvoir, south of Washington's Mount Vernon plantation, to erect batteries on top of the steep banks above the Potomac there. This location was selected because the river narrowed at that point and the bluffs stood thirty to sixty feet above the water. It was thought that cannons could fire down on passing ships and the enemy would be unable to raise their guns properly to return the fire. 2) Captain Oliver Hazard Perry was to set up defensive operations further south at Indian Head, on the Maryland side of the Potomac. 3) Commodore John Rodgers was to cobble together any vessels that he could find at the still smoldering navy yard to use them as fire boats and ram the British ships. In a letter to Jones, Porter described the preparations for the American defense at the White House bluffs:

> "SIR: Agreeable to your orders of the 31st ult I proceeded with the detachment of Sailors and Marines under my command, to the White House on the West bank of the Potomac, there to erect batteries and attempt the destruction of the enemy's ships on their passage down the river. Captain Creighton, Lieut Clack, and several other Navy officers, as well as Mr. Augustus Monroe, Mr. Ferdinand Fairfax, and several other citizens and officers of the Militia and Volunteer companies, hearing of my destination, volunteered their services on the occasion, and ably supported me through the arduous and fatiguing enterprize.
>
> By preceding my men, I arrived in company with the Hon. Secretary of State and Generals Hungerford and Young, on the evening of the 1st instant, at the spot fixed on, where I found a few militia belonging to General Hungerford's army, clearing away the trees to make room for mounting our cannon, which had not yet arrived, but which had been seen on their way down, consisting of three long eighteens and two twelves.
>
> Generals Hungerford and Young had received orders to co-operate with me, to detach men on my requisition, and make such disposition of their forces as would effectually protect me in the rear in the event of the enemy's landing; the positions they were to occupy were also allotted to them by mutual agreement, when the enemy should attempt to pass, as it was believed that concealed by the thick woods on the high bank they would be enabled to clear the enemy's decks with their musquetry, and in a great measure divert his fire from our battery."

Monroe encountered resistance from a colonel who refused the Secretary's written order to move three cannons from Virginia to the southern tip of Mason's Island, and to also move some others closer to Alexandria. Strongly displaying his appointment as acting Secretary of War, Monroe sought out the officer and spoke to him in person, making it very clear that he was acting under the authority of the President in taking charge of the capital's defenses. Rather than receive orders from the acting Secretary of War, Colonel Winder simply retired. There was no further insubordination from the American troops. Monroe later recorded the incident in "Notes Respecting the Burning City in 1814:"

> "He took immediate measures for mounting a battery at Greenleaf's
> Point, another near the bridge, a third at the wind mill point, and sent
> an order to Colonel Winder, who was in charge of some cannon, on
> the opposite shore above the ferry-landing, to move three of the
> pieces to the lower end of Mason's Island, and the others some
> distance below that point on the Virginia shore, to co-operate with the
> batteries on the Maryland side. Colonel Winder refused to obey the
> order, on which Mr. Monroe passed the river, and riding to the
> colonel gave the order in person. The colonel replied that he did not
> know Mr. Monroe as secretary of war or commanding general. Mr.
> Monroe then stated that he acted under the authority of the President,
> and that he must either obey the order or leave the field. The colonel
> preferred the latter."

As did many other residents, a subdued First Lady returned to the ashen capital on Sunday. She had not received her husband's second message alerting her of further terror to the city; however, she must have known that the British reached Alexandria, because the sound of the explosion at Fort Warburton would have reverberated throughout Falls Church. Nothing survived over time indicating Dolley's route back to the capital. Since Minor's Hill and Wren's Tavern had become the ad hoc military headquarters, she would have known that Long Bridge, connecting Washington with Alexandria, had been burnt. Furthermore, the tornado had severely damaged it as a violent gust of wind had broken the chains to its drawbridge. With that bridge destroyed and the enemy north of Fort Warburton, she would not have headed in the direction of Alexandria. The Little Falls Bridge was intact and Mason's Ferry was back in operation transporting troops and citizens to and from Virginia. Dolley would have either used the bridge at the falls or the ferry on her return to Washington. At some point in time a decision was made to abandon her personal carriage, because she arrived at the Cutt's residence in a carriage owned by Richard Parriott. Presumably at least Sukey, Anna and her three children returned to the city with Dolley, because they left Minor's Hill together as later reported by Mrs. Sayrs. Mrs. Thornton kept up her diary during the catastrophic events and recorded her visit with the First Lady and Mrs. Smith during tea the afternoon everyone returned:

> "Mrs. M. came to Mrs. Cutts' in a Parrott's carriage - Mr. Madison,
> Monroe, &c dined there.... Mrs. Smith & family came in & staid to
> tea. We stepped in to see Mrs. Madison; she was very violent against
> the English - & wished we had 10,000 such men as were pafsing (a
> few troopers) <u>to sink our Enemy to the bottomlefs pit</u>. She had better
> attribute the lofs of her palace to the right cause viz want of proper

defence in time."

Returning from Brookville Sunday afternoon were the Smiths, who called upon the Madisons later that day at the Cutts's residence. There they found a very downcast First Lady, who related that she remained at the White House as long as she did because she was confident of an American victory. The Thorntons lived next door to the Cutts, and Mrs. Thornton invited Dolley and Mrs. Smith in for tea. Being absent from the city Tuesday night through late Sunday, Mrs. Smith learned during the tea many vivid details concerning Bladensburg, the brief British occupation, and the burning of the capital as was described to her by the hostess. Mrs. Smith related to her sister Jane:

> "Mr. Smith went to see the President, who was at Mr. Cutts' (his brother in law) where we found Mrs. Madison and her sister Mrs. Cutts. Mrs. M. seen'd much depress'd, she could scarcely speak without tears. She told me she had remained in the city till a few hours before the English enter'd. She was so confident of Victory that she was calmly listening to the roar of cannon, and watching the rockets in the air, when she perceived our troops rushing into the city, with the haste and dismay of a routed force. The friends with her then hurried her away....

> She cross'd into Virginia where she remained until Sunday, when she return'd to meet her husband. Men, soldiers, expresses were round the house, the President was in a room with his cabinet, from whence he issued his orders. The English frigates were laying before Alexandria and as it was supposed only waiting for a wind to come up to the city. The belief was that about 700 or more sailors were to be let loose in the city for plunder, dreadful idea. A universal despondency seem'd to pervade the people, --- we every where met them in scattered groups relating, or listening to their fears.

> We drank tea at Mrs. Thornton's, who described to us the manner in which they conflagrated the President's H. and other buildings, --- 50 men, sailors, and marines were marched by an officer, silently thro' the avenue, each carrying a long pole to which was fixed a ball about the circumference of a large plate, --- when arrived at the building, each man was station'd at a window, with his pole and machine of wild-fire against it, at the word of command, at the same instant the windows were broken and this wild-fire thrown in, so that an instantaneous conflagration took place and the whole building was wrapt in flames and smoke. The spectators stood in awful silence, the city was light and the heavens redden'd with the blaze."

A few months after the burning of Washington, Dolley wrote to her longtime friend Mary Latrobe, whose husband, Benjamin, guided her in decorating the White House. In this letter the First Lady described her feelings and confessed that the Madisons lost much of their personal property in the burning of the President's House. Dolley also related that she had been away from the capital nearly three days, when in fact it was from Wednesday afternoon through late Sunday morning. She wrote:

December 3, 1814

"Two hours before the enemy entered the city, I left the house where Mr. Latrobe's elegant taste had been so justly admired, and where you and I had so often wandered together, and on that *very day* I sent out the silver (nearly all) --- the velvet curtains and Gen. Washington's picture, the cabinet papers, a few books and the small clock --- left everything else belonging to the publick, our own valuable stores of every description, a part of my clothes, and all my servants' clothes &c., &c., in short it would fatigue you to read the list of my losses, or an account of the general *dismay*, or particular distresses of your acquaintance. Mrs. Hunter and Mrs. Thompson were the only ladies who stood their ground. I confess that I was so unfeminine as to be free from fear, and willing to remain in the *Castle*. If I could have had a cannon through every window, but alas! those who should have placed them there, fled before me, and my whole heart mourned for my country!

I remained nearly three days out of town, but I cannot tell you what I felt on re-entering it --- such destruction --- such confusion! The fleet full in view and in the act of robbing Alexandria! The citizens expecting another visit --- and at night the rockets were seen flying near us."

The Joneses also returned Sunday, but did not remain in their Georgetown house. Looters had broken in, destroying much and taking some possessions. Even though they were absent but a short time, there was mildew damage, particularly to the curtains. Mrs. Jones quickly left Washington for Baltimore. The Navy Secretary was able to find space in a boarding house not too long afterwards. Mrs. Jones traveled through Bladensburg on her way north and, in a letter to her husband, written from Baltimore September 1, 1814 she described a nightmarish scene:

"A view of the ground where the battle was fought, and the graves of the fallen men, the cannon near which Com. Barney lost his horse and where they buried it, excited the most painful sensations, particularly on seeing the foot of one above the earth. Passing the hospitals in Bladensburg we saw the wounded, Americans and British, and preparations to bury an English soldier just expired. On the road we met our heroes of the Navy with their crews, the Marines, Cavalry, and 800 regulars. The whole amounting Mr. (Gray) thought to be 2000 at least."

153

Library of Congress

The picture shows the gutted shell of the fire damaged White House with its crooked lightening rod after the fires. The engraving by William Strickland (1787-1854) was done in 1815 after a painting by George Munger. After escaping Washington before the enemy entered, the Madisons were never again to occupy the Executive Mansion. President James Monroe (1758-1831) and his wife Elizabeth Kortwright (1768-1830) moved into an unfinished White House October, 1817. The Monroes were forced to live in the same set of uncomfortable circumstances as John and Abigail Adams faced seventeen years earlier. On New Year's Day, 1818, the Monroes opened the refurbished White House to all and hosted its first public reception since the conflagration, with the full-length portrait of George Washington prominently displayed.

19

GORDON'S CONDITIONS

Sunday passed without any further encounter with Gordon's squadron. The Captain waited until Monday morning, August 29, when his small fleet was safely anchored and well positioned to threaten all parts of Alexandria, before announcing the conditions he required to spare the city and its inhabitants. Israel Thompson, clerk of the Common Council of Alexandria, submitted the following to the Investigative Committee:

> "On the morning of the next day, to wit, the 29th of August, it arranged itself along the town, so as to command it from one extremity to the other. The force consisted of two frigates, to wit: the Seahorse, rating thirty-eight guns, and Euryalus, rating thirty-six guns; two rocket ships, of eighteen guns each; two bomb-ships, of eight guns each; and a schooner of two guns, which were but a few hundred yards from the wharves, and the houses so situated that they might have been laid in ashes in a few minutes."

At 10:00 a.m., Gordon sent one of his officers into the town to notify Mayor Simms of his terms. The Mayor, who was given one hour to accept the conditions, immediately sent for the committee of vigilance while the officer waited for a reply. Gordon's list included such things as surrendering naval and ordnance stores; all goods for exporting, such as tobacco, flour and cotton; all boats and ships, including those that had been sunk; and all merchandise that had been removed from the town after the 19th of August. The committee responded that merchandise sent out of the town during the past ten days could not be recalled and that citizens could not be compelled to raise the sunken vessels. They also inquired whether more merchandise needed to be delivered than could be taken away in the ships. The waiting officer replied that it would not be expected that the merchandise be recalled, that British sailors would raise the sunken ships, and that excess merchandise would not have to be brought to the wharves. The conditions that Gordon's officer delivered to the Mayor were the following:

"GENTLEMEN:
In consequence of a deputation yesterday received from the city of Alexandria, requesting favorable terms for the safety of their city, the undermentioned are the only conditions in my power to offer:

The town of Alexandria, with the exception of public works, shall not be destroyed, unless hostilities are commenced on the part of the Americans; nor shall the inhabitants be molested in any manner whatever, or their dwelling houses entered, if the following articles are complied with:

Article 1. All naval and ordnance stores, public and private, must be immediately delivered up.

Article 2. Possession will be immediately taken of all the shipping, and their furniture must be sent on board by the owners, without delay.

Article 3. The vessels that have been sunk must be delivered up in the state they were in on the 19th of August, the day of the squadron passing the Kettle Bottoms.

Article 4. Merchandise of every description must be instantly delivered up; and, to prevent any irregularities that might be committed in its embarkation, the merchants have it in their option to load the vessels generally employed for that purpose, when they will be towed off by us.

Article 5. All Merchandise that has been removed from Alexandria, since the 19th instant, is to be included in the above articles.

Article 6. Refreshments of every description to be supplied the ships, and paid for at the market price by bills on the British Government.

Article 7. Officers will be appointed to see that Articles Nos. 2, 3, 4, and 5, are strictly complied with; and any deviation or non-compliance, on the part of the inhabitants of Alexandria, will render this treaty null and void."

Negotiating a verbal agreement with the officer sent by Gordon, the committee of vigilance submitted the revised terms to the Common Council, which had little choice but to agree; thus, submitting to the conditions offered by the naval commander. To be more specific --- the town of Alexandria simply surrendered. The August 29th resolution passed by Alexandria's Common Council was as follows:

> "*Resolved*, That the Common Council of Alexandria, in assenting to the conditions offered by the commander of the British squadron, now off the town, has acted from the impulse of irresistible necessity, and solely from a regard to the welfare of the town; that it considers the assent by it given as only formal, inasmuch as the enemy had it already in their power to enforce a compliance with their demand by a seizure of the property required from us; and believing the safety of the persons of the inhabitants, of their dwellings, and of such property as is not comprehended within the requisition, to depend entirely on the observance of the terms of it, the Common Council recommends to the inhabitants as acquiescence, at the same time that it does expressly disclaim the power of doing any act on its part to enforce compliance, its authority, in this particular, being limited to recommendation only."

Mrs. Smith wrote to her sister that Alexandria had capitulated, but Madison had taken a firm stand to defend the capital. Referring to Thornton's interest in a "white flag" delegation, she suggested that some terrified citizens opposed the President's stance because everything they valued was already gone. They had nothing more to lose. There was nothing left to fight for. Her letter indicated that the President, through Monroe, was in charge of the dangerous situation and their orders were being enforced. Troops were being collected and more were on the way. Residents were again fleeing the city. In her view, the terror seemed more real than before:

> "The President is determined on making a resistance in case the enemy returns. But our citizens sent a deputation begging him not to attempt it, as it would be ineffectual, and would only be making them and the roofs that shelter'd them a sacrifice. 'They now,' they said, 'had neither their honor or property to loose. All they valued was gone.' The President's orders however, were enforced and all day yesterday while I was in the city I saw them collecting. Troops are order'd from all around, and 3000 are expected tonight. Alexandria has surrender'd its town with all their flour and merchandize and the frigates are now laying before that town, loading the Alexandria shipping with the goods of the citizens. What will be our fate I know

not. The citizens who remain'd are now moving out, and all seem
more alarm'd than before."

JOHNNY BULL and the ALEXANDRIANS.

City of Alexandria / The Lyceum

This satire by British cartoonist William Charles (1776-1820) depicts citizens of
Alexandria on their knees begging for mercy from England's Johnny Bull. The
Alexandrians on the left are pleading, "Pray Mr. Bull. Don't be too hard with us. You
know we were always friendly, even in the time of our Embargo!" Johnny Bull demands,
"I must have all your Flour...All your Tobacco...All your Provisions...All your
Ships...All your Merchandize...Every thing except your PORTER and PERRY...Keep
them out of my sight. I've had enough of them already..."

20

ARMSTRONG RESIGNS

It was not before one o'clock Monday afternoon that Armstrong, officially the Secretary of War, finally arrived back at the capital city from Fredericktown! This was two days after the return of Madison, Rush and Monroe! He discovered that public opinion was violently against him. Armstrong was blamed for everything and quickly became the scapegoat for what should have been a preventable disaster. *The Enquirer*, a Richmond newspaper, published a letter written by an unknown author from Dumfries, Virginia, dated August 29, 1814, that described a universal animosity towards the Secretary of War:

> "... All the functionaries are greatly censured and vilified, but Armstrong is held in the utmost abhorrence. Tis said that Cockburn planned the scheme and Ross executed it. Private property of every kind except Gale's printing materials was held sacred and inviotable.

> The President, Sec'y. of State and Navy are at Washington. Gen Armstrong is missing, but certainly is not among the valiant slain. The enemy have fallen down to Marlborough. I have given you the facts attendant on this successful attempt of the foe, which will ever be viewed as a national calamity on account of the stigma it affixes to

the American name.

P. S. --- A report has just reached this place that some soldiers hung
up Armstrong in Frederick town, Maryland."

A few tried to blame Madison for the destruction of the capital, and rumors were circulating that his life was in danger. A unit of fifty militia guards was posted around the Cutts' home; however, almost everyone blamed Armstrong as the man responsible for the capture of the city. Residents of the District of Columbia thought that Armstrong, as Secretary of War, did not expend much energy in preparing for a solid defense of the nation's capital. Now that Washington lay in ruins, angry citizens pointed out that it should and could have been defended. His tardy arrival back to the city did not help his situation. Mrs. Smith described the hostility towards Armstrong upon his return:

> "Universal execration follows Armstrong, who it is believed never wished to defend the city and I was assured that had he pass'd thro' the city the day after the engagement, he would have been torn to pieces. The district certainly was not in a state of preparation, whether from want of ability or want of inclination on the part of the administration we can not know. The city was capable of defence and ought to have been defended. But we will retrieve, yes I trust we will retrieve our character and restore our capital."

Matters were brought to a head when Armstrong rode down to Windmill Point on the afternoon he returned in his official position as Secretary of War to inspect the District Militia. He was coldly received by local officers, who where mainly men of property, heavily invested in Washington. Carroll refused to shake Armstrong's hand. Other officers simply laid down their swords, and enlisted men working on ditches threw down their shovels. In a separate incident, officers in the District Militia vowed to rip off their epaulets before receiving orders from Armstrong. Smith, commander of the District Militia, sent a message to the President stating that his officers would serve under any other member of the Cabinet, but not Armstrong. That evening a very concerned President met with Armstrong at the Secretary's residence in the Seven Buildings to discuss the awkward situation and the impending threat of an attack from enemy forces at Alexandria. Madison recorded the conversation in his "Memorandum," August 29, 1814:

> "...that violent prejudices were known to exist against the administration, as having failed in its duty to protect it, particularly against me and himself as head of the War Department; that threats of personal violence had, it was said, been thrown out against us both,

but more especially against him; that it had been sufficiently known for several days, and before his return to the city (which was about one o'clock P.M. of the 29th) that the temper of the troops was such as made it expedient, if possible, that he should have nothing to do with them; that I had within a few hours received a message from the commanding General of the Militia informing me that every officer would tear off his epauletts if Genl. Armstrong was to have anything to do with them; that before his arrival there was less difficulty, as Mr. Monroe who was very acceptable to them, had, as on preceding occasions of his absence, though very reluctantly on this, been the medium for the functions of Secretary of War, but that since his return and presence, the expedient could not be continued, and the question was, what was best to be done."

According to Madison, Armstrong responded by saying that he knew of the talk against him, claiming that there were intrigues against him, but that everything was founded on falsehoods and was groundless. The Secretary thought that his conduct in defending the city proved that there had been no deficiency on his part and remarked that he had not omitted any preparations for the safety of the place of which he was supposed to protect. He offered to give up his appointment, or retire from the scene by setting out immediately to visit his family in the state of New York. The President suggested that a temporary retirement from Washington would placate the inhabitants. Madison continued:

> "I replied that as the conversation was a frank one, I could not admit this justification, that it was the duty of the Secretary of War not only to execute plans, or orders committed to him, but to devise and propose such as would in his opinion be necessary and proper, that it was an obvious and essential part of his charge, and that in what related to military plans and proceedings elsewhere, he had never been scrupulous or backward in taking this course, that on the contrary he well knew from what on another occasion had passed between us, he had taken a latitude in this respect which I was not satisfied with, that it was due to truth and to myself to say, that he had never appeared to enter into a just view either of the danger to the city which was to be apprehended, or of the consequences of its falling into the hands of the Enemy, that he had never himself proposed or suggested a single precaution or arrangement for its safety, everything done on that subject having been brought forward by myself, and that the apparent difference of his views on that subject from mine had naturally induced a reduction of my arrangements to the minimum, in order to obtrude the less on a reluctant execution.

> I reminded him also that he had fallen short of the preparations even decided on in the Cabinet, in some respects, particularly not having arms and equipments brought to convenient depots from the distant ones, some of the militia, when called on for the defence of the City, being obliged to get arms first at Harper's ferry.

The conversation was closed by my referring to the idea of his setting out in the Morning on a visit to his family; and observing that he would of course revolve it further, and if he continued to think on it as he then did, he would consider me as opposing no restraint. We parted as usual in a friendly manner. On the next morning he sent me word by Mr. Parker that he should proceed immediately to visit his family; and on his arrival at Baltimore, transmitted his resignation."

Armstrong left the capital Tuesday morning, but by the time he reached Baltimore he realized the impossibility of his remaining in the Cabinet and sent his resignation to the President. At the same time, he submitted a lengthy letter to the editor of the *Baltimore Patriot* hostilely expressing his reasons for leaving the War Department:

"On the evening of the 29th ultimo, the President called at my lodgings, and stated that a case of much delicacy had occurred; that a high degree of excitement had been raised among the militia of the District; that he was himself an object of their suspicions and manaces; that an officer of that corps had given him notice that they would no longer obey any order coming through me as Secretary of War; and that in the urgency of the case, it might be prudent so far to yield to the impulse, as to permit some other person to exercise my functions in relation to the defence of the District.

To this statement and proposition, I answered substantially as follows - that I was aware of the excitement to which he alluded, that I knew its source & had marked its progress; that the present was not a moment to examine it's more occult causes, objects and agents; that it ostensibly rested on charges known to himself to be false, that it was not for me to determine how far the supposed urgency of the case made it proper for him to yield to an impulse so vile and profligate --- so injurious to truth and so destructive of order; but that for myself, there was no choice; that I could not surrender a part of my legitimate authority, for the preservation of the rest --- that I must exercise it wholly, or not at all; that I came into office, with objects exclusively public; and that to accommodate my principles or my conduct to the humors of a village mob, stimulated by faction and led by folly, was not the way to promote these, and that if his decision was taken in conformity to the suggestions he had made.

I entreated him to accept my resignation. This he declined doing. It was an extent, he was pleased to say, to which he meant not to go; that he knew the excitement was limited, as well with regard to time as to place; that he was now, and had always been, fully sensible of the general zeal, diligence and talent, which I had put into the discharge of my duty, and that it would give him pleasure, were I to take time to consider his proposition. I renewed the assurance of my great personal respect, and my readiness to conform to his wishes on all proper occasions. --- I remarked, that whatever zeal, diligence and talent I possessed, had been employed freely but firmly, and according to my best views of the public good, and that as long as they were left to be so exerted, they were at the service of my country --- but that the moment they were made to bow to military usurpation or political faction, there should be an end of their public exercise. We now parted, with an understanding that I should leave Washington the following morning....

It but remains to exhibit and to answer, the several charges raised against me and which form the groundwork of that excitement, to which the President has deemed it prudent to sacrifice his authority, in declining to support mine. They are as follows, viz.

1st. That (from ill will to the District of Columbia, and a design to remove the seat of government,) I gave orders for the retreat of the army, in the affair of the 24th ult. Under circumstances not making retreat necessary or proper. This charge has not for its support the shadow of truth. The commanding general will do me the justice to say that I gave him no such order, and that he was and is under the impression, that the retreat was made earlier than I believed it to be proper. To the President I appeal, whether I did not point out the disorder and retreat of a part of the first line, soon after the action began, and stigmatise it as base and infamous.

2d. That, in despite of the remonstrances of Gen. Winder, and by the interposition of my authority, I had prevented him defending the Capital. This charge contains in it a total perversion of the truth. When the head of the retiring column reached the Capital, it was halted for a moment. Gen. Winder here took occasion to state to Mr. Monroe and myself, that he was not in condition to maintain another conflict, and that his force was broken down by fatigue and dispersion. Under this representation, we united in opinion, that he should proceed to occupy the heights of Georgetown.

3d. That I had withdrawn the covering party from the rear of fort Washington, and had ordered captain Dyson to blow up the fort without firing a gun. This charge is utterly devoid of truth. The covering party was withdrawn by an order from general Winder and capt. Dyson's official report shews, that the orders under which he acted, were derived from the same source, though, no doubt, mistaken or misrepresented.

4th. That by my orders, the navy yard had been burned. This like it's predecessors, is a positive falsehood. Perceiving that no order was taken for apprising Commodore Tingey of the retreat of the army, I sent Major Bell to communicate the fact and to say, that the Navy Yard could no longer be covered. The commodore was of course left to follow the suggestions of his own mind, or to obey the orders, if orders had been given, of the Navy Department.

5th. And lastly that means had not been taken to collect a force sufficient for the occasion. As the subject of this charge may very soon become one of congressional enquiry, I shall at present make but a few remarks:

1st. That no means within reach of the War Department had been omitted or withheld --- that a separate military district, embracing the seat of government, had been created; that an officer of high rank and character had been placed in charge of it; that to him was given full authority to call for supplies and for a militia force of *fifteen thousand men*; that to this force was added the 36th regt. of the line, a battalion of the 38th, detachments of the 12th, of the artillery, and of the dragoons; the marine corps, and the crews of the flotilla, under the special command of commander Barney ---making a total of 16,500 men.

Gen. Winder's official report of the engagement of the 24th ult. shews, how much of this force had been assembled, and the causes why a greater portion of it had not been got together. These will be found to have been altogether extraneous from the Government, and entirely out of its control: and

2d. That from what is now known of the enemy's force, of the loss he sustained in the enterprise, of the marks or panic under which he retreated &c &c, it is obvious, that if all the troops assembled at Bladensburg had been faithful to themselves and to their country, the enemy would have been beaten, and the Capital saved."

21

GORDON'S DESCENT

Fortunately for Georgetown and the District, Gordon's squadron did not advance any further up the Potomac. Instead, his ships remained moored at Alexandria's docks for several days, while British sailors plundered the surrounding land and warehouses near the wharfs. They loaded their contraband onto twenty-one captured vessels, most of which had been raised from the bottom of the harbor. The inhabitants of the town gave no assistance to the enemy. They remained mere spectators to an event of which they obviously could not prevent. On Wednesday, August 31, another British ship, the *Fairy*, arrived with orders from Cochrane for the force to return to the bay. Its commander, Captain Henry Baker, told Gordon that the trip back down the river would be difficult because the *Fairy* had encountered shelling on its way upriver to Alexandria from Americans who were quickly putting together a battery on top the White House cliffs. Porter wrote:

> "...one of the enemy's vessels of war, a brig of 18 guns, was seen coming up. General Hungerford and his men took their position in the woods; and two small four pounders that instant arriving, I caused them to be planted on the edge of the bank, and on the enemy

arriving abreast of us we opened a brisk fire on him; having a fine breeze he was enabled to pass us, but could fire only one broadside as he crossed the fire of our field pieces and musquetry; the militia continued following him up along the bank and greatly annoyed him by their well directed fire. In this affair we had only one man wounded, and we believe our elevated position rendered breast works useless, as it was remarked that none but the enemy's grape passed over us, his round shot went into the bank below."

Recognizing the danger, Gordon hurried the loading and began a gradual retreat back down the Potomac the following day, Thursday, September 1. He started by sending two ships, the *Meteor* and *Fairy*, ahead to bombard the White House battery in hopes of impeding its construction or destroying it. The remaining British ships departed before dawn Friday morning, taking with them the twenty-one raised vessels now loaded with booty. The bomb ship *Devastation* ran aground before reaching the rubble that had been Fort Warburton. All the other vessels sailed passed without incident, dropping anchor opposite Mount Vernon so that there was support for the *Devastation* if needed. There they remained waiting the arrival of the grounded ship and favorable winds necessary to escape past the American battery and return to the bay. On Saturday Gordon ordered the *Etna* and *Erebus*, plus a captured American barge supporting a long 32-pounder, to proceed downriver and assist the *Meteor* and *Fairy* in their engagement at the bluffs. Porter continued:

> "The evening of our arrival, two eighteen pounders reached our position, and next morning one of the enemy's Bomb Ships and two barges, one carrying a long two and thirty, the other a mortar, commenced their operations upon us, the first throwing shells in front, beyond the reach of our shot; the other flanking us on our right; several shells fell near and burst over our battery, and although the firing lasted all day without intermission, it had no other effect than to accustom the militia to the danger.
>
> In the afternoon I took an eighteen pounder to a more advanced point, about a mile distant, and commenced a fire on the Bomb Ship, which did so much execution as to draw on me the fire of all their vessels, including a schooner and an eighteen gun brig which had dropped down that day. On the 3d the enemy was reinforced from above by another bomb ship and a sloop of war fitted up as a rocket ship."

The *Devastation* remained stranded throughout Saturday. Its exposed predicament offered Rodgers a perfect opportunity to unleash his fire boats. The Commodore ordered that three boats be set ablaze Saturday night and had them set loose in hopes of ramming the stranded bomb ship; but unfavorable winds and British sailors in barges pushed the flaming vessels away, preventing much damage. Rodgers made two more futile attempts at ramming the *Devastation* with other fire boats before it became free Monday morning and sailed down the river, linking up with the squadron preparing to pass the American battery at the White House. Two articles that appeared in the *National Intelligencer* on September 6, discussed Rodgers attempts at ramming the British ship:

> "The enemy's vessels dropt down the river from Alexandria on Friday night; and on Saturday Com. Rodgers had possession of that unfortunate town. On Saturday two or three fireships were sent down to the frigates then lying off Warburton, but did not take effect on them. The river was immediately covered with barges, thirty or forty in number, and these dangerous objects were towed out of the way of the vessels. The scene was witnessed from the high grounds of the city, and was very interesting – the river being covered with vessels and boats of almost every description.
>
> The frigates opened a heavy fire on the ruins of the old fort, or, on the shore near which they were lying, with what view we have not heard, nor have we heard any particulars of the damage done. Rockets were seen, and firing heard down the river, at intervals on Saturday night. Several of the vessels were seen below yesterday. The enemy's vessels evidently expect to be severely handled on their return, and doubtless will be, attempt it when they may."

> "Com. Rodgers on Sunday evening proceeded down the river with four barges, well manned, towards the nearest frigate; when he came within two miles distance, 7 barges full of men were sent to meet him. The barges manoeuvered within gun shot of each other till nine or ten o'clock at night, when a very warm firing of musquetry and large shot commenced between them, which lasted about 15 minutes, and ended in the repulse of the British barges with much loss. A barge was found on shore in the morning, with swords, &c. in it; and at least one barge was destroyed. On our part two or three men only were hurt."

The firing at the White House battery was constant for four days as the foreign ships assembled and waited for the winds to change in order to make a run for it. During this time, the British had been unable to eliminate the American battery because their cannons could not get the required angle due to the heights of the cliffs. On the other hand, the Americans were unable to destroy the British fleet because they did not have enough of the necessary equipment! The British tried landing a few men at night to spike the American guns, but had no success. Meanwhile militia sharpshooters kept the enemy at bay by picking at sailors from the shore. Porter further continued:

"Some thirty-two pounders arrived. Carpenters were employed to make carriages. Two mortars, a large quantity of ammunition and an abundance of shot and shells reached us; two barges were equipping and every thing promised that we should speedily be put in a proper state for annoying the enemy. In the evening two frigates anchored alone above us, making his whole force

GUNS

Two Frigates carrying, 96

Three Bomb Ships, 30

One Sloop of War, fitted as a 26

Rocket Ship,

One Brig, 18

One Schooner, 1

Two Barges, 2

Total, 173

The guns mounted in the battery were three 18 pounders, two 12 pounders, six 6 pounders & two fours. My two mortars were without carriages, as were all my thirty - two's, for notwithstanding every effort was made by the government at Washington to have them made there, as by myself on the spot, they could not be completed in time."

Once the *Devastation* became loose, she rejoined the rest of the squadron. Gordon's fleet, including the prize ships, was now complete. The winds appeared favorable on Monday, so Gordon decided to make a break for it. While waiting, the Captain had figured out a solution to the elevation problem. He had his seamen shift the ballast in his retreating ships. This placed more weight on one side, thus giving his cannons the necessary angle to fire high enough to silence the American guns. Around noon on Monday, September 5, the British undertook a tremendous, deafening cannonading upon the battery, forcing the Americans to evacuate their White House position an hour later. A dejected Porter then ordered his troops to assist Hungerford's riflemen in "picking at the sailors" and prevent them from landing. The constant heavy shelling and flying rockets kept the riflemen from taking advantageous positions in the woods near the heights in order inflict much injury. Gordon, by skillful seamanship, safely slipped past the battery that afternoon with little damage to his squadron. Unfortunately, Porter may have erred in his report by writing that the British ships escaped the White House bluffs on September 6. Gordon's log book and all other accounts indicate that, after heavy cannonading, the enemy slipped passed the cliffs the afternoon of September 5. Otherwise, the facts in the various reports remained the same. Porter continued:

> "On the morning of the 6th, the enemy shewed a disposition to move. I advised Gen Hungerford of the same, and prepared to meet them with hot shot. Abut twelve o'clock the two frigates got under way with a fair wind and tide, and stood down for us. The rocket sloop, bomb vessels, brig, schooner and prizes following in succession, the gun boats endeavoring to flank us on our right....
>
> Finding that the whole of the enemy's fire was directed at my force, and that in a few minutes all his force would be brought to bear on me, and (entertaining no hopes of preventing his passing) as some of my men had already been killed and wounded, I determined not to make a useless sacrifice and when the enemy was on the point of anchoring abreast the battery, after sustaining his fire one hour and a quarter, I directed the officers and men to retire behind a hill on our left, and be in readiness to charge the enemy if he should land to spike our guns. The two frigates anchored abreast, the bombs, sloops and smaller vessels passed outside them, all pouring into the battery and neighboring woods a tremendous fire of every description of missive....
>
> I have understood, that in order to bring their guns to bear on our battery, they cut away the upper part of their ports and took the inner trucks from their gun carriages. When they had passed down, I sent a torpedo after them --- it was heard to explode about nine at night, but I have not learnt the effect it produced."

The *National Intelligencer* printed a descriptive account of the manner in which Gordon's squadron incrementally passed the battery at the White House on Monday, September 5. The writer, who witnessed the event from the Maryland shore, also mentioned hearing firing from Indian Head further down the Potomac later that same afternoon. On September 9 the *Intelligencer* included:

> "The British squadron (assembled at Mr. Marshall's Point a little below Mount Vernon) began to move downwards about two o'clock on Monday at the pitch of high tide and a most favorable fresh wind at N.E. The preceding ship was the Commodore in the Sea Horse frigate of 38 guns with the first division of the prize craft, firing but a few guns towards the Virginia shore, and the high bluff of Belvoir; the fort previously and at the same time constantly and spiritedly annoying them with their shot. The Euryalus frigate of 36 guns went

next, and distinguished herself for the most active firing of any of the fleet.

Those two vessels, after passing the bluff, hauled up in the wind nearer to the Maryland shore and continued their firing, particularly the Euryalus which then became headmost, until all the fleet had passed close in below the Fort, the channel there being deep and close in under the cliff; the third was the Etna Bomb, the Rocket ship, and after them the Manly armed brig of 14 guns, which had passed up the river and joined the lower squadron in the evening of the 1st inst. after receiving some shot (four in number, one of which passed through her) from the Bluff battery; after those went in succession the remaining prizes, the Meteor Bomb and lastly the Devastation; none of the Bombs appearing to fire as they passed the battery on the heights; the result was not known.

A fire ship with a party under Com. Rodgers, could not overtake the rear of the fleet in time for full effect, they being peculiarly favored by a most favorable wind to carry them through the lower reach of the channel. It was on fire and went seemingly in good direction for the Euryalus frigate, but grounded on the point.

From 6 o'clock till dark, firing of heavy cannon from below was heard and supposed to be from Indian Head 10 or 12 miles below the Belvoir Bluff. Some shot hit the Sea Horse, and her mizen top sail was seen to fall on the deck as she passed the point."

Gordon's escape past the White House bluffs was short-lived. The British squadron encountered opposition once again further down river from Perry's battery, firing from Maryland cliffs at Indian Head. This engagement did not last long because the American forces only had one large cannon, few arms, and quickly ran out of ammunition. As darkness approached, Perry withdrew his men out of firing range. The British ships, plus the twenty-one captured vessels, easily sailed past Indian Head without opposition Tuesday morning and reached the Chesapeake Friday, September 9. A copy of the letter written by Perry to the Secretary of the Navy was printed in the *Alexandria Gazette*:

"George-town, Sept 9, 1814

SIR - The Battery under my direction at the Indian Head, was of too small calibre to make much impression on the enemy, as they descended the Potomac on the 5th instant. A single 18-pounder, which arrived only 30 minutes before the firing began, ill supplied with ammunition, was the only gun that could be of much service.

The field pieces (6-pounders) under the direction of that excellent officer Major Peter, of the Georgetown, & Capt. Birch of the Washington volunteers, and Captain Lewis of General Stewart's Brigade, kept up a very spirited fire. These officers, together with

Captain Stull and Davidson, and their brave men, behaved in the handsomest manner, and rendered all the assistance their limited means afforded.

The ammunition of the 18-pounder, and of several of the sixes, being expended; and the fire of the enemy from two frigates, two sloops of war, two bombs, one rocket ship and several small vessels being very heavy: it was thought advisable by Gen. Stewart, Major Peter and myself to retire a short distance in the rear. This was done in good order, after sustaining their fire for more than an hour....

The advantageous situation we occupied prevented the enemy from doing us much injury. Only one man was wounded."

Upon arriving back in the Chesapeake to rejoin the main fleet, Gordon immediately submitted his report to Cochrane. This was written from the *Seahorse*, September 9. In it he stated that on September 5, the decision was made at noon to make a break for it and that the American guns were silenced three hours later. He wrote:

"On the 5th at noon the wind came fair and all my arrangements being made, the Seahorse and Euryalus within short musquet shot of the batteries, the whole of the prizes passed between us and the shoal, the Bombs, the Fairy, and on firing as they passed and afterwards in a favorable position for facilitating means of their fire, the further removal of frigates.

At 3 P.M. having completely silenced the enemy's fire, the Seahorse and Euryalus cut their cables and the whole of us proceeded to the next position taken up by the troops where they had two batteries mounting from 16 to 18 guns on a ray of cliffs of about a mile extent under which we were of necessity obliged to pass very close. I did not intend to make the attempt that evening, but the Erebus grounding within range we were necessarily called into action. On this occasion the fire of the Fairy had the most decisive effect, as well as that of the Erebus, whilst the Bombs threw their shells with excellent precision, and the guns of the batteries were completely silenced by about 8 O'clock. At daylight on the 6th I made the signal to weigh and so satisfied were the whole of the parties opposed to us of their opposition being ineffectual, that they allowed us to pass without further molestation."

The siege of Alexandria was over when the last of the eight British ships left the port. The town had been spared destruction. Yet, its inhabitants remained uneasy, fearful that any American harassment of the enemy on its voyage back down the Potomac, might provoke Gordon to return and lay waste their town; thus, Alexandria did not hoist the American flag! When Rodgers entered the town on Saturday in preparation of implementing use of the fire boats, he was appalled at not seeing the "Stars and Stripes" flying over the city. Before leaving Alexandria, the Commodore made certain that the American flag was proudly flying above the city. Rodgers later described the situation to the Secretary of the Navy:

> "At 9 A.M. in advance of the fire-vessels in my gig, finding no colours displayed at Alexandria, but a Swedish Ensign on board a schooner - being near the wharves, I hailed and ordered the American flag to be hoisted; and after seeing the flag hoisted, I directed the fire-vessels (which were conducted by Lieut. Newcomb, Lieut. Forrest, and Sailing Master Ramage) to proceed to the objects of attack...."

Captain Charles Nourse, aide-de-camp to Monroe, in writing to his mother said that he wished the town had been destroyed because its citizens were fearful of raising the "Stars and Stripes" once the enemy set sail for the Chesapeake:

> "The Alexandrians are ashamed of themselves; I wish the town had been burnt to the ground or blown out of existence = Oh my country: Rodgers had actually to swear he would fire into the town if they did not warrant to his hoisting the American flag which they had objected to even after the British had left the place."

Many residents in Washington and Georgetown branded the citizens of Alexandria as cowards for what they considered as easily surrendering their town to the humiliating terms offered by Gordon. Inhabitants of Alexandria argued that they had no choice in the matter, claiming that if they had resisted, the British would have blown the town to bits with their cannons and set fire to everything that remained. Mrs. Sayrs stated in her *Recollections* that the only option for Alexandria was submission:

> "In a short time we arrived at 'Miss Minor's' ten miles from our house and from Washington. We found the house filled with refugees, families, who like ourselves, had come there for safety from the 'English Ships of War,' who having arrived in the Chesapeake Bay, were hourly expected up the Potomac to attack Washington, the Capital of the U. S. This in a few days accomplished. The town of Alexandria was deserted of women and children who had flown elsewhere for protection.
>
> And now I will say to my grandchildren that our dear old town Alexandria has been accused of cowardice in surrendering her city to the Commander of the English fleet! My father told me that with several others who were physically unable to go in the army remained in Alexandria for the protection of its property. In going out of his house early one morning he found the 4 streets leading up

the town each with a large 'Man of War' anchored and cannon pointed to burn the place unless certain demands were not granted. I only remember flour and tobacco in the public warehouses, principal items! Shorn of her strength by the absence of all able bodied men, nothing was left, but submission."

In response to an article printed in the *New York Star*, Ephraim Gilman wrote an account of his *Reminiscences* of the British siege which was printed in the *Alexandria Advertiser,* October 9, 1851:

"REMINISCENCES - An article in the New York Star lately, speaking of the British army being in Washington *thirty-seven years ago*, wakes up some reminiscences not remarkably gratifying to some of us;...

For permitting this invasion, our town was ridiculed and lampooned by many ignorant simpletons, for suffering what it was totally impracticable to prevent. Our four or five companies of militia were then absent on duty in Maryland and Virginia; but, if present, what could they, or an army of forty thousand veterans, have done against six armed ships (two frigates, two bomb-ketchers, and two rocketeers,) lying a half mile off in the stream, that in five minutes could have set our combustible town in a blaze? The idea of resistance being out of the question, we followed literally the precept of unerring wisdom, and sent an embassy from among our most respectable citizens - Col. Simms, (Mayor,) Rev. D. Muir, and Dr. Dick.

The Commodore received them very politely, expressing his surprise that such a fortress as that (Fort Washington) should have suffered him to pass so quietly; and after the usual interchanges of civility were passed, and a desire intimated to be acquainted with the motive of so important a visit, the Commodore observed that his thousand hungry fellows lived partly by eating, and he would have to trouble us for some *flour*, and as they would always go their death for *tobacco*, he would want some of that also; and if we decided to make no resistance he would take the articles quietly, and no soldier or sailor should be seen in the streets to annoy any one; that some *fresh provisions* would be wanting, which would be *paid for on delivery*. If we would order two or three beeves slaughtered and laid on the wharf, the worth of it in gold would be left in its place when removed This compact was strictly adhered to on both sides, and during the five days' visit there was perfect quietness, almost too much so, for curiosity carried many of us from our own business to the wharves to see the enemy, and when there scarce an incident came off worth relating.

A file of men, and two or three officers to keep order and direct the men while rolling out the flour, was pretty near the amount. I thought one of these officers ill qualified for a warrior, according to Mr. Jefferson's definition: *'the trying which could do the other the most harm.*' This officer, after taking part of the contents of one warehouse, called for the keys of the next, the owner of which expostulated, and asked him why he did not finish the one he was at first. 'Because,' said the officer, 'I want, if possible, to equalize in some measure the losses among the owners. It is an unpleasant duty, and I am opposed to ruining one and leaving his neighbor untouched.' Thinks I to myself, that man has got a soul to be saved....

After the squadron had dropped down, and anchored in the stream near Fort Washington, Com. Rodgers sent one or two small fire-ships after them, which they managed to tow aside; but having to pass under a high bluff at the 'White House,' a mile below Mount Vernon, where preparations were made to tender them a *cold collation*, they looked up to this as something so overwhelming, that they cut their port-holes on the starboard side into port doors to elevate their pieces, if necessary; but waited for a favorable breeze, and escaped with their booty with but little loss.

Yes, it is thirty seven years ago; and yet I should not be surprised (since Amy Darden got paid for her horse, and the French spoliations previous to 1800 *almost* paid for) if these merchants should be paid yet for their flour and tobacco, and *another old gentleman* for his whiskey, sugar, molasses, tea, coffee, chocolate, dry goods, and grubbing hoes, abstracted by the same flotilla."

The loss to the American forces in defending Alexandria and the Potomac shores during the enemy descent was eleven killed and nineteen wounded. Gordon's voyage cost England seven sailors, with thirty-five wounded. He did spare Alexandria from total obliteration. The loss to the port town was the following:

"*Estimate of the loss.* Three ships, three brigs, several bay and river craft, some vessels burned, sixteen thousand barrels of flour taken, one thousand hogsheads of tobacco, one hundred and fifty bales of cotton, five thousand dollars' worth of wine, sugar, &c."

A general court-martial, presided over by the Commander of the District Militia, followed in Washington, to try Dyson for quitting his post at Fort Warburton as the British fleet was approaching Alexandria. Basically, the specifications were that, as the commanding officer of the garrison, he shamefully abandoned the fort as the enemy was approaching, ordered its arms and ammunition destroyed, left the area contrary to orders, and was highly intoxicated. The court found Dyson guilty of all charges, except drunkenness, of which he was acquitted. He was sentenced November 12, 1814, to be dismissed from the service of the United States. As the newly appointed commander of the 10th

Military District, Major General Winfield Scott approved the sentence. The *National Intelligencer* printed the following article:

> "At a General Court Martial held at the City of Washington, whereof Brigadier-General Smith of the Militia of the D.C. was President, the Court on the 12th inst. decided, that Captain SAMUEL T. DYSON, of the United States' Corps of Artillery, being commanding officer of the United States fort, Fort Washington, did on or about the 27th day of August, 1814, when an enemy was approaching said Fort, misbehave himself before the enemy and shamefully abandon the Fort and Post which he then and there commanded, and which it was his duty to defend.
>
> Also, that he did, at the same time and place, cast away and destroy his arms and ammunition, dismantle and destroy the fort; and, without the necessity therefor from the pressure of an enemy, did march off the garrison from the same, in violation of his duty, and contrary to his orders.
>
> And the Court sentenced the said Samuel T. Dyson to be dismissed the service of the U.S.
>
> Which sentence has been approved by Major-General Scott, commander of the 10th Military District."

Fort Belvoir Historian

During the battle that took place at the White House Cliffs, British cannons heavily damaged the White House and reduced to rubble the remaining ruins of the original Belvoir Manor. The property owner at that time was Ferdinando Fairfax (1774-1820), the third son of Bryan, Eighth Lord Fairfax. He inherited the Belvoir estate at the death of his uncle George William Fairfax in 1787. The c.1900 photo shows the White House during the time it was used as a shad fishery. The White House on the Belvoir property was later destroyed by fire.

22

INTRIGUE

While aboard the *Tonnant* still anchored in the Patuxent, Cochrane wrote an ominous message dated Thursday, August 18, 1814 to Secretary of State Monroe, officially announcing the British decision of destructive measures and uncivilized warfare against the United States. Whenever it was actually written, or for whatever reason, Cochrane's letter to the Secretary did not leave the ship until Monday, August 29, six days after the British scorched the capital. The letter was included in a sealed packet to Mason that was irregularly handed to an American go-between on the Patuxent shore, who then took it to an American camp. Mason, Commissioner of Prisoners, received the packet from an American dragoon before daylight Wednesday, August 31. He read the letter addressed to him dated August 29, and quickly sought out Monroe and turned the rest of the packet over to him. It contained a note addressed to the Secretary of State, possibly postdated, that attempted to lay a foundation that justified and suggested British authorization for the devastation inflicted upon Washington and Alexandria. The text of Cochrane's message was printed in the *National Intelligencer*, September 10, 1814:

177

> "SIR __ Having been called upon by the Governor General of the Canadas to aid in carrying into effect measures of retaliation against the inhabitants of the United States, for the wanton destruction committed by their Army in Upper Canada, it has become imperiously my duty, conformably with the nature of the Governor General's application, to issue the naval force under my command, an order to destroy and lay waste such towns and districts upon the coast, as may be found assailable.
>
> I had hoped that this contest would have terminated, without my being obliged to resort to severities which are contrary to the usage of civilized warfare, and as it has been with extreme reluctance and concern that I have found myself compelled to adopt this system of devastation, I shall be equally gratified if the conduct of the Executive of the United States will authorise my staying such proceedings, by making reparation to the suffering inhabitants of Upper Canada: thereby manifesting that if the destructive measures pursued by their army were ever sanctioned, they will no longer be permitted by the Government."

Mason told Monroe that the messenger further reported that an "open note" was also in circulation. The "open note" was thought to be suspicious because it was included with Cochrane's packet that was delivered to the American camp by the go-between. Dated August 28, 1814, "the open note" was written by Rear Admiral Edward Codrington, and addressed to Gordon, advising that his squadron vacate Alexandria. This was the day that the English ships finally reached their destination. The dragoon went on to tell Mason that he thought American officers intended to have a citizen put the "open note" on board one of the enemy ships anchored at Alexandria. The "open note" eventually found its way to Monroe later that afternoon. It read:

> "IPHIGENIA, 28th August, 1814
> The object of the expedition being accomplished, and the inhabitants of the country upon the banks of the Potomac being alarmed for their property, on account of the presence of the British squadron in that river, the commander-in-chief has directed me to forward openly, by the hands of one of the inhabitants, this order, for the ships in the Potomac to retire and rejoin his flag."

Having received both letters the same day, August 31, in a manner that was circumspect, Monroe was cautious. They smelled of intrigue. The enemy had been plundering, sacking, burning houses and destroying public buildings from the moment they first arrived in the Chesapeake the previous year. Monroe thought it best to wait before responding to Cochrane's letter, and, along with the support of Mason, he decided not to acknowledge that the government was aware of

Codrington's message to Gordon, but felt that Alexandrians should be made aware of its content. He, therefore, directed Mason to hand over the "open note" to a resident of Alexandria, who would in turn, give it to the committee of vigilance. This was accomplished within an hour after the discussion; however, rather than being delivered to a member of the committee, it was placed in the letter box in what served as the Alexandria Post Office, removed several miles from the town during the enemy's occupation. Mason stated to the Investigative Committee:

> "The contents of this note, as well as the manner chosen by the enemy for its conveyance, if it did come from him, were thought not a little singular and suspicious. The communication by water was open to him; and to express his anxiety for the fears of the inhabitants about the safety of their property from a force which had been for two years in the constant habit of burning and carrying it off in every direction on these waters, and was which at that moment emptying the stores of Alexandria of private property to an immense amount, could hardly be considered earnest; and particularly when this expression was contrasted with his determination to destroy and lay waste every district of country within his power, made known by the letter of Admiral Cochrane to the Secretary of State, of the 18th August, (since published) which was the letter delivered by me that morning, and with which this note was understood to have come from Admiral Cochrane's fleet.

> Colonel Monroe took this view of the subject, and expressed his suspicions that the note was a forgery, and the possibility, if it was genuine, that, by previous concert, it might be intended to convey something different from, perhaps the very reverse of, what appeared on its face. Under these circumstances, and in the same state of things, a preparation going on to intercept the British chips below Alexandria, some doubts were entertained to the propriety of permitting it to pass to them; he, however, determined that it should be disposed of in such a way as to let the citizens of Alexandria have benefit of it, if benefit there was, and at the same time to keep the enemy in ignorance that the government had any knowledge of it.

> He requested me to take charge of the note, to deliver it to a gentleman of Alexandria, and to ask him to give it such a course immediately. I did accordingly, in about an hour after, put it into the hands of a highly respectable citizen of that town, accompanied by the request enjoined on me.

> He undertook the charge with great cheerfulness, and suggested as the best mode of answering the purpose intended, that he would place it in the post office at Alexandria, under cover, addressed to one of the acting committees of the town, remarking that it would reach them in that way almost as speedily as if he were to deliver it himself, and that by this means the committee and himself would be relieved from embarrassment, if the committee were called upon to answer by

the officers of the enemy, in whose power they were, as to the channel through which it had been received. I thought his reasons good, and approved of the mode he proposed to adopt. That he did so deposit the note, in the course of the same afternoon, I was informed by him on the next day; and I have no question on the fact."

Alexandria's Post Office during the British occupation, operated through a mail box located inside a vacant house in the country. Letters were daily thrown into the letter box and sorted, but Codrington's "open note" was not discovered until after Gordon's squadron had departed for the Chesapeake with their plunder. The postmaster found the Admiral's note Friday, September 2. Enclosing the questionable note was a brief message without a name, date or postmark, addressed to the "committee of vigilance or safety of the town of Alexandria" which simply stated:

> "GENTLEMEN: Motives of a personal nature prevent my delivering the enclosure. You will best judge of the propriety of doing it in your official character, *without loss of time*."

Alexandrians were in an uproar when they learned about Codrington's undelivered note. The townspeople generally thought that further plundering and destruction to their port would have ceased had Gordon received the message. It was some time before it became known that banker Antoine Charles Cazenove was the countryman who had left Codrington's "open note" at the temporary Post Office. Vindictive feelings ran high against him and his character was maligned. The citizens even brought charges against the United States government because Monroe and Mason had handled the letter. It was in this context that the matter of the letter came before the Investigative Committee. The said Committee eventually decided that Mason gave a satisfactory account of the events in his report and so, the matter of Codrington's "open note" officially ended. Mason continued:

> "Whether the enemy received this note, or when, and if received, what influence it may have had on his conduct, I have never learned; but there is one fact notorious on this subject --- that he ceased to levy contributions on the town of Alexandria about the middle of the day Commodore Porter's battery reached the White House (the position below Alexandria selected from which to annoy him in his descent) and that he immediately after began to draw off his ships from the station he had taken before the town. This was on the 1st day of September.
>
> Commodore Porter's artillerists and General Young's brigade crossed the ferry at Georgetown, on the expedition, at the commencement of the night of the 31st of August. That this movement was known to the

enemy on the next day, and instantly arrested his devastations at Alexandria, I have never had the slightest doubt. As to the time and circumstance of the movement, I cannot be mistaken, as I was with both corps during that night, one at their encampment, and the other on the march.

In relation to the remaining part of your letter, there are no particular facts within my knowledge, that I am aware of, pertinent to the inquiry of the honorable committee into the cause of the success of the enemy in his recent enterprises against Washington and Alexandria."

Even though Monroe did not immediately answer Cochrane's letter, announcing authorization for the devastation inflicted upon the Washington metropolitan area, he lost no time in discussing its contents with Madison. The President issued a Proclamation the following day, September 1, appealing to the patriotic feelings and devotion of the American people to their country, and urging them not to forget the independence, recently acquired by their fathers. He severely chastised the British forces for their barbaric conduct, particularly during a time that peace negotiations were underway between the two nations:

"Whereas the enemy by a sudden incursion have succeeded in invading the capital of the nation, defended at the moment by troops less numerous than their own and almost entirely of the militia, during their possession of which, though for a single day only, they wantonly destroyed the public edifices, having no relation in their structure to operations of war nor used at the time for military annoyance, some of these edifices being also costly monuments of taste and of the arts, and others depositories of the public archives, not only precious to the nation as the memorials of its origin and its early transactions, but interesting to all nations as contributions to the general stock of historical instruction and political science; and

Whereas advantage has been taken of the loss of a fort more immediately guarding the neighboring town of Alexandria to place the town within the range of a naval force too long and too much in the habit of abusing its superiority wherever it can be applied to require as the alternative of a general conflagration an undisturbed plunder of private property, which has been executed in a manner peculiarly distressing to the inhabitants, who had inconsiderately cast themselves upon the justice and generosity of the victor; and

Whereas it now appears by a direct communication from the British commander on the American station to be his avowed purpose to employ the force under his direction 'in destroying and laying waste such towns and districts upon the coast as may be found assailable,' adding to this declaration the insulting pretext that it is in retaliation for a wanton destruction committed by the army of the United States in Upper Canada, when it is notorious that no destruction has been committed, which, notwithstanding the multiplied outrages previously committed by the enemy was not unauthorized, and promptly shown to be so, and that the United States have been as constant in their endeavors to reclaim the enemy from such outrages by the contrast of their own example as they have been ready to terminate on reasonable conditions the war itself; and

Whereas these proceedings and declared purposes, which exhibit a deliberate disregard of the principles of humanity and the rules of civilized warfare, and which must give to the existing war a character of extended devastation and barbarism at the very moment of negotiations for peace, invited by the enemy himself, leave no prospect of safety to anything within the reach of his predatory and incendiary operations but in manful and universal determination to chastise and expel the invader."

Monroe, in consultation with the President, waited a week before responding to Cochrane's surreptitious letter. By this time, the invading forces of Ross and Cockburn had reached their shipping and Gordon's squadron had left Alexandria. In his reply, the Secretary wrote that he was amazed to learn that the British destruction to Washington was authorized and its justification based entirely on retaliation. He pointed out that the American actions in Upper Canada were not sanctioned and the perpetrators had been punished. He goes on to discuss the barbaric behavior and numerous destructive outrages committed by the British throughout the Chesapeake and other areas, particularly at the River Raisin, prior to the ruination of America's capital. Monroe remained steadfast that if England continued to wage uncivilized warfare, not consistent with the principles of humanity, it would be met with a determination becoming a free people:

> "Sept. 6, 1814
>
> SIR: I have the honor to receive your letter of the 18th of August, stating, that having been called on by the Governor General of the Canadas, to aid him in carrying into effect measures of retaliation against the inhabitants of the United States, for the wanton desolation committed by their army in Upper Canada, it has become your duty, conforming with the nature of the Governor General's application, to issue to the naval force under your command, an order to destroy and lay waste such towns and districts upon the coast as may be found assailable.
>
> It is seen with the greatest surprise, that this system of devastation which has been practised by the British forces, so manifestly contrary to the usage of civilized warfare, is placed by you on the ground of retaliation. No sooner were the United States compelled to resort to war against Great Britain, than they resolved to wage it in a manner

most consonant to the principles of humanity, and to those friendly relations which it was desirable to preserve between the two nations, after the restoration of peace. They perceived however with the deepest regret that a spirit alike just and humane was neither cherished nor acted on by your Government. Such an assertion would not be hazarded, if it was not supported by facts, the proof of which has perhaps already carried the same conviction to other nations that it has to the people of these states.

Without dwelling on the deplorable cruelties committed by the Savages in the British ranks, and in British pay, on American prisoners at the River Raisin, which to this day have never been disavowed or atoned, I refer, as more immediately connected with the subject of your letter, to the wanton desolation that was committed at Havre-de-Grace, and at George Town, early in the Spring 1813. These villages were burnt and ravaged by the naval forces of Great Britain, to the ruin of their unarmed inhabitants, who saw with astonishment that they derived no protection to their property from the laws of war. During the same season, scenes of invasion and pillage, carried on under the same authority, were witnessed all along the waters of the Chesapeake, to an extent inflicting the most serious private distress, and under circumstances that justified the suspicion, that revenge and cupidity, rather than the manly motives that should dictate the hostility of a high minded foe, led to their perpetration.

The late destruction of the Houses of the Government in this City is another act which comes necessarily into view. In the wars of modern Europe, no examples of the kind, even among nations the most hostile to each other, can be traced. In the course of ten years past, the Capitals of the principal powers of the Continent of Europe have been conquered, and occupied alternately by the victorious armies of each other, and no instance of such wanton and unjustifiable destruction has been seen. We must go back to distant and barbarous ages, to find a paralled for the acts of which I complain.

Altho' these acts of desolation invited, if they did not impose of the Government the necessity of retaliation, yet in no instance has it been authorised. The burning of the village of Newark in Upper Canada, posterior to the early outrages above enumerated, was not executed on that principle. The village of Newark adjoined Fort George, and its destruction was justified by the officer who ordered it, on the ground that it became necessary in the military operations there. The act however was disavowed by the Government. The burning which took place at Long Point was unauthorised by the Government, and the conduct of the officer subjected to the investigation of a military tribunal. For the burning at St. David's, committed by stragglers, the officer who commanded in that quarter was dismissed without a trial, for not preventing it.

I am commanded by the President distinctly to state, that it as little comports with any orders which have been issued to the military and naval commanders of the United States, as it does with the established and known humanity of the American nation, to pursue a system which it appears you have adopted. This Government owes it to itself, to the principles which it has ever held sacred, to disavow, as justly chargeable to it, any such wanton, cruel and unjustifiable warfare.

Whatever unauthorised irregularity may have been committed by any of its troops, it would have been ready, acting on these principles of sacred and eternal obligation, to disavow, and, as far as might be practicable, to repair. But in the plan of desolating warfare which your letter so explicitly makes known, and which is attempted to be excused on a plea so utterly groundless, the President perceives a spirit of deep rooted hostility, which, without the evidence of such facts, he could not have believed existed, or would have been carried to such an extremity.

For the reparation of injuries, of whatever nature they may be, not sanctioned by the law of nations, which the military or naval force of either power may have committed, against the other, this government will always be ready to enter into reciprocal arrangements. It is presumed that your government will neither expect nor propose any which are not reciprocal.

Should your government adhere to a system of desolation, so contrary to the views and practice of the United States, so revolting to humanity, and repugnant to the sentiment and usages of the civilized world, whilst it will be seen with the deepest regret, it must and will be met with a determination and constancy becoming a free people, contending in a just cause for their essential rights, and their dearest interests."

Gales was appalled at Cochrane's aggressive stance. As editor of the *National Intelligencer*, he could not resist commenting on what he claimed was deception on the part of the Vice Admiral. On September 14, his paper printed the following:

"We observe it mentioned in some prints, that the late letter of Admiral Cochrane to the Secretary of State was received before the enemy entered Washington. This is not so. We state the fact, on the most unquestionable authority, that it did not arrive in Washington until late in the night of the 30th of August, and that it was not received by the Secretary of State until the morning of the 31st. The letter was dated on the 18th, probably the very day the Tonnant arrived in the Patuxent. It effects to give previous notice of an intention to destroy and lay waste our towns, and yet is not even *sent off* (although antedated) until *after* this purpose has been accomplished at Washington. This is a very pretty little *trick* played off by the Vice Admiral in his first essay at diplomatic correspondence, and we doubt not has been matter of pleasant chuckling between himself and friend, that accomplished and high bred gentleman admiral George Cockburn. It is worthy of remark, that a near blood relation of the Vice Admiral's has lately been convicted in England and sentenced to the pillory for a deception practiced apon the public there. The vice appears to run through the family,"

Cochrane had the final word in the correspondence on this issue. Not surprising, his position did not change. After reading Monroe's letter of September 6, he replied by claiming that he had no authority to revoke his order of retaliation because it was sanctioned by Prevost. The Vice Admiral's response to Monroe, written from the *Tonnant*, was dated September 19, 1814, five days after the exhilarating American victory at Fort McHenry. This ended the correspondence on this matter between the two adversaries. Cochrane's letter was published in the *National Intelligencer* September 27, 1814, under the heading "Adm. Cochrane's Last Letter:"

"Sir: I had the honor to receive your letter of the 6th inst. this morning, in reply to the one which I addressed to you from the Patuxent.

As I have no authority from my government to enter upon any kind of discussion relative to the points contained in your letter, I have only to regret that there does not appear to be any hope that I shall be authorised to recal my general order; which has been further sanctioned by a subsequent request from Lieut. General Sir George Prevost.

A copy of your letter will this day be forwarded by me to England, and until I receive instructions from my government the measures which I have adopted must be persisted in; unless remuneration be made to the inhabitants of the Canadas for the injuries they have sustained from the outrages committed by the troops of the U. States."

Library of Congress

Vice-Admiral Sir Alexander Cochrane was appointed British Commander of the North American station in 1814 and quickly initiated a three pronged plan for the British campaign to capture the city of Washington.

Courtesy Gunston Hall

General John Mason (1766-1849) built his home on Mason's Island and owned the ferry that served the President in his escape across the Potomac to Virginia.

23

A SMALL VICTORY

Parker's diversionary force sent to the northern area of the Chesapeake Bay, was smaller than Gordon's fleet. It consisted of the thirty-eight gun frigate *Menelaus* and two tenders. The purpose of his mission was to draw attention away from the principal objective. The plan was for his forces to commit sufficient mayhem along the Eastern Shore to tie up the local militia and prevent them from reinforcing troops at Washington. His destructive raids began Saturday, August 20, the same day Ross left Benedict to begin his march towards the capital. The British committed as much damage as possible along the Eastern Shore, wantonly burning numerous farms and fields. There was little opposition until information reached the *Menelaus* the evening of August 30 that a small American force was encamped about a mile from the shore. At 11:00 p.m. Parker landed 134 sailors and Royal Marines near the village of Moorfields, and recklessly led them against a contingent of prepared local militia. The nighttime engagement was short. It began after midnight and became known as the Battle of Caulk's Field. The 170 Yankee force, led by Lieutenant Colonel Philip Reed, was waiting and ready. While leading a charge, Parker was mortally wounded. The Redcoats quickly withdrew, taking their Captain's body with them, but leaving behind 9 dead on the field. The British casualties also included 25 injured, some of whom later died. The Americans reported 3 men wounded. The *National Intelligencer* reported the skirmish September 6:

"HUZZA FOR THE MILITIA!

We do not recollect ever to have read of a more brilliant and decisive exploit by a handful or militia hastily rallied by a partizan officer, than that described in the following extract of a letter, on the correctness of which the fullest reliance may be placed:

Chester Town, Md. Sept. 1.
On or about the 20th ult. the British frigate Menelaus, rating 38, carrying 49, and pierced for 54 guns, commanded by Sir Peter Parker, Bt. made her appearance in view of Rock Hall, upon which Lieut. Col. Reed called out the 21st regiment of the Maryland militia.

On Sunday the 28th the enemy came on shore at the farm of Mr. Henry Waller, being on the Chesapeake Bay about seven miles above Rock Hall, and burnt his dwelling house, barns, all other out-houses, wheat in the granary and stack, and in short destroyed everything by fire that they possibly could --- his loss is estimated at 8 or 10 thousand dollars.

On Tuesday the 30th they went to the farm of Richard Frisby, Esq. adjoining Waller's (he now resides near Baltimore) and committed the same disgraceful and degrading acts; his loss is supposed to be about the amount of Waller's. At each of the aforesaid places they set fire to the property and made their escape to the frigate before the militia could get down to attack them.

On Tuesday morning also they landed and went to the house of James Frisby, it is supposed for the purpose of burning him out. However Mrs. Frisby prevailed upon them to spare the property. They took with them some poultry and said they intended that day to attack and defeat Col. Reed and his militia near Bell Air, and then to go and get supper in Chester town.

True in part to their promise, about half past 11 o'clock that night they landed between 2 and 300 men, headed by Sir Peter Parker; having a few days before taken 4 of Richard Frisby's negroes, they made one of said negroes pilot them to the American encampment about two and a half miles from the bay shore.

Though very recently made, our videttes observed their movements, and gave information thereof to the Colonel, who prepared for action and did fight them with from 150 to 160 militia men, not one of whom except himself had ever been in an engagement; the action lasted a half an hour or upwards.

On the American side there were three privates wounded, not supposed dangerously, and one taken prisoner. On the British one Master's Mate, one Midshipman, 8 privates killed, and 5 wounded left on the field of battle, two of them died of their wounds yesterday, one deserter - Sir Peter received two wounds, the last of which was in the head, and killed him instantaneously; he fought in front of the marines (such bravery merited a better cause). One of the prisoners, the captain of the fore-top, who received only a flesh wound in the thigh, says he fought be the side of Sir Peter when he was killed. On their retreat they called at a house some distance from the field of battle & got a blanket and sheet, it is supposed to wrap Sir Peter in...."

The report about the militia victory at Caulk's Field was printed in the *Intelligencer* the very day Gordon's squadron reached the Bay. Something positive had finally happened for the Americans and the news lifted their dejected spirits. On the other hand, the defeat, combined with the loss of their dashing Captain, was an unexpected setback for the British. Parker was shot in the thigh severing the femoral artery and, not taking the wound seriously, he continued to lead the fight. He fell due to a loss of blood and expired before medical help could be obtained. Reed's report to Brigadier General Benjamin Chambers spoke of running out of ammunition, and varied slightly from the article printed in the *Intelligencer* regarding the figures for the casualties. Reed's report included the following:

"...about half past eleven o'clock on the night of the 30th ult., I received information that the barges of the enemy, then lying off Waltham's farm were moving in shore. I concluded their object was to land and burn houses, etc., at Waltham's and made the necessary arrangements to prevent them and to be prepared for an opportunity which I had sought for several days, to strike the enemy. During our march to the point threatened, it was discovered that the blow was aimed at our camp.

Orders were immediately given to the Quarter Master to remove the camp and baggage, and to the troop to countermarch, pass the road by the right of our camp, and form on the rising ground about three hundred paces to the rear – the right towards Caulk's House, and the left retiring on the road, the artillery in the centre, supported by the infantry on the right and left.

I directed Captain. Wickes and his Second Lieutenant Beck, with a part of the rifle company to be formed so as to cover the road by which the enemy marched, and with this section I determined to post myself, leaving the line to be formed under the direction of Major Wickes and Captain Chambers.

The head of the enemy's column soon presented itself and received the fire of our advance party at seventy paces distance, and, being pressed by numbers vastly superior, I repaired to my post on the line, having ordered riflemen to return and form on the right of the line. The fire now became general along the whole line and was sustained by our troops with the most determined valor. The enemy pressed our front; foiled in this he threw himself on our left flank which was occupied by Capt. Chambers' company. Here, too, his efforts were equally unavailing. His fire had nearly ceased when I was informed that in some parts of our line the cartridges were entirely expended, nor did any of the boxes contain more than a few rounds, although each man brought twenty into the field. The artillery cartridges were entirely expended.

Under these circum-stances I ordered the line to fall back to a convenient spot where part of the line was fortified when the few remaining cartridges were distributed amongst a part of the line, which was again brought into the field, where it remained for a considerable amount of time, the night preventing a pursuit. The artillery and infantry for who there were no cartridges were ordered to this place (Belle Air).

The enemy having made every effort in his power, although apprized of our having fallen back manifested no disposition to follow us up, but retreated about the time our ammunition was exhausted. When it is recollected that very few of our officers or men had ever heard the whistling of a ball; that the force of the enemy, as the most accurate information enables us to estimate, was double ours; that it was commanded by Sir Peter Parker of the Menelaus, one of the most distinguished officers in the British navy and composed (as their officers admitted in subsequent conversation) of as fine men as could be selected from the British service, I feel justified in the assertion that the gallantry of the officers and men engaged on this occasion, could not excelled by any troops....

You will be surprised sir, when I inform you that in an engagement of so long continuance, in an open field, when the moon shone brilliantly on the rising ground occupied by our troops, while the shade of the neighboring woods, under the protection of which the enemy fought, gave us but an indistinct view of anything but the flash of his guns; that under the disparity of numbers against us and the advantage of regular discipline on the side of the enemy, we had not one man killed, and only one sergeant, one corporal and one private wounded, and those slightly. The enemy left one midshipman and eight men dead on the field and nine wounded; six of whom died in the course of a few house. Sir Peter Parker was amongst the slain: he was mortally wounded by a buck-shot, and died before he reached the barges to which he was conveyed by his men."

24

AN ANTHEM IS BORN

The British invasion of America's seat of government was over once Gordon's fleet sailed passed the battery at Indian Head. The entire episode lasted twenty-three days. Americans, yearning for something positive to talk about, spoke of the Battle at Caulk Fields as if it were a major military victory; but it was a relatively small affair when compared with the rout at Bladensburg, the burning of the capital and the sacking of Alexandria. The English had taken and still held many prisoners. One of the remaining captives continued to be Beanes, the elderly doctor seized at Upper Marlboro. Alarmed that Beanes would be taken to Bermuda or Halifax for trial, and possibly hanged, residents of Prince George's County pressured Ross for his freedom. Many letters were sent to the British General pleading for the release of the physician. One such request was written by Levin Winder, Governor of Maryland and cousin to General Winder, who contacted Ross inquiring about the case and expressing the opinion that Beanes was a just and honorable man. He mistakenly thought that his interest in the matter would induce Ross to immediately relinquish the prisoner. Along with his letter was included a second document marked "enclosure," bearing the same date:

"Annapolis, August 31, 1814

Sir: I am informed that a party from your army a few nights ago, took Dr. Beanes, a respectable and aged old man, out of his house, treated him with great rudeness and indignity, carried him to your camp, and that he is now on ship board. The bearer of this, Mr. ______, goes to your camp for the purpose of conveying some necessaries to the doctor for his accommodation, and to ascertain what has occasioned this procedure, so unusual, in warfare amongst civilized nations.

I am persuaded it will only be necessary to enquire into this case, to cause the doctor to be released. I am informed he is an honorable man, and would not have been guilty of any act intentionally and knowingly, contrary to the usages of war, or derogatory to the character of a man of honor.

I hope sir, on enquiry, justice and humanity will induce you to permit the doctor to return to his family and friends as speedily as may be."

"The bearer hereof, Mr. Richard West, has permission to pass to the enemy's camp for the purpose of carrying a despatch to General Ross and some necessaries to Doctor Beans, Doct Hill and Phillip Weems, a prisoner with the enemy."

Except for Beanes, Ross reluctantly released the Upper Marlboro prisoners. The General remained adamant that the doctor had broken his earlier promise of neutrality by jailing British stragglers, even though they were destroying everything in their path. Beanes continued to remain in confinement aboard the flagship *Tonnant*, during which time preparations were being drawn up for an offensive operation against Baltimore. Mrs. Thornton's diary included:

"Two or three other gentlemen who were taken at the same time were liberated, as they had made no promises and were not in the town when the first entered it."

Friends of Beanes approached Key, a Georgetown lawyer who fought with Peter's artillery at Bladensburg, requesting him to negotiate the release of the doctor. Key spoke with the President and received permission to deal directly with the enemy regarding Beanes under a flag of truce. He undertook the mission jointly with Colonel John Skinner, an American prisoner-of-war exchange officer. The two men set sail from Baltimore, Monday, September 5, waving a white flag and headed down the Patapsco River seeking the *Tonnant*. It was two days before they finally sighted the British flagship. The two men boarded the vessel

192

somewhere near Tangier Island. Roger Taney, brother-in-law to Key, recalled in 1856:

> "On the evening of the day that the enemy disappeared, Mr. Richard West arrived at Mr. Key's and told him that after the British army passed through Upper Marlboro, on their return to their ships, and had encamped some miles below the town, a detachment was sent back, which entered Dr. Beanes's house about midnight, compelled him to rise from his bed, and hurried him off to the British camp, hardly allowing him time to put his clothes on; that he was treated with great harshness, and closely guarded; and that as soon as his friends were apprized of his situation, they hastened to the headquarters of the English army to solicit his release, but it was peremptorily refused, and they were not even permitted to see him; and that he had been carried as a prisoner on board the fleet.
>
> And finding their own efforts unavailing, and alarmed for his safety, his friends in and about Marlboro thought it advisable that Mr. West should hasten to Georgetown and request Mr. Key to obtain the sanction of the government to his going on board the admiral's ship, under a flag of truce, and endeavoring to procure the release of Dr. Beanes, before the fleet sailed. It was then lying at the mouth of the Potomac, and its destination was not at that time known with certainty."

After an elaborate meal, discussions took place concerning the fate of Beanes. The Americans presented documents provided by British prisoners wounded at Bladensburg, praising the care they were receiving. Ross reluctantly decided that Beanes could be released; however, it would not be immediate. The British were in the midst of finalizing their plans to invade Baltimore, and so it was decided to detain the three Americans because they certainly would inform their government of Cochrane's intentions. The trio was transferred to another warship, the frigate *Surprise* commanded by Captain Thomas Cochrane, son of the Admiral. Aboard the *Surprise*, the men sailed up the Patapsco, along with fifteen other heavy British vessels, five of which were bomb ships. On September 11, the trio was allowed to return to their American cartel sloop. Still under guard, they remained aboard it several days. From its deck they witnessed the naval bombardment of Fort McHenry, under the command of Colonel George Armistead. Taney's account continued:

> "Mr. Key and Mr. Skinner continued on board the *Surprise*, where they were kindly treated by Sir Thomas Cochrane, until the fleet reached the Patapsco, and preparations were making for landing the troops. Admiral Cochrane then shifted his flag in the frigate, in order that he might be able to move further up the river, and superintend in person the attack by water, on the fort. And Mr. Key and Mr. Skinner were then sent on board their own vessel, with a guard of

sailors or marines to prevent them from landing. They were
permitted to take Dr. Beanes with them, and they thought themselves
fortunate in being anchored in a position which enabled them to see
distinctly the flag of Fort McHenry from the deck of the vessel."

However, before Cochrane ordered the cannonading of the fort, Ross and Cockburn landed with their forces at North Point during the morning darkness of September 12. A march began towards Baltimore, about fourteen miles distant. Brigadier General John Stricker posted his Third Maryland Militia Brigade in line awaiting the enemy approach. Ross and Cockburn, in advance, halted at the farm of Robert Gorsuch to wait for the rest of their force. Learning they were at the farm, Stricker sent riflemen and some cavalry ahead to harass the invading army but they ran into British scouts. A "fire, load and run" style of fighting broke out. The riflemen were forced to retreat, but a few remained. Taking a small advance guard, Ross rode ahead to reconnoiter. He was mortally wounded from a musket ball fired by one of two soldiers from Captain Edward Aisquith's Maryland Militia Rifle Company. The General died shortly thereafter in the arms of Captain Duncan McDougall. The two snipers also died in the skirmish. Not knowing who actually killed Ross, credit was given to both privates Daniel Wells and Henry G. McComas. Colonel Arthur Brooke then took over as the new commander of the British land forces. The American papers had little to say about the death of Ross. The *National Intelligencer* printed the following article on September 20, without identifying the writer:

"I have just seen Dr. Beans from Upper Marlboro', (who has for some time been a prisoner on board the enemy's fleet) who states that General Ross was killed in the early part of the engagement on Monday; the force that they landed was about eight thousand, including 3000 marines – they are much disappointed in not being able to carry Baltimore. Major Armistead in his defence of fort McHenry has immortalized Himself, in withstanding an incessant fire from the enemy, of upwards of 24 hours – Our militia all behaved well. The disaster at Washington, I hope is a little softened by our defence here – at least the hero of Washington is no more."

About sunrise September 13, from a distance of about two miles, Cochrane began a heavy bombardment of the fortress that guarded the entrance to Baltimore's harbor. The fog was dense and it was raining. Both sides kept up the cannonading intermittently for nearly twenty-five hours. The trio observed at best they could the engagement from the deck of their boat, but had no way of knowing how the battle was going. As long as they could hear the boom of the cannons and the screaming Congreve rockets, they knew the fort had not surrendered. It was not until dawn of the following day, when, through the smoke and haze they saw the large American flag, thirty feet wide and forty two feet long, still triumphantly flying, that they realized Fort McHenry had held firm. Taney further related:

> "While the bombardment continued, it was sufficient proof that the fort had not surrendered. But it suddenly ceased some time before day; and as they had no communication with any of the enemy's ships, they did not know whether the fort had surrendered, or the attack upon it had been abandoned. They paced the deck for the residue of the night in painful suspense, watching with intense anxiety for the return of the day, and looking every few minutes at their watches to see how long they must wait for it; and as soon as it dawned, and before it was light enough to see objects at a distance, their glasses were turned to the fort, uncertain whether they should see the stars and stripes or the flag of the enemy. At length the light came and they saw that 'our flag was still there.'
>
> And as the day advanced, they discovered from the movements of the boats between the shore and the fleet, that the troops had been roughly handled, and that many wounded men were carried to the ships. At length he was informed that the attack on Baltimore had failed, and the British army was re-embarking, and that he and Mr. Skinner and Dr. Beanes would be permitted to leave them and go where they pleased, as soon as the troops were on board and the fleet ready to sail."

The victory and sight of the American flag triumphantly flying was a tremendous emotional experience for the three men. Key, a poet, was so inspired that he immediately jotted down on the back of an envelope what he had witnessed during the night. The land assault on Baltimore, as well as the naval attack, had been abandoned. When the British fleet retired the trio was released, and before reaching Baltimore, Key's thoughts had turned into a finished poem. Later that evening, in his lodgings at the Indian Queen Hotel, a song developed from the poem. The meter and melody of a well known English drinking song "To Anacreon in Heaven" were added to Key's verses. The next morning, Key showed his composition to another brother-in-law, Judge Joseph Nicholson, one of the defenders of Fort McHenry. The judge was enthusiastic and promptly had the poem taken to a printer, who struck off handbills for immediate circulation throughout the city. Skinner was responsible for taking Key's composition to Baltimore's leading newspaper, *The Baltimore Patriot,* for publication. In 1849 Skinner related in the *National Intelligencer* the following:

> "'The rocket's red glare, the bombs bursting in air,' and the song, which was written night after we got back to Baltimore, in the hotel

then kept at the corner of Hanover and Market streets, was but a versified and almost literal transcript of our expressed hopes and apprehensions, through that ever memorable period of anxiety to att, but never of despair. Calling on its accomplished author the next morning, he handed it to the undersigned, who passed it to the Baltimore Patriot, and through it to immorality.

Your obedient servant, J. S. S.
(J. S. SKINNER, Agent for Prisoners)"

The Baltimore Patriot published Key's composition September 20, 1814, under the caption "Defence of Fort McHenry." The poem/song was immediately popular and the following month it was sung during a theatrical performance in Baltimore under the name "The Star-Spangled Banner." The inspirational song was officially sung by the guests in Washington on December 14, 1814 at the McKeown Hotel during the retirement party for Jones, who resigned as Secretary of the Navy. "The Star-Spangled Banner" remained just one of several patriotic songs until March 3, 1931, when Congress approved it as the National Anthem of the United States. The following was printed in *The Baltimore Patriot*:

"DEFENCE OF FORT McHENRY

The following beautiful and animating effusion, which is destined long to outlast the occasion, and outlive the impulse, which produced it, has already been extensively circulated. In our first renewal of publication, we rejoice in an opportunity to enliven the sketch of an exploit so illustrious, with strains, which so fitly celebrate it.

Tune - ANACHEON IN HEAVEN

O! say can you see, by the dawn's early light,
What so proudly we hail'd at the twi-
ights last gleaming,
Whose broad stripes and bright stars through
the perilous fight,
O'er the ramparts we watch'd, were so gal-
lantly streaming;
And the Rocket's red glare, the Bombs burst-
ing in air,
Gave proof through the night that our Flag
was still there;
O! say, does that star-spangled Banner
yet wave,
O'er the land of the free
and the home of the brave?

On the shore, dimly seen through the mists of the

196

the deep,
    Where the foe's haughty host in dread
        silence reposes,
What is that, which the breeze o'er the tow-
        ering steep,
    As it fitfully blows, half conceals, half dis-
        closes?
Now it catches the gleam of the morning's
        first beam,
In full glory reflected now shines on the
        stream.
            'Tis the star-spangled banner; O! long
                may it wave
            O'er the land of the free and the home
                of the brave.

And where is that band who so vauntingly
        swore
    That the havoc of war and the battle's con-
        fusion,
A home and a country should leave us no
        more?
    Their blood has wash'd out their foul foot-
        steps' pollution.
No refuge could save the hireling and slave,
From the terror of flight or the gloom of
        the grave;
            And the star-spangled banner in tri-
                umph doth wave,
            O'er the land of the free and the home
                of the brave.

O! thus be it ever when freemen shall stand,
    Between their lov'd home, and the war's
        desolation,
Blest with victory and peace, may the Heav'n-
        rescued land,
    Praise the power that hath made and pre-
        serv'd us a nation!
Then conquer we must, when our cause it
        is just,
And this be our motto – 'In God is our
        Trust!'
            And the star-spangled banner in tri-
                umph shall wave,
            O'er the land of the free and the home
                of the brave."

Lawyer Francis Scott Key (1780-1843) served at Bladensburg in the Georgetown Light Field Artillery. While under guard aboard a cartel boat in the Patapsco River, he witnessed the British bombardment of Fort McHenry. As daylight approached September 14, the shelling ended. Key was so inspired to see the American flag still standing that he put down his thoughts in words in the form of a poem, which later became known as the "Star Spangled Banner."

25

CONCLUSION

The burning of Washington, the lowest point in the history of the United States, turned out to be the pivotal point of the war. Madison had previously been dealing with a country divided on the war issue; but by delivering a decisive blow to America's capital, England succeeded in bringing together a plethora of outraged citizens in a universal wave of anti-British sentiment. The conflict was now justifiable; after all, the Redcoats had reduced the dreams and plans representing aspirations for a new republic into an ashen village. Linked with the heroic defense of Fort McHenry, Key's inspirational song, and a victorious naval battle at Plattsburg, a surge of national pride and patriotic exuberance exploded throughout the country. To keep this patriotic energy in motion and to keep the New England Federalists off its back, the government needed to show strength. On September 19 the Thirteenth Congress, third session, convened in temporary quarters using Post Office space in Blodget's Hotel. The issue of relocating the seat of government, whether it would be temporary or permanent, was quickly addressed. Obviously, everyone was concerned for the security of the capital, its leaders and remaining public records. Few felt that the national government would remain at

Washington. Those who had invested in building or improving the infant city, lost a great deal due to the invasion, and were not desirous of relocation because they would lose even more. Those who had never been pleased with the swampy, wooded site between the Potomac shores clamored for relocation. An old wound had reopened. Soon after the British marched from the burned city, Mrs. Smith expressed concern that the government would never return to Washington. She was hopeful that its citizens would follow the example of the Romans and not be driven from their homes. She wrote:

> "Oh that I a feeble woman could do something! This is not the first capital of a great empire, that has been invaded and conflagrated; Rome was reduced still lower by the Goths of old, than we are, and when its senate proposed removing the seat of government, they were answered, Romans would never be driven from their homes, Rome should never be destroy'd. May a Roman spirit animate our people, and the Roman example be followed by the Americans."

Madison delivered his Presidential message to Congress on, September 20, the day after it convened. In it he stated that the British attack, "which had interrupted for a moment only the ordinary public business at the Seat of Government," had not stopped the operations of the government of the United States. He insisted that everything was operating normally. Nevertheless, expectations ran high that a northern city such as Philadelphia or New York, or even possibly Cincinnati in the West, would house a relocated government. Reasons given for moving government operations were security, proximity to financial centers, stronger military protection, better living conditions for the officials, and space where a government could operate with better efficiently. On the other hand, patriotic sentiments ran high that the location of the government should not be determined by the barbaric actions of the enemy. The *National Intelligencer* printed:

> "We have heard some indistinct suggestions buzzed abroad of a design to endeavor, in consequence of the recent events, to remove the seat of government, temporarily or permanently, from this place. We cannot find language to express our abhorrence and astonishment at the suggestion of a *permanent* removal of the seat of government. Besides being a violation of the constitution establishing a permanent seat of government, it would be injustice so great to the people of this district, to those who have enriched the public offices with population and laid out fortunes in the purchase of property in and about the city, as Congress cannot, dare not sanction. There is besides something of cruelty in the idea of robbing the citizens of their all, because they have already greatly suffered by the incursion of the enemy.

Even though the British no longer posed an immediate threat to
Washington, concerns for the safety of government operations were quite
real. The United States continued to be embroiled in the war with Great
Britain. Peace negotiations continued, but there appeared to be no end in
sight. Other cities were undoubtedly targeted by the enemy for attack.
Where best to operate the functions of the government, yet reduce the
threat of another assault upon it, proved challenging. The space at
Blodget's Hotel was cramped. On September 26, the House agreed to
consider a resolution to remove the seat of government during the current
session, but did not name a location. The resolution read:

The resolution's wording suggested a temporary removal only,
but there were fears that any move would lead to a permanent change
and the government would never return to Washington. It was pointed
out that to relocate America's seat of government would undermine the
1790 compromise locating the capital in a federal district along the
shores of the Potomac River, in exchange for passing legislation of
assumption and funding supported by Alexander Hamilton. Southerners
threatened that national unity was at stake if the government moved
north. The President made it known that he would veto any legislation
regarding moving the capital. There were several alternations to the
original resolution, but in the end, it was determined that America's seat
of government would remain at Washington. The *National Intelligencer*
printed that it hoped this discussion was put to bed forever:

"The decision of the House of Representatives has, as we had anticipated, put to sleep now, and we trust for ever, the project of a removal of the Seat of Government from Washington, the seat designated, and the city planned by the immortal Hero and Patriot whose name it bears. This decision, viewed in its proper light, as the rejection of the prelude to a permanent removal, we believe will receive the cordial approbation of nine-tenths of all the People of the U. States, interested persons excepted....

The interests of the Union were involved in it. It was a question as interesting to the Province of Maine as to the State of Georgia. The seat of government was solemnly located with a view to its central position, and to other circumstances intimately connected with certain early acts of the government which entered into their compact or compromise, in consequence of which the seat of government was settled here. To remove it now would be almost to deracinate the principle of several of the most important of the first acts of the government, and would have warranted their abrogation, if a majority could be found so regardless of the honor and good faith of the nation as to have sanctioned it."

Once the relocation question was settled, Congress was able to tackle issues involving the reconstruction of the city itself. Eventually it passed a bill that approved appropriating $500,000 for repairing or rebuilding the President's House, the Capitol and other public offices on their present sites in Washington. At the same time, it also addressed replacing the burnt volumes that made up the Library of Congress. Using Smith, the founder of the *National Intelligencer*, as an agent, Jefferson offered to sell his personal library to Congress. He was willing to accept any price set by that body, but requested that the collection be preserved in its entirety. Along with this offer, he volunteered to make an alphabetical index of the author's names to help find the works in the catalogue. Jefferson wrote to Smith:

"Monticello, Sep 21. 14

I ask your friendship, therefore, to make for me the tender of it to the library committee of Congress, not knowing myself, of whom the committee consists; I enclose you a catalogue, which will enable them to judge of its contents, nearly the whole are well bound, abundance of them elegantly, and of the choicest editions. They may be valued by persons named by themselves, and the payment made convenient to the public; it may be for instance, in such annual instalments as the law of Congress has left at their disposal, or in stock of any of their late loans, or of any loan they may institute at this session so as to spare the present calls of our country, and await its days of peace and prosperity. They may enter nevertheless, into immediate use of it, as 18 or 20 wagons would place it in Washington in a single trip of a fortnight....

I do not know that it contains any branch of science which Congress would wish to exclude from their collection. There is in fact no subject to which a member of Congress may not have occasion to refer. But such a wish would not correspond with my views of preventing its dismemberment. My design is either to place it in their hands entire, or preserve it so here.

I am engaged in making an Alphabetical Index of the author's names to be annexed to the catalogue, in order to facilitate the finding their works in the catalogue, which I will forward to you as soon as completed. Any agreement you shall be so good as to take the trouble of entering into with the committee, I hereby confirm."

Jefferson's library at Monticello was a total library. Its contents went beyond the bounds of a legislative library devoted primarily to legal, economic or historical works, and included over twice the number of volumes that had been destroyed in the fires. It was not an easy sell. Serious debates occurred about the wisdom of purchasing such a library. Some Congressmen were concerned that many of the volumes were written in a foreign language and other books contained material not thought germane for the use of Congress. Naturally, there was a question of the cost to purchase. The *Annals of Congress* recorded in October, 1814:

"The objections to the purchase were generally its extent, the cost of the purchase, the nature of the selection, embracing too many works in foreign languages, some of too philosophical a character, and some otherwise objectionable. Of the first description, exception was taken to Voltaire's works, &c, and of the other to Callender's Prospect Before Us.

On the other hand, those who advocated the purchase proposed to be made, contended that so valuable a library, one so admirably calculated for the substratum of a great national library, was not to be obtained in the United States; and that, although there might be some works to which gentlemen might take exception, there were others of very opposite character; that this, besides, was no reason against the purchase, because in every library of value might be found some books to which exceptions would be taken, according to the feelings or prejudices of those who examined them."

Congress eventually realized that Jefferson's library was too important a collection to pass up and approved appropriating $23,950 to purchase the collection in its entirety. It consisted of 6487 volumes. The financial figure was based on a good faith estimate by Joseph Milligan, a Georgetown book dealer. Madison signed the bill on January 30, 1815.

Upon receiving the news that Congress had approved the purchase of his library, Jefferson requested that Milligan travel to Monticello to supervise the packing and transportation of the books to Washington. Ten wagon loads of books were sent to Washington. This collection of rare volumes formed the nucleus of the new Library of Congress. Once the last wagon left Monticello, Jefferson sat down and wrote to Smith, thanking him for his service:

> "Monticello May 8. 15.
> When I first proposed to you to make the overture to the library committee, I thought that the only trouble you would have had, was they would have said yea or nay directly, have appointed values, and spared you all further intermediation; and I saw with great regret this agency afterwards added to the heavy labors of your office. It is done however, and an interesting treasure is added to your city, now become the depository of unquestionably the choicest collection of books in the US; and I hope it will not be without some general effect on the literature of our country."

In his Presidential Message to Congress, Madison also pointed out that many policies regarding the militia needed to be reformed for America to win the ongoing war on the field and survive as a nation. There simply needed to be a much stronger military organization. The President, in the thinking of Jefferson, had never supported a standing army. Both men had always held the opinion that America could be best defended by militia troops; but from the beginning, the War of 1812 demonstrated that dependence upon the militia proved ineffective. The policies governing militia forces in general were the problem. The main difficulty was not planning for an army, but in actually raising one. The rapid defeat at Bladensburg, and the wrath of the citizens afterwards, brought to a head many of the problems officials faced throughout the war concerning the use of militia troops; and, in spite of Armstrong's stubbornness, the difficulties incurred by Winder, were not unknown to other commanders. Problems such as collecting a force, poorly trained troops, men not adequately armed, regular officers refusing to serve under militia officers, states not releasing their portion of the call, and troops who would not stand to the last to defend hearth and home suggested that the militia situation needed an overhaul. Madison stated:

> "To meet the extended and diversified warfare adopted by the enemy, great bodies of militia have been taken into service for the public defence, and great expenses incurred. That the defence everywhere may be both more convenient and more economical, Congress will see the necessity of immediate measures for filling the ranks of the regular Army, and of enlarging the provision for special corps, mounted and unmounted to be engaged for longer periods of service

than are due from the militia. I earnestly renew, at the same time a recommendation of such changes in the system of the militia, as, by classing and disciplining for the most prompt and active service the portions most capable of it, will give to that great resource for the public safety all the requisite energy and efficiency."

Congress acted promptly in addressing the militia issue, but little happened. Bills and amendments were submitted that would increase the size or length of militia service, particularly when it came to defending the frontier, but the old issue of conscription was at issue. The proposed bills did not pass. The *National Intelligencer* commented:

> "With much respect and deference for honest prejudice, we are at a loss to conceive in what respect, as regards the constitutional rights or civil liberty of the citizen, this bill differs from the bill which is annually or biennially passed, without debate or opposition, for authorizing a draft of 100 thousand militia.

> The main question presented by the bill is, in our view, whether it is not wise that the militia should be called into service for a term of twelve months in preference to six months, as now provided by law? Indeed the bill rather confers privileges than abridges civil rights, because it gives the people subject to the draft the right of procuring substitutes, in the shape of regulars, which shall entirely exempt them from militia service."

With the ratification of the peace treaty, Congress focused on necessary changes within the current military establishment. Basically the issue was whether the size of the military should be reduced. Both legislative branches felt that military operations should be consolidated into a peacetime force, but there was bickering between them about the size of the reduction. Congress hotly debated whether to keep a sizeable standing army, while recognizing that the expense of maintaining such a force would be costly. The Military Committee of the Senate asked Secretary of War Monroe his opinion. He replied:

> "In reducing our force to a peace establishment, it is incumbent on the United States to afford to our fellow citizens all the relief which may be consistent with their permanent and best interests. All useless expenditures should be retrenched. It will be admitted however that a force should be retained for every necessary national purpose....

> From the view which I have taken of the subject I am of the opinion that not less than 20,000 troops ought for the present to be retained in service, to be composed of every species of force, that is of infantry, (including riflemen) cavalry and artillery. It will be recollected that the corps will never be complete, that they will seldom contain more than two thirds, and often not more than one half, their legal

complement. Important works have already been erected in different parts of the United States on which vast sums have been expended. Those ought to be completed. Should they be neglected they will go to decay, and the money lost....

By retaining a part of every species of force now in service the knowledge which has been acquired in the science of war may be preserved and improved. This may be done on either of the plans which have been suggested.

Two modes have occurred by which to regulate the reduction. One by retaining the skeleton of every corps now in service, dismissing as many officers and men in each as will reduce the establishment to the proposed number; the other by reducing the number of regiments down to that standard."

Monroe did not get his 20,000 troops. The compromise reached by Congress and signed by Madison March 3, 1815, created a peacetime army of 10,000 men, consisting of artillery, infantry and riflemen as the President judged proper. This was a reduction of two-thirds the strength of the wartime forces. On the other hand, most of the wartime fleet was maintained after the armistice. There were many unhappy veterans (militia and regular) who were not pleased with the move to reduce the size of the army. Feelings ran high that the government was now in a position to draw upon their experience. Furthermore, they questioned the wisdom of America's continued reliance upon the militia for emergency situations. They pointed out that an army needed to be prepared. A disgruntled soldier wrote to the *National Intelligencer*:

"I cannot forbear expressing my surprise on observing the late bill for the reduction of the army.

The sufferings of the country have scarce terminated by a peace, when we hasten to place ourselves in a situation similar to that in which we were, so unfortunately, at the commencement of the war, as if determined that the nation should again experience the loss of blood, of treasure and of time, which characterized our military operations before the intelligence and discipline of the army had arrived at a height to render victory probable. Experience appears to lose all effect upon us....

That a militia force is not an organization adequate to such an emergency, we appeal to the experience of other nations as well as our own, and, if a particular instance is required, we will point to the ruins of our capitol – there we may weep over our folly and learn wisdom for the future....

Of what use are our seminaries of military science, if their fruits are to be scattered to the winds before they have yet ripened? And what inducement is there for men of genius and intelligence to devote themselves to the profession of arms, if, on every occasion of temporary quiet, they are turned adrift to begin the world anew. It is a fallacious economy. The mere inducement to obtain a soldier costs the nation more than his support for two years. We have been every year raising an army and have never yet had one, and now, when officers have acquired experience and know how to preserve the health of their men and themselves – for disease has been more fatal to our ranks than the enemy – we disband them. And why? Forsooth most wisely; that we may enjoy the same waste of treasure and of life hereafter. O Tempora!"

The War of 1812 ended with the signing of the "Treaty of Peace and Amity Between His Britannic Majesty and the United States of America" at Ghent, Belgium, December 24, 1814; exactly four months after the burning of Washington. Since information traveled slowly, the conflict continued for several weeks, culminating with the Battle of New Orleans, where American militia troops, led by General Andrew Jackson, crushed British regulars on January 8, 1815. Reports of the victory reached Washington February 4, 1815. This was followed ten days later on February 14, 1815, by the news of peace and a copy of the Treaty of Ghent. By the terms of the treaty, the war was not officially over until ratifications were exchanged and the treaty proclaimed. This was quickly done. On February 16, 1815, the Senate unanimously advised ratification and the President ratified it the following day, at which time the ratifications were exchanged. The ratifications took place in the Octagon House, the temporary White House for the nation's President and First Lady. Madison then proclaimed the Treaty on February 18, 1815. Hostilities between Great Britain and the United States were now officially over. Wharton described the peace celebrations at the Octagon House, but incorrectly gave the impression that the news of Jackson's glorious victory reached the capital after the Treaty of Ghent:

"Amid general rejoicings the season of 1815, 'the peace winter,' opened. The Madisons were established in the Octagon, which, having formed the habit of opening wide its doors during the residence of its hospitable owners, now as the home of the President and his wife closed them to none. Especially wide were these portals swung to admit the messengers of peace, whose good tidings, if not published upon the mountains, were noisily heralded across the plain by a coach-and-four that thundered along Pennsylvania Avenue one afternoon in February. Cheers greeted the carriage as it sped on its way to the Octagon, where a warm welcome awaited those who brought with them the Treaty of Ghent.

In the hours of rejoicing that followed the arrival of the peace commissioners, hospitality reigned in the house, which was crowded with visitors until midnight. Mrs. Madison received in the large parlor to the right of the entrance hall, while in the dining-room to the left good cheer was dispensed with a liberal hand. Tradition relates that the household servants were not overlooked in the general merry-making, as Miss Sally Coles flew to the basement stairs, crying, 'Peace, peace,' while the distribution of meats and drinks in their quarters was so bountiful and the good cheer was partaken of so joyously that French John was incapacitated for service for some days.

While the President and his Cabinet officers were engaged with the commissioners, Mrs. Madison flitted from room to room and from guest to guest, her face reflecting the happiness that warmed every heart. Whatever mistakes the President may have made were forgotten in the gladness of the hour, and more than one writer has said that Mrs. Madison was at that time the most popular person in the United States. Friends old and new gathered around her to offer their congratulations, the soldiers marching home stopped before the house to cheer her, and the special ambassador from Great Britain, Sir Charles Bagot, declared that the wife of the republican President looked every inch a queen.

The rejoicings over the signing of the Treaty of Ghent had scarcely subsided when news of General Jackson's victory over the British at New Orleans reached the capital and called for renewed festivities. Washington was so gay during the winter of 1815 that it would have been difficult to believe it had so recently known war and devastation had it not been for those silent witnesses, the ruined Capitol and White House, whose charred remains were blots upon the smiling plain."

The treaty basically reverted everything back to the *status quo ante bellum*, or rather, the same conditions that had existed before the hostilities. In other words, no one won the war. Many felt that lives had been lost in vain. It was considered more of a cessation of hostilities than a treaty, yet the United States learned a great deal from the war and gained intangible results far beyond anything that could be included in a written document. For one thing, America emerged from the conflict a more mature nation. England's former colony had now twice defeated the mother country, giving the young nation much needed esteem abroad. Gallatin, writing to Jefferson in 1815, pointed out that the United States had gained European respect due to the war, but more importantly, was now recognized as a naval power on the high seas. Gallatin wrote:

"In every other respect I must acknowledge that the war has been useful. The character of America stands now as high as ever on the European Continent, and higher than ever it did in Great Britain. I may say that we are favorites everywhere, except at courts; and even there, although the Emperor of Russia is perhaps the only sovereign who likes us, we are generally respected, and considered as the nation designed to check the naval despotism of England."

However, the main achievement resulting from the war was a unification of the nation. A new feeling of national pride swept across the country; and nothing did as much to unleash that patriotic spirit as the barbaric destruction of the peoples capital, quickly followed by the same enemy forces being repulsed at Baltimore and a new inspirational song. Combined with the fantastic victories at Plattsburg and New Orleans, citizens in all fifteen states recognized that they were no longer colonists. They had discovered their true identity. They were Americans! Louis Serurier, the French Minister, commented that "Finally the war has given the Americans what they so essentially lacked, a national character founded on a glory common to all." Madison included a special message to Congress when he sent the Treaty of Ghent to be ratified. In it he spoke of American patriotism:

> "The late war, although reluctantly declared by Congress, had become a necessary resort to assert the rights and independence of the nation. It has been waged with a success which is the natural result of the wisdom of the Legislative councils, of the patriotism of the people, of the public spirit of the militia, and of the valor of the military and naval forces of the country. Peace, at all times a blessing, is peculiarly welcome, therefore, at a period when the causes for the war have ceased to operate; when the Government has demonstrated the efficiency of its powers of defence; and when the nation can review its conduct without regret and without reproach.
>
> I recommend to your care and beneficence the gallant men whose achievements, in every department of the military service, on the land and on the water, have so essentially contributed to the honor of the American name, and to the restoration of peace. The feelings of conscious patriotism and worth will animate such men under every change of fortune and pursuit; but their country performs a duty to itself, when it bestows those testimonials of approbation and applause which are at once the reward and the incentive to great actions."

This concludes one of the most inglorious episodes in the history of the United States: the capture and burning of Washington. This horrific disaster was obviously preventable. The capital city of the United States was unprepared. No one person was to blame; the guilt was universal. The country had a major "wake up call" that it needed to be vigilant in the future and ready to protect its borders, homeland and capital; yet, after the War ceased the United States continued to rely on militia forces for its land defense. It will always remain inexcusable that nothing was done to impede the enemy's advance or retreat along the Patuxent or Gordon's fleet as it struggled up the Potomac. The nation would have accepted, no matter how difficult, the swift defeat at Bladensburg because of the superiority of the enemy, but Winder's forces shamelessly abandoning the field and leaving the capital unprotected will always remain an unconscionable act in the annals of American history. Perhaps the young British Subaltern Gleig summed it up best by writing "that the capture of Washington was more owing to the blindness of the Americans themselves than to any other cause." He concluded:

> "With respect to the Americans, again, criticism necessarily degenerates into unqualified censure. From the beginning to the end of the affair, they acted in no one instance like prudent or sagacious men. In the first place, they ought on no account to have risked a general action in an open country, however strong and steep; and, secondly, they deserved to suffer much more severely than they did suffer, for permitting an enemy's army to penetrate beyond Nottingham. In allowing us to land without opposition, they were perhaps guilty of no great mistake; but having done so, instead of concentrating their forces in one place, they ought to have harassed us with continual skirmishing; felled trees on each side, and thrown them across the road; dug deep ditches at certain intervals; in a word, it was their wisdom to adopt the mode of warfare to which their own habits, as well as the nature of their country, invited them.

> In America, every man is a marksman from his very boyhood, and every man serves in the militia; but to bring an army of raw militia-men, however excellent they might be as marksmen, into a fair field against regular troops, could end in nothing but defeat. When two lines oppose each other, very little depends upon the accuracy with which individuals take aim. It is then that the habit of acting in concert, the confidence which each man feels in his companions, and the rapidity and good order in which different movements can be executed, are along of real service. But put these raw militia-men into thick woods, and send your regular troops to drive them out, and you will immediately lose all the advantages of discipline, and reduce your battle to so many single combats.

> Here, therefore, lay their principal error; had they left all clear, and permitted us to advance as far as Nottingham, then broken up the roads, and covered them with trees, it would have been impossible for us to go a step beyond. As soon as this was effected, they might have skirmished with us in front, and kept our attention alive with part of their troops, till the rest, had got into our rear, and, by a similar mode of proceeding, cut off our retreat. Thus we should have been taken in a snare, from which it would have been no easy task to extricate ourselves, and might, perhaps, have been obliged in the end to surrender at discretion.

But so obvious and so natural a plan of defence they chose to reject; and determining to trust all to the fate of a battle, they were guilty of a monstrous error again. Bladensburg ought not to have left unoccupied. The most open village, is resolutely defended, will cost many men before it falls; whereas Bladensburg, being composed of substantial brick houses, might have been maintained for hours against all our efforts. In the next place, they displayed great want of military knowledge in the disposition of both their infantry and artillery. There was not, in the whole space of their position, a single point where an enemy would be exposed to a cross fire. The troops were drawn up in three straight lines, like so many regiments upon a gala parade; whilst the guns were used as connecting links to a chain, being posted in the same order, by ones and twos, at every interval.

In maintaining themselves, likewise, when attacked, they exhibited neither skill nor resolution. Of the personal courage of the Americans there can be no doubt; they are, individually taken, as brave a nation as any in the world. But they are not soldiers; they have not the experience nor the habits of soldiers. It was the height of folly, therefore, to bring them into a situation where nothing except that experience and those habits will avail; and it is on this account that I repeat what I have already said, that the capture of Washington was more owing to the blindness of the Americans themselves than to any other cause."

NOTES & OPINIONS

CHAPTER 2

The figures given for the loss of life, or for those wounded as a result of the magazine blowing up at York, are inconsistent and tend to vary with each account of the horrific event. A general description is often presented to the effect that the explosion produced at least 250 American causalities. In 1882, Theodore Roosevelt's classic *The Naval War of 1812* was published. In his account of the Battle at York and the explosion of its fort, the twenty-three year old future President wrote the following:

> "An explosion immediately afterward killed or wounded 250 of the victors, including General Pike. The Americans lost, on board the fleet, 4 killed, including midshipmen Hatfield and Thompson, and 8 wounded, and of the army, 14 killed and 32 wounded by the enemy's fire, and 52 killed and 180 wounded by the explosion; total loss, 288."

CHAPTER 4

There has been considerable controversy over Monroe's message to the President reporting the pullback of Winder and that the papers had better be secured. This confusion stems from the *American State Papers* because Monroe's note is mentioned twice, but with different dates. His report, page 538, included his letter stating, "Monday, nine o'clock. You had better remove the records." Armstrong's account, page 539, claimed that Madison forwarded Monroe's letter to him late Tuesday night; thus, "Tuesday, 9 o'clock" was also placed in the *American State Papers*. To clear up the issue, a copy of the original document was obtained through the National Archives, Washington D. C. Monroe's letter was obviously written in haste. It failed to include a date, or from where it was sent, but it very clearly shows "Monday, nine o'clock" as a quick addendum. This can only be Monday morning during the time Ross was dithering about what to do at the fork in the road near Oden's farm. Later that evening Madison, Monroe and other Cabinet members were with the army at Old Fields. There would have been no need for Monroe to write Madison at that time. Monroe did not stay overnight in the camp, but went back to the city, taking with him a message for Dolley that the President wrote from the Williams' farm.

CHAPTER 5

Pleasonton's narrative of packing national documents for hiding definitely included the original Declaration of Independence. Many accounts claim that the Constitution, Bill of Rights and Articles of Confederation were also among the treasurers that he removed to Virginia. This is not unreasonable. These priceless documents defined the structure of the young government and were considered the birth certificates of the country. One would assume that they were all kept at the same location, which would have been the Department of State in 1814. Although I have not been able to verify that Pleasonton placed all four documents into his linen bags, I believe one should keep an open mind here.

CHAPTER 7

On Tuesday, August 23, 1814, Dolley started her descriptive narrative of her last hours in the Executive Mansion with "Dear Sister." Unfortunately, many confuse the sibling to whom she was writing. Anna Payne Cutts left the White House with the First Lady and Anna's husband traveled behind in a separate carriage. Dolley's youngest sister Lucy, the widow of George Steptoe Washington, married Judge Thomas Todd at the first White House wedding in March, 1812, and was living in Kentucky. Dolley was writing to Lucy Payne Washington Todd.

In actuality, Dolley's original letter to her sister of August 23, 1814 no longer exists. Two decades after the White House was burned, Mrs. Smith asked the former First Lady to submit some of her documents for a biographical sketch that she was putting together for publication in a new book *The National Portrait Gallery of Distinguished Americans.* Dolley complied. The two day narrative beginning with "Dear Sister" was selected to be printed. What became of the original letter is unknown. It appears that the only surviving version in Dolley's handwriting was later copied out of the book from the printed text. This extract is among the most famous documents in the history of the United States and is what historians have used in describing the First Lady's flight from the nation's capital. The tone of the letter suggests that there was an original document and that Dolley did not verbally relate to Mrs. Smith twenty years later what she remembered in writing to Lucy Todd before fleeing. At the top of the unsigned letter above the date is the following in Dolley's handwriting:

214

CHAPTER 9

The redeployment of Stansbury's Baltimore Militia by Monroe remains an unfortunate blemish on his otherwise illustrious career. The Secretary of State was the first Cabinet official to reach Bladensburg. Before heading for the battle site, Winder first rode to the navy yard so that he could order the forces there to rush to Bladensburg and reinforce Stansbury's troops. With the battle imminent and the General in charge not yet on the field, Monroe on his own initiative took on leadership responsibilities. Winder had not drawn up any prearranged plans. Had the enemy reached the battle site before Winder and the remaining Americans, Stansbury's 2200 troops would have been unable to fend off the approaching attack no matter where they were stationed. Monroe turned out to be a poor tactician. His rearrangement of Stansbury's line was certainly not the cause for the American disaster, but because the new positions were unable to adequately support the front line, it added to the confusion and was a principal reason for the rapid flight from the engagement.

Contrary to the opinions of many historians, Madison showed a great deal of courage at Bladensburg. He remains the only President in the history of the United States who was ever actually on the field in the midst of combat. Others fought battles, but that was before they served in the position of the Chief Executive. Enemies, particularly the Federalists, chastised Madison for leaving the center of the engagement for safer ground. The President was a scholar, not a warrior. He knew little about warfare, but he did recognize that as Commander in Chief he served only in an advisory position. The British would have given anything to have captured and made an example of him. Considering the later fate of Beanes, the suggestion to reposition and leave the fighting to those who knew what they were doing was a prudent thing to do. This was not done in a cowardly fashion. The President did not exit the field, but bravely remained at the rear of the battle viewing the unfolding disaster. According to Rush, the possibility of a move to the rear was established ahead of time on the ride out to Bladensburg. It was only when Madison received the message that Winder had ordered a retreat, that he turned his horse and, along with the Attorney General, slowly made his way back to Washington.

The often told story about the First Lady saving Washington's portrait is sprinkled with legends. One version suggests that "French John," the White House's indispensable domestic servant, used his penknife to cut the picture from its frame. Another account claims that Dolley, using a carving knife, cut the linen canvass with her own hands, rolled it up and carried it with her during her escape. There is even a variation that the First Lady used an axe and broke the outside frame herself. To set the record straight, Jennings recollection is correct – the canvass was never removed from its stretcher. The outside gilded frame was broken, but the frame that the canvass was stretched upon was never shattered. This was confirmed during the Nineteenth Century when the White House first had the painting cleaned and the restorer discovered that the canvass remained intact on its original frame. This fact was further verified by William G. Allman, Curator of the White House in 2004, who pointed out that "conservators working on this portrait in 1978 found no evidence that the painting had ever been cut from its frame and the canvas rolled." Laura Langford wrote in *Ladies of the White House*:

> "Half a century later, when the White House was undergoing a renovation, this portrait was sent, with many others subsequently added to this solitary collection, to be cleaned and the frame burnished. The artist found on examination that the canvas had never been cut, since the rusted tacks, time-worn frame, and the size compared with the original picture, was the most conclusive evidence that Mrs. Madison did not cut it out with a carving knife, as many traditions have industrially circulated."

As generally reported, Charles Carroll did not leave Washington the night the British set it ablaze. He remained in the city to keep an eye on his various properties. William Jones headed up the entourage of women and children that fled Carroll's Bellevue mansion. This included at least Dolley, Sukey, Edward DuVall and the families of Jones, Carroll and Cutts. It is thought that Richard Cutts accompanied the group into Virginia, but returned to Washington the following morning. Carroll's son Daniel L. (not to be confused with Daniel Carroll of Duddington) included the following in a letter to the *New York Herald* January, 1848:

> "It is well known that Mr. Charles Carroll, of Bellevue, remained that night, and was at this place in Georgetown when the British burned the capitol."

Barker offered that Dolley's response to DePeyster's request for her account of the events relating to saving Washington's portrait was printed in the *New York Express*. I searched unsuccessfully for her letter in that publication at the Library of Congress. Unfortunately, only a few copies of that newspaper have survived over the years. A "good faith" effort was also made searching through the *New York Herald* for the printed letter, but again I was unsuccessful.

CHAPTER 13

Monroe did not escape Washington in the company of Madison on Mason's Ferry. It would appear that he crossed into Virginia on horseback over the Little Falls Bridge (Chain Bridge), before stopping at Rokeby looking for the President. Supposedly Ringgold was with him. Wiley's Tavern has always been offered as the place where Monroe spent the night of August 24. He recrossed the Potomac River on Conn's Ferry, before the violent storm erupted Thursday afternoon, and joined Winder's army.

A date c.August 24, 1814 is generally given to Madison's paper "Notes on the Battle of Bladensburg." This date certainly seems like a reasonable guess; however, given the difficulty of Madison's day, it would seem unlikely that it was actually composed on the 24th. The summarization clearly was written sometime after Wednesday's battle and before his encounter with Armstrong Monday evening. A more likely consideration for the writing might be during the hours on Friday, c.August 26, while the Presidential party was waiting above the Great Falls for the Potomac to become navigable. Madison certainly would have had an opportunity to quietly put his thoughts on paper until the ferryman was able to take everyone across the river.

An unfortunate error was made by Irving Brant in his volume *James Madison: Commander in Chief, 1812-1836*. Brant incorrectly used the first name John in citing the owner of the 466 acre Salona property located in what became McLean, Virginia. Using the mistake subsequent scholars created confusion over the years. Salona, where both of the Madisons presumably stopped briefly in their flights from the nation's capital, was the home of the Reverend William Maffitt, a Presbyterian minister. This can be confirmed by Fairfax County, Virginia, Deed Book L2:368.

An often cited, though incorrect version of Dolley's escape, was related by Mrs. Smith in a letter to her sister Jane Kirkpatrick who lived in New Jersey. She told her sister that First Lady followed the retreating army to Tenleytown and spent Wednesday night, August 24, 1814, in an encampment there with guards around her tent. There is an indication that Mrs. Thornton and Mrs. Cutting were amongst Dolley's entourage, which was not the case. This account appears to be a combination of conversations Mrs. Smith had during tea with Dolley and Mrs. Thornton late Sunday after everyone was back in the city. For the record, Mrs. Smith wrote:

> "The friends with her then hurried her away, (her carriage being previously ready) and she with many other families, among whom was Mrs. Thornton and Mrs Cutting with her, retreated with the flying army. In George town they perceived some men before them carrying off the picture of Genl. Washington (the large one by Stewart) which with the plate, was all that was saved out of the President's house. Mrs. M. lost all her own property. The wine, of which there was a great quantity, was consumed by our own soldiers. Mrs. M. slept that night in the encampment, a guard being placed round her tent, the next Day she cross'd into Virginia where she remained until Sunday, when she return'd to meet her husband."

Fortunately, Mrs. Thornton's diary has survived. She wrote that when leaving the city, her group went to the President's House and found that Dolley had already left. The Thorntons were then escorted by the army from the capital, and they saw the portrait of Washington being carted from the city while they were en route to their farm in Maryland. Mrs. Thornton escaped by carriage in the company of Mrs. Cutting while Mr. Thornton traveled on horseback. The Thorntons had separated by the time they reached Georgetown. The two women listened to rumors that the British army was headed in the direction of Tenleytown and, fearful of going any further in that direction, stopped at Tudor Place, the Georgetown Heights residence of Thomas and Martha Custis Peter, designed by Thornton in 1795. A servant was sent ahead to find Thornton and bring him back to Georgetown. There everyone spent a terrified night. Mrs. Thornton entered into her diary August 24, 1814:

"At last saw a man riding hard as possible towards the President's House – we shut up soon after & found that Mrs. M. was gone. We set down to dinner but I couldn't eat nothing & we dilly dally'd till we saw our retreating army come away, and were <u>escorted</u> out of town by our defeated troops. Genl. Washington's picture & a cart load of goods from the President's House in company – (it was supposed that Mr. Custis got some of the soldiers to take out this picture).

When we got to the upper part of Georg T. we met Mr Richardson who advised us not to proceed up the road, as it was crowded with troops &c & that there was a rumor that the British were to send them that way & give them battle. Dr. T. having gone round by Mr. Peters we did not know what step to take, but decided to go to Mrs. Peter's & wait till we could send for him – I sent off John on one of the carriage horses & he did not overtake him till he got to Tenley Town. He supposing we were before him. We staid all night at Mr. Peter's (Mrs. Cutting with us) and there witnessed the conflagration of our poor undefended and devoted city."

There is nothing in Mrs. Thornton's diary entry to indicate that the First Lady was traveling with her or that Dolley had spent the night in Tenleytown. In fact, the First Lady had already vacated the White House by the time Mrs. Thornton stopped by. At Tenleytown Winder was struggling to collect his forces. He had enough trouble enough keeping any semblance of an army together, let alone supplying guards for the First Lady, her family and friends. The General had few supplies. Where did the tent come from? Winder collected what remained of his militia forces at Tenleytown and began the march to Montgomery Court House before midnight. Dolley and her group would have been left without guards. The protection that Mrs. Smith referred to undoubtedly was the guard unit of one hundred that was placed around the White House on Monday. If anything, Mrs. Thornton's story indicates that the First Lady would be desirous of heading in any direction but Tenleytown. Very simply, Mrs. Smith, who left the capital long before the battle began at Bladensburg, passed on to her sister what she thought she heard during tea. Unfortunately, it was erroneous information.

CHAPTER 14

Any account of the Madisons escapes into Northern Virginia would be remiss by not addressing a 1905 article that appeared in the *Washington Star* newspaper. A lengthy narrative was given the reporter by Harriet Smoot suggesting that both of the Madisons stayed at Salona during their flight from Washington. The story apparently originated with Miss Smoot's grandmother Mary Carter Jones, who as a child of twelve was living at Salona when the British burned the city. In reading the article, one has to recognize that correctness of information generally gets lost in accounts that have been verbally handed down in families over many decades. Miss Smoot's romantic account of the Madison's flights of August 24, 1814 is inaccurate because none of her facts support the evidence. What she is describing appears to be the following day, Thursday, August 25, combined with ninety years of hearsay and legend. Using a scenario of August 25, Miss Smoot's descriptive story would place Dolley at Salona after leaving Rokeby. She told the reporter that the President arrived later in the company of Maffitt. This would have been after Madison left Wren's, heading in the direction of Salona where he expected to find Dolley. This makes sense. Everyone rushing to watch the fire from the hill in back of the house may possibly have viewed the well explosion at Greenleaf's Point. Booth, in his account of the Crossroads, only wrote that the President learned there that Dolley had passed by earlier. There is no indication that Madison was aware or unaware of the destination of his wife. Even thought Miss Smoot's story is full of misleading "facts," the author feels certain that both of the Madisons received hospitality at Salona, but Dolley was only there a brief time during the second day of her flight. Miss Smoot stated:

> "Only six miles distant from Washington, three miles above the Chain bridge, in Fairfax county, Va., on the estate known as Salona, in the Langley tract, stands an old house that is of historic interest.... It was this old house that in 1814 sheltered Dolly Madison, wife of the President of the United States, on her flight from Washington in 1814 to escape from the British invaders.

> One of the owners of Salona is Miss Harriet E. Smoot, who resides on the old estate at this time. Miss Smoot recently gave to The Sunday Star an account of the flight of Dolly Madison from the British, the story having been told to her by persons possessed of reliable information relative to the incident. The story as related by Miss Smoot is as follows:

> Dolley Madison fled from Washington August 24, 1814. She was passed over the Potomac River by an order from Chief Clerk Homans of the State Department, who also flew the city about the same time, taking with him the State Department papers. Mrs. Madison was accompanied by a man servant who succeeded in getting a carriage to bear his master from the capital. The wife of the President had with her a small, but valuable, trunk containing the original Declaration of Independence and other important cabinet papers. It is said she also had with her, Stuart's portrait of Washington, cut from its frame by her own hand, in such haste as to leave the artist's signature on the remaining frame. She applied at two houses for shelter, but was refused. Such was the fear of the enemy which possessed the capital.

The third place at which Mrs. Madison sought refuge was Salona, of the Langley tract. This was the home of the Rev. William Maffitt, commonly called Parson Maffitt. Mrs. Maffitt instantly granted Mrs. Madison's request, and she was quickly installed in the home.

Parson Maffitt had gone out early in the day to gain some information relative to the enemy and had just returned when Mrs. Madison arrived. Night was approaching and his wife was (with) us. She seated herself near the window. Suddenly, just about dark, a clatter of horse's hoofs was heard. Mrs. Maffitt (went to) the door, opened it and beheld the Parson on his white horse in front of the (can't read) in hiding President Madison and most of his cabinet. There was a hasty meeting between the President and his wife, who were thankful for their escape.

While seated at the supper table some of the slaves came into the dining room crying 'Fire! Fire!'

All rushed out of the house and stationed themselves on a little hill at the rear of the house and they watched the burning of Washington by the British troops.

The next day the President and cabinet left Salona and Mrs. Madison remained there. She had intimate friends near by, the family of Senator Charles Cutts. I have seen a beautiful ladies ring with her name on it, which she presented to Charles Cutts' daughter Maria, and which is now in the possession of his granddaughter Hebe. The story of (can't read) was told over and over to me when a child by Mrs. Thomas Ap. Catesby Jones, wife of Commodore Jones. Before her marriage she was Mary Walker Carter and was twelve years old and living at Salona at the time of Mrs. Madison's stay with her mother Mrs. Maffitt. Mrs. Maffitt before her marriage to the parson was the widow Carter. Mrs. Jones was married when sixteen to Thomas As. Catesby Jones (can't read) and moved from Salona to her home Sharon adjoining Salona."

<hr>

The roads and bridges are difficult to follow because the names have changed over the years. The bridge near the Little Falls became known as Chain Bridge and the Rochambeau Bridge replaced the Long Bridge. Today the Falls Road is called Chain Bridge Road, Great Falls Road became Great Falls Street, and the Alexandria & Leesburg Road is recognized as Leesburg Pike or Route 7. The Alexandria & Leesburg Road was realigned after Madison's flight by the Middle Turnpike Company, which was created by the Virginia General Assembly in 1818. Its original junction with the Falls Road (the Crossroads where Madison possibly waited out the storm) is located at the western edge of the

Tysons Corner complex at Chain Bridge Road and Old Courthouse Road in what became Vienna, Virginia.

CHAPTER 15

The Washington Navy Yard was the largest ship building and ship fitting facility in the nation. Most of it was destroyed by the fires or looters; however, the recently built schooner *Lynx*, the hulk of a new frigate the *New York*, the main entrance gate designed by Latrobe and two residences, one of which was Tingey's own quarters, survived the flames.

The Tripoli Monument is the oldest outdoor military monument in the United States. Lieutenant David Porter (Captain Porter of the White House Battery) raised $3000 from his shipmates for a monument to honor their fallen comrades. Made of white marble, it was originally erected at the Washington Navy Yard, but was moved to the grounds of the U. S. Capitol in 1831. There it stood in front of the Capitol's west front terrace staircase for nearly three decades, until 1860 when it was relocated to the United States Naval Academy at Annapolis.

CHAPTER 17

Porter's hastily assembled battery on top the White House Cliffs, also known as the Heights of Belvoir, should not be mistaken for the Presidential Mansion. The White House referred to here was built by Ferdinando Fairfax, third son of Byron Fairfax, Eighth Lord Fairfax.

CHAPTER 24

The cartel sloop used by Key and Skinner was not named in this book. It is thought to have been the *Minden*. Historians have never reached agreement on this issue and so its name was purposely left out.

SOURCES

PROLOGUE

1. L'Enfante to Washington. *L'Enfant and Washington*. Page 14.

2. Albert Gallatin. *The City of Washington*. Page 87

3. Mrs. Adams to Mrs. Smith. *Letters of Mrs. Adams*. Page 381.

4. Payment to Lee. Office of the Curator the White House.

5. Latrobe to Mrs. Madison. *The Correspondence and Miscellaneous Papers of Benjamin Henry Latrobe*. Volume II. Page 711.

6. Mrs. Madison to Coles. *Memoirs and Letters of Dolly Madison, Wife of James Madison, President of the United States*. Page 89.

CHAPTER ONE - ALARM

1. Jones. *American State Papers*. Page 540.

2. Gallatin to Monroe. *Writings of Albert Gallatin*. June 13, 1814. Page 627.

3. Jones. *American State Papers*. Page 540.

4. Johnson. *American State Papers*. Page 524.

5. Johnson. *Ibid*.

6. Winder to Armstrong. *American State Papers*. Page 543.

7. Armstrong to Winder. *A Sketch of the Events Which Preceded the Capture of Washington by the British on the Twenty-Fourth of August, 1814*. Page 12.

8. Armstrong to Winder. *Ibid*.

9. Boileau. *American State Papers*. Page 551.

10. Van Ness. *American State Papers*. Page 580.

11. Thompson. *American State Papers*. Page 590.

12. Armstrong. *American State Papers*. Page 539.

13. Madison to Armstrong. *The Writings of James Madison*. Volume VIII. Page 290.

14. Winder to Armstrong. *Official Letters of the Military and Naval*

Officers of the United States During the War with Great Britain in the Years 1812, 13, 14, & 15. Page 400.

15. Monroe to Jefferson. *The Political Writings of James Monroe.* Page 470.

CHAPTER TWO – THE ENEMY LANDS

1.   Brant. The Fourth President: *A Life of James Madison.* Page 540.

2.   Cochrane to Croker. *London Times.* September 28, 1814.

3.   Cochrane to Croker. *Ibid.*

4.   Gleig. *The Campaigns of the British Army at Washington and New Orleans.* Page 51.

5.   {Gleig}. *A Subaltern in America.* Page 14.

6.   {Gleig}. *Ibid.* Page 21.

CHAPTER THREE – ACTING SCOUT MONROE

1.   Monroe. *American State Papers.* Page 536.

2.   Monroe to Armstrong. *The Political Writings of James Monroe.* Page 463.

3.   Winder. *American State Papers.* Page 554.

4.   Barney to Jones. *A Sketch of the Events Which Preceded the Capture of Washington by the British on the Twenty-Fourth of August, 1814.* Appendix 18.

5.   Monroe to Madison. *American State Papers.* Page 537.

6.   Monroe to Madison. *The Political Writings of James Monroe.* Page 464.

CHAPTER FOUR – BARNEY'S FLOTILLA DESTROYED

1.   Gleig. *The Campaigns of the British Army at Washington and New Orleans.* Page 57.

2.   Jones. *American State Papers.* Page 532.

3.   Monroe to Winder. *American State Papers.* Page 537.

4.   Monroe. *Ibid.* Page 536.

5.   *Richmond Enquirer.* August 23, 1814.

6. Madison to Monroe. *The Writings of James Madison.* Volume VIII. Page 291.

7. Gleig. *The Campaigns of the British Army at Washington and New Orleans.* Page 57.

8. Stansbury. *American State Papers.* Page 560.

9. Law. *American State Papers.* Page 585.

10. Monroe to Madison. National Archives, Washington D. C.

11. {Gleig}. *A Subaltern in America.* Page 41.

12. Law. *Ibid.* Page 585.

13. Winder. *American State Papers.* Page 555.

14. Madison to Monroe. *The Writings of James Madison.* Volume VIII. Page 291.

15. Cockburn to Cochrane. Cockburn Papers. August 22, 1814. Library of Congress.

16. Barney to Pleasants. *Niles Weekly Register.* Volume VII. Page 142.

CHAPTER FIVE – PANIC IN WASHINGTON

1. Mrs. Smith to Mrs. Kirkpatrick. *Forty Years of Washington Society.* Page 98.

2. Brown. *Social Life in the Early Republic.* Page 163.

3. Homans. *American State Papers.* Page 255.

4. Booth to Tingey. *Letter and Communication to Commodore Thomas Tingey from Mordecai Booth, His Clerk.* Mary Riley Styles Public Library, Falls Church,Virginia.

5. Pleasonton. *A Sketch of the Events Which Preceded the Capture of Washington by the British on the Twenty-Fourth of August, 1814.* Appendix 10.

6. Pleasonton. *Ibid.*

CHAPTER SIX – WINDER RETREATS

1. {Gleig}. *A Subaltern in America.* Page 45.

2. Madison to Mrs. Madison. *The Writings of James Madison.* Volume VIII. Page 293.

3. Winder. *American State Papers.* Page 555.

4. McKenney. *Memoirs, Official and Personal.* Page 44.

5. Gleig. The *Campaigns of the British Army at Washington and New Orleans.* Page 59.

6. McKenney. *Ibid.* Page 45.

7. Law. *American State Papers.* Page 585.

8. Barney to Jones. *Official Letters of the Military and Naval Officers of the Unite States During the War with Great Britain in the Years 1812, 13, 14, and 15.* Page 405.

CHAPTER SEVEN – ROSS'S DECISION

1. Mrs. Madison to Mrs. Todd. The Papers of Dolley Madison. Library of Congress.

2. Mrs. Jones to Mrs. Madison. *Memoirs and Letters of Dolly Madison.* Page 105.

3. Monroe. *American State Papers.* Page 536.

4. Minor. *American State Papers.* Page 568.

5. Winder. *American State Papers.* Page 557.

6. Scott. *Recollections of a Naval Life.* Page 281.

7. Scott. *Ibid.* Page 282.

8. Skinner. *National Intelligencer.* June 4, 1849.

9. Ross. "Official British Account of the Capture of Washington." *London Times*, September 28, 1814.

CHAPTER EIGHT – AMERICAN UNCERTAINTY

1. Gleig. *The Campaigns of the British Army at Washington and New Orleans.* Page 61.

2. Winder to Armstrong. *American State Papers.* Page 548.

3. Armstrong. *American State Papers.* Page 539.

4. Madison. "Memorandum on the Battle of Bladensburg." *The Writings of James Madison.* Volume VIII. Page 294.

5. Barney to Jones. *American State Papers.* Page 579.

6. Madison. *Ibid.* Page 295.

7. Madison. *Ibid.* Page 297.

8. Armstrong. *American State Papers*. Page 539.

9. Mrs. Madison to Mrs. Todd. *Ibid.*

CHAPTER NINE - THE BLADENSBURG RACES

1. Winder. *American State Papers*. Page 557.

2. Law. *American State Papers*. Page 586.

3. {Gleig}. *A Subaltern in America*. Page 67.

4. Madison. *Ibid*. Page 297.

5. Rush. *American State Papers*. Page 542.

6. Winder. *American State Papers*. Page 558.

7. __________. *Incidents in the Life of Jacob Barker, New Orleans, Louisiana*. Page 121.

8. Barney to Jones. *American State Papers*. Page 579.

9. Jennings. *A Colored Man's Reminiscences of James Madison.* James Madison University. Page 9.

10. Ball. *Slavery in the United States, A Narrative of the Life and Adventures of Charles Ball, A Black Man.* Page 468.

10. Minor. *American State Papers*. Page 569.

11. Winder. *American State Papers*. Page 559.

12. Smith to Johnson. *American State Papers*. Page 565.

13. Lavall to Johnson. *American State Papers*. Page 571.

14. Winder to Armstrong. *American State Papers*. Page 548.

CHAPTER TEN - THE ESCAPES

1. Mrs. Madison to Mrs. Todd. *Ibid.*

2. Mrs. Cutts to Mrs. Madison. *The Selected Letters of Dolley Payne Madison.* Page 194.

3. Jennings. Ibid. Page 10.

4. Mrs. Madison to Mrs. Todd. *Ibid.*

5. Jennings. *Ibid.* Page 11.

6. Barker. *New York Herald.* June 13, 1847.

7. DePeyster. *New York Herald.* June 13, 1847.

8. Mrs. Madison to DePeyster. *Incidents in the Life of Jacob Barker, New Orleans, Louisiana.* Page 110.

9. Cutts. *Memoirs and Letters of Dolly Madison.* Page 107.

10. Clark. *Life and Letters of Dolly Madison.* Page 178.

11. __________. *Incidents in the Life of Jacob Barker, New Orleans, Louisiana.* Page 121.

12. Jones to Johnson. *American State Papers.* Page 576.

13. Jones to Johnson. *Ibid.* Page 577.

14. Monroe. *The Political Writings of James Monroe.* Page 465.

CHAPTER ELEVEN- FIRING THE NAVY YARD

1. Jones to Anderson. *American State Papers.* Page 361.

2. Jones to Johnson. *American State Papers.* Page 577.

3. Armstrong. *Baltimore Patriot.* September 3, 1814.

4. Booth to Tingey. *Letter and Communication to Commodore Thomas Tingey from Mordecai Booth, His Clerk.*

5. Tingey Report. *American State Papers.* Page 578.

CHAPTER TWELVE - THE TERROR

1. Brown. *Social Life in the Early Republic.* Page 163.

2. Shiner. *The Diary of Michel Shiner – The Early History of Washington D.C., Dating from 1813 to 1865.* Library of Congress.

3. Gleig. *The Campaigns of the British Army at Washington and New Orleans.* Page 69.

4. Shiner. *Ibid.*

5. Scott. *Recollections of a Naval Life.* Page 297.

6. Scott. *Ibid.* Page 300.

7. Shiner. *Ibid.*

8. Ross. *Dictionary of National Biography.* Voulme XVII. Page 276.

9. Smith. *The Autobiography of Lieutenant-General Sir Harry Smith.* Chapter XX.

10. Gleig. *The Campaigns of the British Army at Washington and New*

Orleans. Page 71.

11. Scott. *Ibid.* Page 305.

12. Mrs. Smith to Mrs. Kirkpatrick. *Ibid.* Page 112.

CHAPTER THIRTEEN - THE FLIGHTS

1. Rush. *The Life and Letters of Dolly Madison.* Page 170.

2. Jennings. *Ibid.* Page 12.

3. Templeman. *Arlington Hertiage.* Page 146.

4. Sayrs. *Recollections.* Lloyd House.

5. Booth to Tingey. *Ibid.*

6. Jennings. *Ibid.* Page 12.

7. Jennings. *Ibid.* Page 13.

8. Love. *Reminiscences.* Page 291.

9. Wharton. *Social Life in the Early Republic.* Page 172.

10. Winder. *American State Papers.* Page 559.

11. {Gleig}. A Subaltern in America. Page 81.

CHAPTER FOURTEEN - WILEY'S TAVERN

1. Booth to Tingey. *Ibid.* Page 19.

2. Jennings. *Ibid.* Page 13.

3. Ingersoll. *Historical Sketch of the Second War Between the United States of America and Great Britian.* Page 208.

4. Booth to Tingey. *Ibid.* Page 20.

5. Booth to Tingey. *Ibid.*

6. Booth to Tingey. *Ibid.* Page 22.

CHAPTER FIFTEEN – THE RUSES DE GUERRE

1. Williams. *History of the Invasion and Capture of Washington.* Page 267.

2. Thornton. *National Intelligencer.* September 7, 1814.

3. Mrs. Smith to Mrs. Kirkpatrick. *Ibid.* Page 112.

4. Scott. *Ibid.* Page 313.

5. *National Intelligencer.* August 31, 1814.

6. Mrs. Thornton. *Journal and Diaries of Mrs. William Thornton.* Page 678.

7. Gleig. *The Campaigns of the British Army at Washington and New Orleans.* Page 75.

8. *National Intelligencer.* September 1, 1814.

9. *Ibid.*

CHAPTER SIXTEEN – BRITISH WITHDRAWAL

1. Smith. *Ibid.*

2. Smith. *Ibid.*

3. Ross to Bathurst. *Columbian Centennial.* December 7, 1814.

4. Cattlett. *American State Papers.* Page 584.

5. Mrs. Thornton. *Ibid.* Page 686.

6. Gleig. *The Campaigns of the British Army at Washington and New Orleans.* Page 80.

7. Smith. *Ibid.*

8. Mrs. Smith to Mrs. Fitzpatrick. *Ibid.* Page 117.

CHAPTER SEVENTEEN – RETURN TO THE CAPITAL

1. Madison to Monroe. *The Writings of James Madison.* Page 298.

2. Mrs. Love. *Ibid.* Page 291.

3. Young. *American State Papers.* Page 567.

4. Thornton. *National Intelligencer.* September 7, 1814.

5. Blake. *National Intelligencer.* September 10, 1814

6. Monroe. *The Political Writings of James Monroe.* Page 465.

7. Madison to Jones. August 27, 1814. William Jones Papers. Ulsema Clark Smith Collection. Historical Society of Pennsylvania.

8. Madison to Mrs. Madison. *The Writings of James Madison 1808-1819.* Page 300.

9. Mrs. Smith to Mrs. Kirkpatrick. *Ibid.* Page 107.

10. Jennings. *Ibid.* Page 13.

11. Sayrs. *Childhood in 1812-A True Story.*

CHAPTER EIGHTEEN – ALEXANDRIA SURRENDERS

1. Gordon. *Log of Proceedings, HMS Seahorse.*

2. Dyson to Armstrong. *American State Papers.* Page 591.

3. Lee. *Alexandria Gazette.* September 3, 1814.

4. Madison to Mrs. Madison. *Life and Letters of Dolly Madison.* Page 172.

5. Monroe to Jefferson. *The Political Writings of James Monroe.* Page 471.

6. Thornton. *National Intelligencer.* September 7, 1814.

7. Monroe. *The Political Writings of James Monroe.* Page 465.

8. Porter to Jones. *National Intelligencer.* September 12, 1814.

9. Monroe. *The Political Writings of James Monroe.* Page 466.

10. Mrs. Thornton. *Ibid.* Page 683.

11. Mrs. Smith to Mrs. Kirkpatrick. *Ibid.* Page 110.

12. Mrs. Madison to Mrs. Latrobe. *The Life and Letters of Dolly Madison.* Page 166.

13. Mrs. Jones to Jones. September 1, 1814. William Jones Papers. Uselma Clark Smith Collection. Historical Socicty of Pennsylvania.

CHAPTER NINETEEN –GORDON'S CONDITIONS

1. Thompson. *American State Papers.* Page 591.

2. Thompson. *Ibid.* Page 592.

3. Thompson. *Ibid.*

4. Mrs. Smith to Mrs. Kirkpatrick. *Ibid.* Page 114.

CHAPTER TWENTY - ARMSTRONG RESIGNS

5. *The Enquirer.* August 31, 1814.

6. Mrs. Smith to Mrs. Kirkpatrick. *Ibid.* Page 115.

7. Madison. "Memorandum, August 29, 1814." *The Writings of James Madison.* Page 300.

8. Madison. *Ibid.*

9. Armstrong. *Baltimore Patriot*. September 3, 1814.

CHAPTER TWENTY-ONE – GORDON'S DESCENT

1. Porter to Jones. *National Intelligencer*. September 12, 1814.

2. Porter to Jones. *Ibid*.

3. *National Intelligencer*. September 6, 1814.

4. *Ibid*.

5. Porter to Jones. *Ibid*.

6. *National Intelligencer*. September 9, 1814.

7. Perry to Jones. *Alexandria Gazette*. September 22, 1814.

8. Rodgers to Jones. *National Intelligencer*. September 14, 1814.

9. Nourse to Mother. September 10, 1814. University of Virginia.

10. Sayrs. *Childhood in 1812-A True Story*.

11. Gilman. *Alexandria Advertiser*. October 9, 1851.

12. Johnson. *American State Papers*. Page 533.

13. *National Intelligencer*. November 21, 1814.

14. Gordon. *British Warships at Alexandria, Virginia, 1814. The English Viewpoint as Recalled by the Log of H.M.S. Seahorse*. Page 155.

CHAPTER TWENTY TWO - INTRIGUE

1. Cochrane to Monroe. *National Intelligencer*. September 10, 1814.

2. Codrington to Gordon. *American State Papers*. Page 594.

3. Mason to Johnson. *American State Papers*. Page 595.

4. Committee of Vigilance. *American State Papers*. Page 594.

5. Mason to Johnson. *American State Papers*. Page 595.

6. Hunt. *The Writings of James Madison*. Volume VIII. Page 304.

7. Monroe to Cochrane. *National Intelligencer*. September 10, 1814.

8. Cochrane to Monroe. *National Intelligencer*. September 27, 1814.

9. *National Intelligencer*. September 14, 1814.

CHAPTER TWENTY-THREE – A SMALL VICTORY

1. *National Intelligencer.* September 6, 1814.

2. Reed to Chambers. September 3, 1814. Historical Society of Kent County, Maryland.

CHAPTER TWENTY-FOUR – AN ANTHEM IS BORN

1. Winder to Ross. *The British Invasion of Maryland 1812-1815.* Page 189.

2. Winder to Ross. *Ibid.* Page 190.

3. Mrs. Thornton. *Ibid.* Page 686.

4. Marine. *The British Invasion of Maryland.* "Taney Letter, 1856." Page 183.

5. Marine *Ibid.* Page 186.

6. *National Intelligencer*, September 20, 1814.

7. Marine. *Ibid.* Page 187.

8. Skinner. *National Intelligencer.* June 4, 1849.

9. *Baltimore Patriot.* September 20, 1814.

CHAPTER TWENTY-FIVE – CONCLUSION

1. Mrs. Smith to Mrs. Kirkpatrick. *Ibid.* Page 115.

2. *National Intelligencer.* September 2, 1814.

3. *Annals of Congress.* Page 312.

4. *National Intelligencer.* October 18, 1814.

5. Jefferson to Smith. Library of Congress.

6. *Annals of Congress.* Page 398.

7. Madison to Congress. *Ibid.* Page 14.

8. *National Intelligencer.* December 10, 1814.

9. Monroe to Military Committee of the Senate. February 22, 1815. *The Writings of James Monroe.* Page 324.

10. *National Intelligencer.* March 3, 1815.

11. Wharton. *Ibid.* Page 179.

12. Gallatin to Jefferson. *Writings of Albert Gallatin.* September 6, 1815. Page 651.

13. Madison. *Annals of Congress*. Page 255.

14. Gleig. *The Campaigns of the British Army at Washington and New Orleans*. Page 83.

NOTES AND OPINIONS

1. Roosevelt. *The Naval War of 1812*. Page 219.

2. Mrs. Madison to Mrs. Todd. *Ibid.*

3. Langford. *Ladies of the White House.*

4. Smith. *The First Forty Years of Washington Society*. Page 110.

5. Thornton. *Journal and Diaries of Mrs. William Thornton*. Page 682.

6. *Washington Star*. November 12, 1905.

BIBLIOGRAPHY

Adams, Charles (Editor). *Letters of Mrs. Adams.* Fourth Edition. 1848.

Adams, Henry. Editor: Major H. A. DeWeerd. *The War of 1812.* Cooper Square Press: New York, 1999.

Adams, Henry. Editor: Harbert. *History of the United States of America during the Administrations of James Madison.*

Adams, Henry. *The Writings of Albert Gallatin.* Antquarian Press: New York, 1960.

Alden, Robert Ames. *The Flights of the Madisons.* Fairfax County Council of the Arts: Fairfax, Virginia, 1974.

Ames, William E. *A History of the National Intelligencer.* The University of North Carolina Press: Chapel Hill, 1972.

Ammon, Harry. *James Monroe, The Quest for National Identity.* University Press of Virginia: Charlottesville, 1990.

Armstrong, John. *Notices of the War of 1812.* Vol. II. Wiley and Putnam: New York, 1840.

______________. *Incidents in the Life of Jacob Barker New Orleans, Louisiana.* Washington, 1855.

Ball, Charles. *Slavery in the United States: A Narrative of the Life and Adventures of Charles Ball, A Black Man.* John S. Taylor: New York, Brick Church Chapel, 1837.

Barney, Mary. *Commodore Joshua Barney: From Autobiographical Notes and Journals.* Boston: Gray and Bowen, 1832.

Brant, Irving. *James Madison: Commander in Chief, 1812-1836.* Indianapolis: Bobbs Merrill, 1961.

Brant, Irving. *The Fourth President: A Life of James Madison.* The Bobbs-Merrill Company: Indianapolis and New York, 1970.

Clark, Allan. *Life and Letters of Dolly Madison.* Washington D.C.: Roberts, 1914.

Colbert, David (Editor). *Eyewitness to America.* Pantheon Books: New York, 1997.

Coles, Harry. *The War of 1812.* The University of Chicago Press:

Chicago, 1965.

Cresson, W. P. *James Monroe.* University of North Carolina Press: Chapel Hill, 1946.

Cutts, James Madison. "Dolly Madison." *Records of the Columbia Historical Society.* Volume 3. Columbia Historical Society: Washington: 1900.

Flexner, James Thomas. *George Washington and the New Nation (178 - 1793).* Little, Brown and Company: United States, 1970.

Fogle, Jeanne. *Two Hundred Years, Stories of the Nation's Capital.* Vandamere Press: Arlington, Virginia, 1991.

Froncek, Thomas (Editor). *The City of Washington: An Illustrated History.* By the Junior League of Washington. Wings Books: New Jersey, 1992.

Gapp, Frank W. *The Commodore and the Whale.* Vantage Press: New York, 1996.

Gleig, George. *The Campaigns of the British Army at Washington and New Orleans in the Years 1814-1815.* Solar Press Limited: Yorkshire, England, 1972.

{Gleig, George}. *A Subaltern in America Comprising His Narrative of the British Army at Baltimore, Washington, &c, &c, During the Late War.* Baltimore: Carney, Hart and Company, 1833.

Goodwin, Maud Wilder. *Dolly Madison.* Charles Scribner's Sons: New York, 1896.

Green, Constance. *Washington Village and Capital, 1800-1878.* Princeton University Press: Princeton, 1976.

Groene, Bertram H. *A Trap for the British-Thomas Brown and the Battle of the "White House."* Virginia Cavalcade. Volume XVIII. Virginia State Library: Richmond, Virginia, Summer, 1968-Spring, 1969.

Hamilton, Stanislaus Murray. *The Writings of James Monroe.* Volume V. AMS Press: New York, 1969.

Hatch, Winslow. *Old Roads and New Insights-Adventures in Discovery.* Reston Copy Center: Reston, Virginia, 1985.

Hildt, John C. *Letters Relating to the Capture of Washington.* The South Atlantic Quarterly. Volume VI. Durham: North Carolina, 1907.

Howarth, Stephen. *To Shining Sea, A History of the Untied States Navy*

1776-1991. Random House: New York, 1991.

Hunt, Gaillard (Editor). *Writings of James Madison 1808-1819.* G. P. Putnam's Sons: Knickerbocker Press, New York, 1908.

Ingersoll, J. Charles. *Historical Sketch of the Second War Between the United States of America and Great Britain.* Philadelphia: Lea and Blanchard, 1849.

Ingraham, Edward D. *A Sketch of the Events Which Preceded the Capture of Washington by the British on the Twenty-Fourth of August, 1814.* Philadelphia: Casey and Hart, 1849.

James, William. *Naval History of Great Britain.* Volume VI. London: Richard Bentley, New Burlington Street, 1837.

Key-Smith, F. S. *Francis Scott Key author of the Star Spangled Banner.* Key-Smith and Company: Washington D. C., 1911.

Kilmer, Kenton and Sweig, Donald. *The Fairfax Family in Fairfax County.* Fairfax, Virginia: Fairfax County Office of Comprehensive Planning, 1975.

King, Horatio. *The Battle of Bladensburg. Magazine of American History.* Volume XIV. Pages 438-457. Reinsch Library. Marymount University, Virginia.

Kite, Elizabeth. *L'Enfant and Washington.* Johns Hopkins Press: 1929.

Larner, James B. (Editor). *Records of the Columbia Historical Society.* Volume 24. The Columbia Historical Society: Washington: 1922.

Leckie, Robert. *From Sea to Shining Sea.* HarperCollins Publishers: New York, 1993.

Long, David F. *Nothing Too Daring – A Biography of Commodore David Porter 1789-1843.* United States Naval Institute: Annapolis, 1970.

Longacre, James Barton and Herring, James (Editors). *The National Portrait Gallery of Distinguished Americans.* Volume III. Arno Press and *The New York Times*: New York, 1970.

Lord, Walter. *The Dawn's Early Light.* The Johns Hopkins University Press: Baltimore, 1972.

Lossing, Benson J. *Pictorial Field Book of the War of 1812.* New York: Harper and Brothers, 1869.

Lucier, James P. *The Political Writings of James Monroe.* Regnery

Publishing, Inc.: Washington D. C., 2001.

McKenney, Thomas L. *Memoirs, Official and Personal.* University of Nebraska Press: Lincoln, 1973.

McNamara, Robert. "In Search of the Carrolls of Belle Vue." *Maryland Historical Magazine.* Volume 80, No. 1. Spring, 1985.

Madison, Dolley. *Memoirs and Letters of Dolly Madison, Wife of James Madison, President of the United States.* Editor, Lucia Beverly Cutts. 1886. Reprint, Port Washington, New York: Kennikat Press, 1971.

Mahon, John K. *The War of 1812.* University of Florida Press: Gainesville, 1972.

Marine, William M. *The British Invasion of Maryland 1812-1815.* Tradition Press: Hatboro, Pennsylvania, 1965.

Mattern, David B. "Dolley Madison Has the Last Word-The Famous Letter." *White House History.* White House Historical Association: Washington D. C., Fall, 1998.

Mattern, David B. and Schulman, Holly C. (Editors). *The Selected Letters of Dolley Payne Madison.* University of Virginia Press: Charlottesville, 2003.

Morris, Maud. "The Life and Times of Pontius D. Stelle." *Records of the Columbia Historical Society*, Volume 7. Columbia Historical Society: Washington, 1904.

Myer, Donald Beekman. *Bridges and the City of Washington.* Washington, D. C.: U. S.Commission of Fine Arts, 1974 (Reprinted 1983, 1992).

Ordway, Colonel Frederick Ira. (Editor) *General Society of the War of 1812-Register 1972.* Society of the War of 1812: Washington D. C.: 1972.

Pitch, Anthony. *The Burning of Washington-The British Invasion of 1814.* Naval Institute Press: Annapolis, Maryland, 1998.

Pratt, Sherman W. *Northern Virginia in the War of 1812.* The Arlington Historical Magazine. Volume XII. Number 2. Arlington Historical Society: Arlington, Virginia, October, 2002.

_____________. *Dictionary of National Biography.* Volume XVII. Oxford University Press: Ely House, London, 1973.

Roosevelt, Theodore. Editor: Sweetman, Jack. *The Naval War of 1812.* Naval Institute Press: Annapolis, 1987.

Schulman, Holly and Mattern, David. Dolley Madison-*Her Life, Letters and Legacy*. The Rosen Publishing Group: New York, 2003.

Scott, Captain James. *Recollections of a Naval Life*. Volume 3. London: Samuel Bently, Dorset Street, Fleet Street, 1834.

Smith, Henry (Harry), Sir. *The Autobiography of Lieutenant-General Sir Harry Smith*. London: J. Murray, 1903.

Smith, Margaret Bayard. *The first Forty Years of Washington Society*. Charles Scribner's Sons, 1906.

Stagg, J. C. A. *Mr. Madison's War*. Princeton University Press: Princeton, 1985.

Stanton, Richard L. Potomac Journey. Smithsonian Institution Press: Washington, 1993.

Templemen, Eleanor. *Arlington Heritage*. Avenel Books: New York, 1959.

Thornton, Anna Marie. *Journal and Diaries of Mrs. William Thornton*. Library of Congress.

Thornton, Anna Marie. "Diary of Mrs. William Thornton. Capture of Washington by the British." *Records of the Columbia Historical Society*. Volume 19. Columbia Historical Society: Washington: 1916.

Van Horn, John. *The Correspondence and Miscellaneous Papers of Benjamin Henry Latrobe*.

Wharton, Anne Hollingsworth. *Social Life in the Early Republic*. J. B. Lippincott Company: Philadelphia and London, 1902.

Whitehorne, Joseph A. *The Battle for Baltimore 1814*. The Nautical & Aviation Publishing Company of America, Inc: Baltimore, 1943.

Williams, John S. *History of the Invasion and Capture of Washington*. New York: Harper and Brothers, 1857.

Wright: Larner, John B. (Editor). "Sketch of Elias Boudinot Caldwell." *Records of the Columbia Historical Society*. Volume 24. Columbia Historical Society: Washington: 1922.

SPECIAL COLLECTIONS

Booth, Mordecai. *The Capture of Washington in 1814*. Mary Riley Styles Public Library, Falls Church, Virginia.

Carroll, Daniel of Duddington (papers). Library of Congress.

Cochrane, Sir Alexander Cochrane (papers). Library of Congress.

Cockburn, Sir George (papers). Library of Congress

Gordon, James Captain. *British Warships at Alexandria, Virginia, 1814. The English Viewpoint as Recalled by the Log of H.M.S. Seahorse.* Lloyd House. Special Collections. Alexandria Public Library. Alexandria, Virginia.

Gordon, James Captain. *Log of Proceedings, HMS Seahorse.* Lloyd House. Special Collections. Alexandria Public Library. Alexandria, Virginia

Jennings, Paul. *A Colored Man's Reminiscences of James Madison.* Brooklyn: George C. Beadle, 1865. James Madison University. Special Collections.

Jones, William (papers). Historical Society of Pennsylvania. The Uselma Clarke Smith Collection. Philadelphia, Pennsylvania.

Madison, Dolley. "The papers of Dolley Madiosn." Library of Congress. Manuscript Division. Container 1.

Madison, James. "The Papers of James Madison." Library of Congress.

Nourse Family Papers. University of Virginia Library. Charlottesville, Virginia.

Sayrs, Matilda Roberts. *Childhood in 1812-A True Story.* Alexandria Public Library. Lloyd House. Special Collections. Alexandria, Virginia.

Sayrs, Matilda Roberts. *Recollections.* Alexandria Public Library. Lloyd House. Special Collections. Alexandria, Virginia.

Shiner, Michael. *The Diary of Michel Shiner – The Early History of Washington D.C., Dating from 1813 to 1865.* Library of Congress.

NEWSPAPERS

Alexandria Gazette. Alexandria, Virginia.
Baltimore Patriot. Baltimore, Maryland.
Columbian Centennial. Boston, Massachusetts
London Times. London, England.
National Intelligencer. Washington D. C.
New York Express. New York
New York Herald. New York City, New York.
Niles Weekly Register. Baltimore, Maryland.
Richmond Enquirer. Richmond, Virginia.
Washington Star. Washington D. C.

INDEX

242

248